Challenge Klasse 11

Englisch für Berufliche Gymnasien
Bundesausgabe

von
Annely Humphreys
Jason Humphreys

Ernst Klett Verlag
Stuttgart · Leipzig

Challenge ^{Klasse 11}

Englisch für Berufliche Gymnasien
Bundesausgabe

Autorinnen und Autoren: Annely Humphreys, Jason Humphreys
Beratung: Regina Keller, Sachsen; Susanne Loeser, Rheinland-Pfalz; Arnd Nadolny, Niedersachsen;
Ines Schumacher, Hessen

Werkübersicht:

Schülerbuch, Klasse 11, 978-3-12-809208-9
Schülerbuch, Klassen 12/13, 978-3-12-809209-6
Workbook und EXAM TRAINING mit Audio-CD, Klassen 11-13, 978-3-12-809213-3
Vocabulary Notebook, Klassen 11-13, 978-3-12-809214-0
Schülerbuch-Paket: Schülerbuch Klasse 11 + Schülerbuch Klassen 12/13, 978-3-12-809215-7
Arbeitsmaterial-Paket: Workbook/EXAM TRAINING + Vocabulary Notebook, Klassen 11-13, 978-3-12-809216-4
Lehrerhandbuch inkl. Digitalem Lehrer-Service, Klassen 11-13, 978-3-12-809212-6

1. Auflage   1 ⁶ ⁵ ⁴ ³ ² | 18 17 16 15 14

Alle Drucke dieser Auflage sind unverändert und können im Unterricht nebeneinander verwendet werden.
Die letzte Zahl bezeichnet das Jahr des Druckes.

Projektleitung: Matthias Rupp
Redaktion: Astrid Keller
Herstellung: Angelika Lindner

Satz und Gestaltung: Ulrike Promies, Metzingen
Umschlaggestaltung: Projektteam des Verlages
Reproduktion: Meyle + Müller Medien-Management, Pforzheim
Druck: Druckhaus Götz GmbH, Ludwigsburg

Printed in Germany
ISBN 978-3-12-809208-9

Das Lehrwerk **Challenge Bundesausgabe** entspricht den Lehrplänen für die Jahrgangsstufen 11 bis 13 des Beruflichen Gymnasiums. Alle zu erreichenden Kompetenzen und Prüfungsformate werden intensiv trainiert.

1. Mit jedem Topic Schritt für Schritt sicher zum Abitur

- Einstiegsdoppelseite Topic: Vorbereitung auf das jeweilige Thema
- 5 Doppelseiten mit **aktuellen, authentischen Texten** – begleitet von **englisch-deutschen Wortangaben** für einen schnelleren Zugang zum Text und **differenzierten Aufgaben**, die ausgewogen alle Kompetenzbereiche trainieren und auf die in der Abiturprüfung vorgesehenen Prüfungsformate vorbereiten
- Fokusseite Spot on grammar: Wortschatzübungen und Vertiefung der wichtigsten **Grammatikkenntnisse**
- Fokusseite Hotspot: Handlungsorientierte Themenbearbeitung **mit vielen Projekt- und Internetaufgaben**
- Doppelseite Exam practice: **Testaufgabe im Abiturformat**
- `Video lounge` : Authentische BBC-Videos zum Training des Hör- / Sehverstehens

2. „Your challenge" bietet umfangreiches Material zur individuellen Förderung

- **Self-assessment:** Kategorien zur Selbsteinschätzung
- **Assessment tests:** Thematisch verknüpfte Aufgaben zur Selbsteinschätzung und zur Lernwegdokumentation
- **Helping hand:** Differenzierungsangebot zu komplexen Aufgabenstellungen
- **Grading grid:** Bewertungsbogen für Englisch
- **Skills files:** Alle Kompetenzen prägnant und mit vielen *Phrases* (Redewendungen)
- **Grammar files:** Kompaktgrammatik zum Wiederholen und Nachschlagen
- **Dictionary:** Alphabetisches Vokabelverzeichnis

3. Training und Prüfungsvorbereitung

- **Challenge-Code:** Über den Challenge-Code können Sie sich das *Talking vocabulary* (vertonte Wortlisten) als MP3-Dateien zum Anhören der korrekten Aussprache kostenlos unter www.klett.de herunterladen.
- **3-in-1-Workbook:** Für die Jahrgangsstufen 11 bis 13 bieten wir Ihnen ein Workbook zzgl. Prüfungsvorbereitung und Audio-CD:
  - Grammatikintensivtraining im Arbeitsheft zum Hineinschreiben
  - Hörverstehensübungen mit beiliegender Audio-CD
  - intensive Prüfungsvorbereitung mit Hinweisen zum Abitur und Wiederholung der wichtigsten *Skills* mit Prüfungsaufgaben auf Abiturniveau im *EXAM TRAINING*
- **Vocabulary Notebook:** Das Vokabellernheft für die Jahrgangsstufen 11 bis 13 ist der thematische Aufbauwortschatz, der gebündelt nur die wichtigen Vokabeln aus den Texten sowie zusätzlichen Wortschatz mit vielen Aufgaben zum Hineinschreiben trainiert.

Inhalt

Symbole und Abkürzungen

⊕ p9v2et	Challenge-Code mit *Talking vocabulary*: vertonte Wortlisten als MP3-Download	👥👥	Partneraufgabe
A1.1 💿	Audio: Für den Lehrer auf den Audio-CDs im Lehrerhandbuch. Für die Schüler teilweise auf der Audio-CD im Workbook.	👥👥👥	Gruppenaufgabe
		→	Verweise auf die *Skills* und *Grammar files* im Anhang
		🖥	Aufgaben zur selbstständigen Recherche im Internet
[1] **to improve** – (sich) verbessern	Lernvokabular ist in den Topics schwarz hervorgehoben	p.84 ◭	Aufgaben mit Differenzierungsangeboten im Anhang (*Helping hand*)

Topic 1
Being young today

A

B

C

D

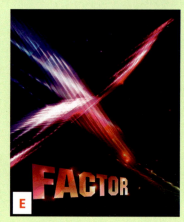

E

F

Getting started

1 Work on your own. Look at the photos and collect words that both describe and summarise what each photo shows. → Describing pictures, p. 128

2 Now get together with your neighbour and compare your results. Then agree on another photo that should be added. Give reasons for your choice.

3 Exchange your ideas and your "new photos" in groups. Make a word cluster containing key terms you need to describe young people's lives.

4 Vocabulary → Working with a dictionary, p. 142

  a) Collect adjectives that describe what you like/dislike about people your age.

  b) In groups, use your list of positive and negative adjectives and make sentences which describe what you like/dislike about people your age, e.g. "I like people who are reliable because it is important that you can trust someone who is your friend."

"Don't call me a teenager.
From now on, I want to be referred
to as a pre-adult."

A survey about growing up in England

In an online survey respondents were asked to name the best thing about being a child or young person living in England. This was an open-ended question, so that the respondents could reply exactly as they wanted to. Their answers were grouped together in the broad themes shown here.

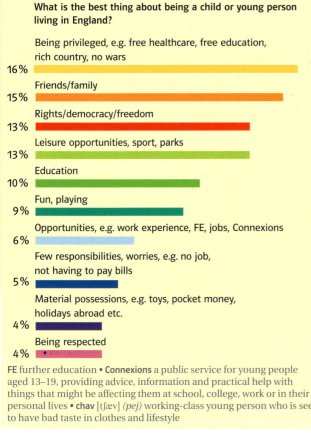

What is the best thing about being a child or young person living in England?

Being privileged, e.g. free healthcare, free education, rich country, no wars
16%

Friends/family
15%

Rights/democracy/freedom
13%

Leisure opportunities, sport, parks
13%

Education
10%

Fun, playing
9%

Opportunities, e.g. work experience, FE, jobs, Connexions
6%

Few responsibilities, worries, e.g. no job, not having to pay bills
5%

Material possessions, e.g. toys, pocket money, holidays abroad etc.
4%

Being respected
4%

What is the worst thing about being a child or young person living in England?

Age restrictions
11%

Lack of respect for teenagers
10%

Violence, crime and not feeling safe
9%

Bullying
7%

Nothing
7%

Not being listened to
7%

Lack of sports, leisure and play facilities, places to hang out
6%

Other young people (gangs, "chavs")
6%

Weather
4%

School
4%

Educational expectations/pressure
4%

Pollution, environment, traffic, litter
4%

FE further education • **Connexions** a public service for young people aged 13–19, providing advice, information and practical help with things that might be affecting them at school, college, work or in their personal lives • **chav** [tʃæv] *(pej)* working-class young person who is seen to have bad taste in clothes and lifestyle

5 Summarise and comment on the survey results above. Compare them to what you and your classmates would have expected.

6 In groups, draw up a survey to find out the best things and the worst things about being a young person in Germany. Ask your classmates to do the survey, then discuss the results. → Questionnaires and surveys, p. 149

7 Projects → see Hotspots 1 and 2, p. 19

Word bank

The survey results show/indicate/prove/suggest that … •
A (high) percentage of … •
A majority/minority of … •
A significant number of … •
Compared with/to … •
A surprising number of …

A   Growing up

1   **Before you read** → Brainstorming, p. 140
Have a look at the following headlines and facts about a Facebook party in Germany. Have you ever been to a flash mob party? What do you think happened? Why do you think all the people came?

> A Hamburg girl used Facebook to organise her 16th birthday party but unknowingly broadcast the invitation for all Facebook users to see, leading to more than 1,500 guests turning up for the event.

> A spontaneous party in the city of Wuppertal attracted some 800 people.

> A flash mob of 5,000 invaded the small North Sea island of Sylt and the community was left to clean up the mess.

> The costs of the party (cleaning up, damages, etc.) are estimated to be around €20,000.

2   **Comprehension** → Understanding non-fictional texts, p. 109
Collect the information mentioned in the text which speaks against Facebook parties.

p.100

3   **Role play** → Discussions, p. 133
Prepare a panel discussion with the following roles. Collect arguments and examples that can help you to support your position.

a) A teenager who attends Facebook parties. ("Simply celebrating is not a crime.")

b) The mayor of a town who tries to prevent Facebook parties. ("We cannot guarantee the safety of the teenagers and our citizens.")

1   **interior minister** – Innenminister
2   **recent** – kürzlich, letzte(r/s)
2   **social networking site** – Internetseite eines sozialen Netzwerks
4   **phenomenon** – Phänomen
5   **monitoring** – Beobachtung
7   **inadvertently** – irrtümlich
8   **public order** – öffentliche Ordnung
8   **to ban** – verbieten
8   **in advance** – im Vorfeld
12   **evidence** – Beweis
13   **duty** – Pflicht
14   **municipal** – städtisch
15   **to fuel** – anheizen
16   **appropriate** – angemessen
17   **to intervene** – intervenieren, einschreiten

DW-WORLD.DE
DEUTSCHE WELLE
Search [ ] GO

Home | Your link to Germany | DW-World | DW Radio live | DW TV Europe live |

Interior ministers speak out against 'dangerous' Facebook parties
Recent months have seen parties organized over social networking site Facebook overrun by thousands of party crashers who were accidentally sent invitations. Now, German state interior ministers want an end to the phenomenon.
5   German interior ministers have called for increased monitoring of house parties organized on the social networking site Facebook after several small events organized on the site inadvertently attracted thousands of guests.
"If public order and safety are put at risk then Facebook parties must be banned in advance," Lower Saxony Interior Minister Uwe Schünemann told the weekly *Welt am*
10   *Sonntag* newspaper.
North Rhine-Westphalia Interior Minister Ralf Jäger echoed these thoughts, telling the newspaper that "if there is concrete evidence of potential danger to participants or innocent third parties ahead of a planned Facebook party, then it is the duty of the municipal police to prohibit the event."
15   However, Malte Spitz from the Greens said the interior ministers were fueling a "sham debate" with their comments, adding that "police already have appropriate powers to intervene in cases of danger arising from Facebook parties."

c) A representative of a parent organisation. ("As long as they all celebrate together and are monitored by the police, we know what they are doing.")

d) A social worker of a town with fewer than 150,000 inhabitants. ("There's often not much to do for teenagers who aren't 18 yet; Facebook parties that are controlled by local authorities are a good way for them to get to know teenagers from other towns.")

e) Another representative of a parent organisation. ("Parties organised by social networking sites attract all kinds of people; we need to protect those who are underage and so we should forbid such parties.")

f) Any other role you believe is missing in this discussion.

4 **Text production: Writing an email** → Writing an email, p. 118
On a social networking site you read an invitation to a flash mob pool party in which teenagers in California are called upon to come to an address of a property with a large swimming pool. The person who wrote this invitation used google maps to locate this house. Write an email to this person in which you tell him what you think of the invitation.

5 **Mediation** → Mediation, p. 132
Summarise the following information in German. Do not translate it.

> The amount of time that people from all over the world spend on social networking sites is increasing. According to recent reports, Russians spend an average of over 6 hours per month on these sites compared to Germans (over 4 hours). Facebook alone is said to have about one billion active users. Twitter, MySpace, etc. are popular, too. Spending on online advertising on such sites is predicted to rise to $2.6 billion by 2012 for the USA alone.

Party to remember

In early June, a Hamburg girl used Facebook to organize her 16th birthday party but un-
20 knowingly broadcast the invitation for all Facebook users to see, leading to more than 1,500 guests turning up for the event and forcing some 100 police officers to intervene to keep the crowd under control.
Eleven people were detained during the party and one police officer was injured, as well as dozens of people wearing flip-flops who had stepped on shards of glass from broken
25 bottles. Two small fires had to be extinguished and the birthday girl, identified only as Thessa, was forced to flee as the party got out of control.
Shortly after, a spontaneous party in the western city of Wuppertal attracted some 800 people, 41 of whom were taken into police custody and 16 injured.
Hamburg authorities are currently also bracing themselves ahead of a Facebook party
30 planned for September 30 and an expected influx of up to 19,000 partygoers on the city's transport grid.
Schünemann said that in order to prevent such events from occurring, young people using Facebook needed an "Internet drivers license" to educate them about the potential dangers of using the website.
35 "Young people often don't know what they're getting themselves into," he told *Welt am Sonntag*. "They have to pay for any damages and necessary rubbish collection, and this can cost thousands of euros."   (413 words)

20 **to broadcast** – senden, übertragen
22 **crowd** – Menschenmenge
23 **to detain** – in Gewahrsam nehmen
24 **shard** – Scherbe
25 **to extinguish** – löschen, auslöschen
28 **police custody** – Polizeigewahrsam
29 **to brace oneself** – sich rüsten
30 **influx** – Zustrom, Einfall
36 **rubbish** – Müll

B Teenagers and technology

1 Before you read → Brainstorming, p. 140

a) Have a look at the picture. Imagine you had to describe it to someone who doesn't know what mobile phones are.

b) "I'd rather give up my kidney than my phone." What do you think the text is about? What is your first reaction to this quote?

2 **kidney** – Niere

7 **enslaved** – versklavt

7 **social inadequates** – sozial Benachteiligte

9 **to deadpan** – witzeln

11 **carrier pigeon** – Brieftaube

28 **to swap** – tauschen

29 **communication hub** – Kommunikationszentrum

31 **to weld** – schweißen

33 **prevalent** – vorherrschend

35 **senior research specialist** – leitende(r) Forscher(in)

36 **developmental needs** – Entwicklungsbedürfnisse

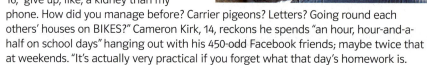

theguardian

News | Sport | Comment | Culture | Business | Money | Life&Style | Travel | Environment

Comment is free ▸ Society   Search [   ] GO

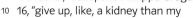

Teenagers and technology: 'I'd rather give up my kidney than my phone'

Text, text, text, that's all they think
5 about: but are all those hours on the
phone and Facebook turning teenagers into screen-enslaved social
inadequates? Jon Henley finds out.
"I'd rather," deadpans Philippa Grogan,
10 16, "give up, like, a kidney than my
phone. How did you manage before? Carrier pigeons? Letters? Going round each
others' houses on BIKES?" Cameron Kirk, 14, reckons he spends "an hour, hour-and-a-
half on school days" hanging out with his 450-odd Facebook friends; maybe twice that
at weekends. "It's actually very practical if you forget what that day's homework is.
15 Unfortunately, one of my best friends doesn't have Facebook. But it's OK; we talk on
our PlayStations."
Emily Hooley, 16, recalls a Very Dark Moment: "We went to Wales for a week at half term
to revise. There was no mobile, no TV, no broadband. We had to drive into town just to
get a signal. It was really hard, knowing people were texting you, writing on your Wall,
20 and you couldn't respond. Loads of my friends said they'd just never do that." […]
75% of all teenagers (and 58% of 12-year-olds) now have a mobile phone. Almost 90% of
phone-owning teens send and receive texts, most of them daily. Half send 50 or more
texts a day; one in three send 100. In fact, in barely four years, texting has established
itself comfortably as "the preferred channel of basic communication between teens and
25 their friends".
But phones do more than simply text, of course. More than 80% of phone-owning teens
also use them to take pictures (and 64% to share those pictures with others). Sixty per
cent listen to music on them, 46% play games, 32% swap videos and 23% access social
networking sites. The mobile phone, in short, is now "the favoured communication hub
30 for the majority of teens".
As if texting, swapping, hanging out and generally spending their waking hours welded
to their phones wasn't enough, 73% use social networking sites, mostly Facebook – 50%
more than three years ago. Digital communication is not just prevalent in teenagers'
lives. It IS teenagers' lives.
35 There's a very straightforward reason, says Amanda Lenhart, a Pew senior research
specialist. "Simply, these technologies meet teens' developmental needs," she says.
"Mobile phones and social networking sites make the things teens have always done

– defining their own identity, establishing themselves as independent of their parents, looking cool, impressing members of the opposite sex – a whole lot easier."

40 Flirting, boasting, gossiping, teasing, hanging out, confessing: all that classic teen stuff has always happened, Lenhart says. It's just that it used to happen behind the bike sheds, or via tightly folded notes pressed urgently into sweating hands in the corridor between lessons. Social networking sites and mobile phones have simply facilitated the whole business, a gadzillion times over.

45 For Professor Patti Valkenburg, of the University of Amsterdam's internationally respected Centre for Research on Children, Adolescents and the Media, "contemporary communications tools" help resolve one of the fundamental conflicts that rage within every adolescent. Adolescence, she says, is characterised by "an enhanced need for self-presentation, or communicating your identity to others, and also self-disclosure

50 – discussing intimate topics. Both are essential in developing teenagers' identities, allowing them to validate their opinions and determine the appropriateness of their attitudes and behaviours."

But, as we all recall, adolescence is also a period of excruciating shyness and aching self-consciousness – which can make all that self-presentation and self-disclosure

55 something of a perilous, not to say agonising, business. So the big plus of texting, instant messaging and social networking is that it allows the crucial identity-establish-ing behaviour, without the accompanying embarrassment. "These technologies give their users a sense of increased controllability," Valkenburg says. "That, in turn, allows them to feel secure about their communication, and thus freer in their interpersonal

60 relations."

"Controllability", she explains, is about three things: being able to say what you want without fear of the message not getting through because of that humungous spot on your chin or your tendency to blush; having the power to reflect on and change what you write before you send it (in contrast to face-to-face communication); and being

65 able to stay in touch with untold hordes of friends at times, and in places, where your predecessors were essentially incommunicado. […]   (726 words)

40	**to boast** – angeben
41	**bike shed** – Fahrrad-schuppen
44	**gadzillion** – Unmenge
49	**self-disclosure** – Selbst-offenbarung
51	**to validate** – bestätigen
53	**to excruciate** – quälen
55	**perilous** – gefährlich
55	**agonising** – quälend
62	**humungous** – riesig
62	**spot** – *hier:* Pickel
63	**to blush** – erröten
65	**untold** – unermesslich
66	**predecessor** – Vor-gänger(in)
66	**incommunicado** – isoliert

2 **Comprehension** → Understanding non-fictional texts, p. 109

a) Summarise each paragraph in a single, simple sentence.

b) Outline why – according to Professor Valkenburg – these communication tools are so popular with teenagers.

c) "[…] being able to say what you want without fear of the message not getting through because of that humungous spot on your chin or your tendency to blush." (ll. 61–63) Explain this sentence in your own words.

3 **Listening comprehension: Teens, cell phones and texting** → Listening, p. 108
Listen to the text about US teenagers and text messages.

a) When you listen for the first time, write down the central ideas / topics which are mentioned in the text.

b) When you listen for the second time, arrange these central ideas into a cluster and add as much information as possible.

4 **Comment** → Writing a comment, p. 116
"Digital communication […] IS teenagers' lives." (ll. 33–34) Comment on this statement.

C Young people and families

1 Before you read: Do you agree with the following statements? Why (not)?

a) Parents should be role models for their children and should always behave accordingly. (dementsprechend)

b) Parents should immediately drop their hobbies when their children need their time and attention.

c) Growing up with two parents is always better than living in a one-parent family.

d) The family will always be at the core of western societies.

e) Fathers should always appear strong and confident.

f) Parents should never criticise each other or even argue in the presence of their children.

g) Mothers often have to be tougher than fathers.

h) Families in which the parents do not serve as role models are very likely to be the homes disadvantaged children come from.

Willy Russell
(English writer, born in 1947)

Raymond Marks ("a normal boy from a normal town") is the protagonist of the novel "The Wrong Boy". He grows up living with his mother who split up with her husband when Raymond was still a baby. The following scene tells us why.

5 **to hum** – summen
6 **to acquire** – erwerben
7 **dedicated** – engagiert
7 **determined** – entschlossen
7 **nowt** (northern English dialect) – nichts
8 **to bleed dry** – ausbluten
9 **pram** – Kinderwagen
10 **hire-purchase bills** – Rechnungen über Ratenkäufe

bill- Rechnung
Apparently- obvious
- evident
- offensichtlich
debts- Schulden

The wrong boy

Apparently my Dad was always coming home with musical instruments that he could never ever play. And at first, my Mam said, she didn't mind.
'That was the reason I fell in love with him,' she said, 'because he was a man who had so much melody in his heart.'

5 But for all the melody that apparently hummed within the heart of my father and regardless of how fine the instruments he acquired, no matter how dedicated and determined his efforts, he could never wring a tune out of nowt. 'And it was bleeding us dry,' my Mam said. 'You were just a little baby then, still in your pram; and with me just doin' part time at the Kwiky we'd hardly a pair

10 of pennies to knock together. We'd gas bills and electricity bills, hire-purchase bills and the rent to pay. But it never made any difference. We'd all the debts in the world but they were as nowt to your father. I'm not saying it was his fault. It was like a sickness that he had. Johnny just couldn't help himself. With whatever money we did manage to scrape together, he'd set off with the best of

15 intentions in the world, telling me how he was off to the gas showroom or the electricity board to pay off the bills. And me,' my Mam said, 'I always believed Johnny, always believed your father because your father believed himself. But he'd never get to the showroom or the electricity board. He'd turn up back here with a big bass fiddle or a saxophone or flute. And he'd have that dreamy look

20 in his eye again.'

2 **Comprehension** → Understanding fictional texts, p. 111
In your own words, summarise the role musical instruments play in the family's life.

3 **Analysis** → Text analysis, p. 115

   a) Explain the phrase "it's an addiction and it's bleeding us dry" (ll. 32–33) in your own words.

   b) Analyse the language the author uses to contrast the worlds the parents live in. Collect relevant words and passages from the text in a table. Indicate the lines as well.

Dad	Mam

   c) Taking into account the changing meaning of "a man with melody in his heart" in this extract, outline the relationship the parents have to each other.

4 **Partner interview**
Interview your partner about the role a family will play in his or her future. The phrases in the box should give you some ideas, but you can and should include your own questions as well.

> regularly seeing your brothers and sisters • looking after your parents • getting married • having children • your parents' house • blood is thicker than water

And that's what started the rows [Kampf] between my Mam and my Dad. My Mam said that at first, after the shouting was over, she always found it in herself to forgive him for spending all the money on a Hammond Organ or a xylophone or a trumpet or a bass trombone. […]

25 And then my Mam came home from the KwikSave one day and saw him with the Rickenbacker guitar that he'd said was an absolute steal at four hundred and thirty-four pounds; my Mam watched him as he stood there, in the middle of the parlour [Halle], the guitar strapped around his shoulders as he pretended to play, as he mimed along to an Eric Clapton record, his fingers skittering up and down
30 the fretboard in a wildly haphazard [planlos] but passionate frustrated frenzy. And my Mam said there were tears dropping down from my father's eyes. And she told him, 'You've got to give this up, Johnny; it's an obsession, it's an addiction and it's bleeding us dry.'

And my Dad did give up the guitar. But when he took it back to the shop he
35 saw a button-key chromatic accordion. He said he got a fantastic part-exchange deal on it.

And that's when my Mam started seeing the holes in the carpet and the flaking paint on the window frames; and with each new instrument my Dad brought home, the flaky paint got flakier, the holes in the carpet grew and my Mam had
40 to work harder and harder at the KwikSave just to keep us all standing still. And that's when my Mam first started to think; that a man with melody in his heart could also be a millstone around a person's neck.   (567 words)

24 **trombone** – Posaune
26 **absolute steal** – Schnäppchen
29 **to skitter** – rutschen
30 **fretboard** – Griffbrett
30 **haphazard** – planlos
30 **frenzy** – Rausch
37 **flaking** – abblättern
42 **to be a millstone around sb.'s neck** – jmdm ein Klotz am Bein sein
mim – nachmachen

D   Binge drinking

1   **Before you read**

a) Work with a partner and ask them the following questions:
- How often do you drink alcohol?
- What kinds of alcoholic drinks do you like?
- How much do you usually drink?
- How do you decide when you've had enough?

b) What is 'binge drinking'? With the same partner, come up with a definition and report back to the class.

1	**binge drinking** – bewusstes Rauschtrinken
2	**to throw up** – sich übergeben
3	**humiliating** – demütigend
4	**sociable** – gesellig
4	**undisputed** – unumstritten
4	**appeal** – Anziehung(skraft)
5	**target** – *hier:* Zielgruppe
6	**to tackle** – etw. angehen
16	**to restrict** – begrenzen
19	**shot** – Kurzer
19	**to encourage** – jdn ermutigen
26	**telesales** – Verkauf über das Telefon
26	**pint** – Britische Maßeinheit; 1 Pint = 568ml
27	**to be conscious of sth.** – sich etw. bewusst sein
27	**to affect** – beeinflussen, sich auswirken auf
28	**long-term** – Langzeit-
28	**to discourage** – abschrekken, abhalten

theguardian

News | Sport | Comment | Culture | Business | Money | Life&Style | Travel | Environment

Comment is free   Society   Search [   ] GO

What teenagers think about binge drinking

Units of alcohol are a complicated matter, cheap drinks are welcomed and throwing up is a humiliating but accepted part of growing up. But while teenagers believe they could be better informed about the dangers of alcohol, the sociable side of drinking still holds undisputed appeal.

5   Young people in the UK, among the heaviest drinkers in Europe, are the target of both government and industry campaigns to tackle binge and under age drinking – so the Guardian went out onto the streets of Britain to speak to them about their experiences with alcohol.

Outside a bar called Cuba Libre in Islington's Upper Street in north London, where the bars are wall to wall and happy hour

10   – lasting three conventional hours – is just finishing, Zoe Spittle, 18, says there was "no downside" to cheap drinks offers. "If there wasn't happy hour, we could go to Tesco to get drinks. But it's better to be in a bar where it's more sociable," she says.

15   Happy hour

Her friend Charlotte Peel, 18, agreed that restricting happy hours "just drives people into their homes to drink." But, she says: "Club nights [in Tottenham Court Road] where it's £1.50 for a shot, encourage binge drinking. I think the

20   answer is more police and more security." [...]

Warnings not taken seriously

In Nottingham, Grace Ennis, 18, who drinks once a week at most, agrees binge drinking needed tackling. She says: "Warnings about binge drinking help, but they're not taken seriously by people because it's a

25   lifestyle – and when people see the news they don't think it's about them."
But telesales worker Alex Wilby, 19, from Beeston, who drinks six or seven pints on a Friday night, is conscious of how much he drinks. "I think it will affect my health more because I'm young," he says. "I think people should be shown the long-term consequences more to discourage them from drinking."

30   Krishna Owen, 18, also from Nottingham, drinks about five pints when he goes out with friends. "If I went out more I may be concerned about my health, but as it is I'm not worried, though technically, I could be described as a binge drinker," he says. "But I think beer should be

labelled with units alongside alcohol percentage: I don't know how many units are in a pint". […]
In Leeds, Holly Makin, 20, is a banker who drinks vodka and coke, was recovering from a house
35 party. "There's a big drinking culture here," she says. "There's a club night every night, and house
parties all the time. If I wake up with a hangover, I wonder why I drank so much but then go out
and do the same again." She says there is pressure to drink: "It's considered the norm. I have a
teetotal friend who is constantly being offered alcohol by friends."
Mikey Harrington, 21, from Leeds and a barman, says peer pressure decreases with age. "When
40 I was young I wanted to drink at dinner like my dad. There's pressure to drink at a young age: it's
seen as a sign of maturity and adulthood. Now, I just drink because I want to."
He thinks alcohol education in schools needs improving. "Kids should be taught responsibility and
how to deal with alcohol properly," he says. Alex Ford, 19, from Leeds, a singer in a post-punk
band, agrees. "People should be taught the importance of knowing their limits: it's reckless to get
45 drunk to the point of being paralytic," he says.

Under-age drinkers

Among under-18s, who mainly drink in parties at each other's houses, there was a consensus that
"almost everyone drinks." Henry Willmore, 16, lives in north London and drinks beer occasionally
with friends – or vodka or Malibu if he's trying to get drunk. "There's no peer pressure to drink,
50 but there's definitely a drinking culture. At parties, everyone's doing it, so some people probably
feel left out if they don't drink." Alcohol can help with confidence. "I think it's more if you feel shy
or nervous around girls. But I don't feel nervous."
Buying alcohol is no problem, says James Burton, 16. "It's easy to get fake ID that works in off
licenses, though not in big pubs or clubs." Lilit Batikyan, 16, from Camden, agreed it's easy to get
55 alcohol. "Older friends supply it, or there are some off licenses in Camden that sell to underage
people." […]
In contrast, Lana Rowlett, from Hackney, is enthusiastic about the joys of drinking. The 19-year-
old Stella and cocktail drinker, who works with children with learning difficulties, says: "During
the holidays I drink more than 50 drinks a week. I know I can stop drinking so it doesn't worry
60 me; it's socialising for me. But if I was still doing this in a few years, I'd have a problem." […]

(800 words)

33	**to label** – beschriften
33	**unit** – *hier:* Alkoholeinheit
33	**alongside** – neben
34	**to recover** – sich erholen
36	**hangover** – Kater
37	**pressure** – Druck
37	**to consider** – ansehen als
38	**teetotal** – abstinent
39	**peer pressure** – Gruppen-zwang
39	**to decrease** – zurückgehen, sinken
41	**maturity** – Reife
41	**adulthood** – Erwachsenen-alter
42	**to improve** – (sich) ver-bessern
44	**reckless** – leichtsinnig
45	**paralytic** – betrunken
47	**consensus** – Übereinstim-mung
51	**confidence** – Selbstver-trauen, Sicherheit
51	**shy** – scheu
53	**fake ID** – gefälschter Aus-weis
53	**off license** – Wein- und Spirituosengeschäft

2 Comprehension

In the text above, a number of young people give their thoughts on binge drinking. Choose at least 6 people from the text and summarise their attitudes towards drinking. Use a table like this one.

Name	Age	Attitude towards drinking
Zoe	18	- likes 'happy hour' because of the cheap drinks - would buy alcohol from the supermarket if bars were more expensive
Charlotte	…	…

3 Text production

A British magazine for teenagers wants to write an article about young people and alcohol in Europe. Write a letter to the magazine in which you give your opinion on drinking among people your age in Germany.

4 Comment

"There's pressure to drink at a young age: it's seen as a sign of maturity and adult-hood." (ll. 40–41) Do you agree with this statement?

 5 Presentation → Presentation, p. 151

"Kids should be taught responsibility and how to deal with alcohol properly."
(ll. 42–43) Work in small groups and come up with a set of rules for responsible drinking. Create a poster and present it to the class. Include pictures and a slogan.

E Young people and the future

1 Think – pair – share

a) Work on your own. Collect the dreams and fears young people have. What are your strategies to achieve what you want in life?

b) Exchange your list with a partner. Which dreams and fears have you both listed? Also compare the strategies you believe can help to achieve what you want in life.

c) Exchange your lists in class and make a cluster on the board. What are the dreams and fears most young people have? How do you believe you can make these dreams come true?

5 **shameless** – schamlos

8 **to be on the right track** – auf dem richtigen Weg sein

13 **to be taken over by fear** – von Angst übermannt werden

15 **to cuss** – beschimpfen

18 **weapon** – Waffe

18 **consumption** – Konsum

The Fear
by Lily Allen

I want to be rich and I want lots of money
I don't care about clever I don't care about funny
I want loads of clothes and fuck loads of diamonds
I heard people die while they are trying to find them

5 And I'll take my clothes off and it will be shameless
Cause everyone knows that's how you get famous
I'll look at the sun and I'll look in the mirror
I'm on the right track yeah I'm on to a winner

[Chorus]
10 I don't know what's right and what's real anymore
I don't know how I'm meant to feel anymore
When do you think it will all become clear?
'Cause I'm being taken over by the fear

Life's about film stars and less about mothers
15 It's all about fast cars and cussing each other
But it doesn't matter cause I'm packing plastic
and that's what makes my life so fucking fantastic

And I am a weapon of massive consumption
And its not my fault it's how I'm programmed to function
20 I'll look at the sun and I'll look in the mirror
I'm on the right track yeah we're on to a winner

[Chorus]
I don't know what's right and what's real anymore
I don't know how I'm meant to feel anymore
25 When do you think it will all become clear?
Cause I'm being taken over by the fear

28 **ammunition** – Munition
30 **saint** – Heilige(r)

[Bridge]
Forget about guns and forget ammunition
Cause I'm killing them all on my own little mission
30 Now I'm not a saint but I'm not a sinner
Now everything's cool as long as I'm gettin thinner

[Chorus]
I don't know what's right and what's real anymore
I don't know how I'm meant to feel anymore
35 When do you think it will all become clear?
'Cause I'm being taken over by the fear

(307 words)

2 Comprehension → Dealing with songs, p. 114

a) In your own words, summarise what the girl in the song wants to achieve in life. Which strategies does she want to employ?

b) Explain the following sentences in your own words:
- 'Cause I'm being taken over by the fear (l. 13)
- Life's about film stars and less about mothers (l. 14)
- Now everything's cool as long as I'm gettin thinner (l. 31)

3 Analysis → Text analysis, p. 115
Analysing the sentence structure and the choice of words, compare the chorus and the five verses. In which way are they different? What is the effect of this?

4 Classroom discussion → Discussions, p. 133
What do you think is the message of Lily Allen's song? Compare it with your list of dreams and strategies (see task 1c).

5 Comment → Writing a comment, p. 116
"Lily Allen's song 'The Fear' is typical of the way teenagers think about their future." Comment on this statement.

6 Mediation → Mediation, p. 132
Summarise the following information in English. Do not translate it.

In einer globalen Studie (14 Länder, 5 600 Befragte, Alter zwischen 8 und 34) waren zentrale Ergebnisse: Die Befragten glauben, dass Eltern, Intelligenz und Freunde im Leben weiterhelfen, die Regierung, Arbeitgeber und Religion dagegen einschränken. Dennoch glaubten sie mehrheitlich, dass sie selbst verantwortlich für ihr Leben seien. Weniger als jeder Zweite ist aber der Meinung, dass er/sie einmal mehr als die eigenen Eltern verdienen wird. Zentrale Sorgen der Befragten waren: Bekomme ich einmal einen guten Job? Wie finde ich heraus, was ich wirklich will? Wer bin ich überhaupt? Bin ich attraktiv?

7 Project → see Hotspot 3, p. 19

Revision of tenses

→ Grammar, p. 154

a) What is the tense used in the following sentences? Try to explain the correct rule and the appropriate usage. If you need help, look up the grammar section.

1. Today, almost every teenager is familiar with the Internet and communicates by email and text messages. Some even believe they cannot survive without Facebook and online games.
2. In the future, there probably won't be any picture post cards written by teenagers during their holidays anymore.
3. Over the past few decades, teenagers have had more and more freetime.
4. Some even say that teenagers have never had so little responsibility.
5. When the Internet was invented, very large portable phones had already been on the market for quite some time. However, they weren't used for sending SMS.
6. At this very moment, mobile phone users all over the world are sending and receiving more than 200,000 text messages. It might be interesting to know how many of these are being sent by teenagers …

b) Which tenses have not been mentioned? Make sure that you know these rules as well. Come up with more sentences about teenagers and the way they live.

c) Copy the email and fill in the correct words in the correct verb forms.

✕

Hi,

I **1** (write) to you because of a problem I **2** (like) some help with. **3** (you • remember) that I **4** (meet) this good-looking boy at Sophie's party last week? Now he **5** (send) me a text message asking me out on Saturday. He **6** (suggest) we could go to the cinema. I **7** (not be) to the cinema for ages, but that's not the real problem.

He's nearly 18, and at the moment he **8** (prepare) for his driving licence. He already **9** (have) a car of his own which is kind of cool as this **10** (make) him very independent from his parents.

But the thing that I **11** (find) difficult really is that he already **12** (have) a son! He and his ex-girlfriend **13** (have) a child last summer, shortly after which they **14** (split) up. They **15** (seem) to get along OK, but **16** (stop) going out with each other half a year ago. I **17** (know) from a friend of mine that he regularly **18** (see) his son and **19** (spend) a lot of time with him over the weekends.

Now I **20** (be) really confused and **21** (not know) what to do. I think I **22** (like) him but I **23** (not know) if I **24** (should) go out with someone who already **25** (have) a child. Perhaps I **26** (fall) in love with him. What **27** (say) my parents?

28 (like) his son me? What **29** (say) his ex? I **30** (not know) yet if I **31** (want) children at all, I **32** really (not think) about that … **33** (you • think) I should **34** (forget) him before I even get to know him?

Confused, Ann

1 **Project: Time to think of your lifestyle** → Projects and group work, p. 148

Think of the following questions and develop a personal fact sheet:
- How would you describe yourself? Include positive and negative characteristics of yourself.
- Who are your idols and how do they influence your lifestyle?
- What is your idea of a "best friend"?
- What do you hope to achieve in your life and how do you want to reach your aim?
- What is your motto in life?

Take your time answering the questions and be honest to yourself. Afterwards choose two classmates you'd like to share your personal facts with and present your results to them.

 2 **Project: What to expect from life** → Presentation, p. 151

Work in groups and prepare a presentation for your classmates on one of the following topics:
- a school / university or a company you want to attend after school
- your dream profession: job profile, requirements and companies you could apply to
- a year off: different possibilities (travelling, voluntary work, advantages and disadvantages)

Collect information and prepare a computer presentation telling your classmates all your main points. Don't forget to illustrate your findings with pictures, diagrams and charts.

> **Finding information**
> - Ask for information at schools and universities in your area.
> - Contact companies in your area (by email, etc.).
> - Look for information on the Internet. Use a search engine and try the following search words: study abroad • internship • apprenticeship • gap year • voluntary work

 3 **Project: Youth studies (Mediation)** → Internet research, p. 147

a) Go online and search for youth studies that deal with the following topics: the future, relationships, communication/the media. Prepare a German summary of the main findings of your study and present it to the class.

b) Go online and search for results of the German youth study *Shell Studie Jugend 2010*. Choose one aspect you find interesting (e.g. diagrams, questions asked, interviews with experts, etc.) and summarise it in English.

A1.4

TheObserver

What's wrong with today's youth?

In Boston, Lincolnshire, 70 teenagers trashed a 380-acre farm. They crashed 10-ton lorries through a gate on David Benton's farm to deliver alcohol, sound equipment and generators for an all-night rave. Halfway round the world in Australia, firemen in Sydney blamed bored children for the bushfires threatening the city. Fourteen of the 21 arrested were juveniles. Add to these so-called revelries the countless news stories about schoolkids killing each other […] and you can't help but echo the age-old refrain: what's wrong with today's youth? […]

To explain their thrill at causing mayhem on a farmer's property or at setting fire to Sydney's national parks, we need to look […] at the social network they inhabit. And what a threadbare set-up this is; once upon a time, teenagers at a loose end after school could join the Scouts or go to the youth club down the road, where they came face to face with peers and authority figures, and were expected to get on with them all. Here they sampled the give and take of compromise, politeness and demands that colours every encounter within a community. It's an emotional bartering that comes naturally to only a few, and must be learned by the rest of us.

But where can today's youngsters learn to say 'please' and wait patiently in the queue rather than growl and elbow their way to the front? Taking their cues from their disaffected parents, who opt out of politics, clubs

---

2 **to trash** – verwüsten

3 **gate** – Tor

8 **to blame sb.** – jmdm die Schuld geben für

10 **juvenile** – Jugendliche(r)

11 **revelry** – ausgelassene Feier

17 **mayhem** – Chaos

21 **threadbare** – schäbig

22 **to be at a loose end** – nicht wissen, was man mit sich anfangen soll

28 **to sample** – ausprobieren

30 **encounter** – Begegnung

32 **bartering** – Austausch

37 **to growl** – sich mürrisch geben

39 **to take one's cue from sb.** – jmds Beispiel folgen

40 **to opt out** – aussteigen

and churches, teenagers of all classes have turned away from organised and collective leisure that would have once taught them social skills, and taken up 45 the solo pleasures of the internet.

In virtual chatrooms and through video games, today's generation engages in a new kind of interaction. Yes, you make connections with 50 others – but wholly on your own terms. Should the invisible interlocutor *unsichtbarer Gesprächspartner* 55 fail to amuse you or to confirm your prejudices or heap sufficient praise upon you, you can simply click your mouse and they're off your screen, to be replaced with someone more amiable or more malleable. [...] *Einmischung* Free of parental interference, and 60 unrestrained by traditional social relationships, young people are turning into socially autistic beings who can only log on and tune out.   (375 words)

48 **to engage in sth.** – sich mit etw. befassen

51 **interlocutor** – Gesprächspartner

53 **to heap sufficient praise (up) on sb.** – jmdn überschwänglich loben

57 **amiable** – liebenswürdig, freundlich

57 **malleable** – gefügig

59 **unrestrained** – uneingeschränkt

1 **Comprehension**

   a) Outline in your own words which problems teenagers in England and Australia caused.

   b) Summarise the reasons given in the text for the teenagers' behaviour.

   c) In your own words, explain the teenagers' "new kind of interaction" (l. 48).

2 **Analysis** → Describing cartoons, p. 129
Analyse the cartoon and state as to whether it is a suitable illustration of the text.

3 **Comment: Choose one of the following tasks**

   a) "[…], young people are turning into socially autistic beings who can only log on and tune out." (ll. 60–62) Discuss.

   b) Today's teenagers are said to be faced with many problems former generations did not have. In your opinion, what are the most urgent problems to be dealt with in order to make young people's lives worth living? Discuss, including possible solutions.

Topic 2
Personal identities and social relationships

 i7kk55

A

B

C

Robert Herrick

Dreams

Here we are all, by day;
by night we're hurled
By dreams, each one,
into a several world.

Getting started

1 Look at the photos and collect as many words as possible that express social relationships, e.g. mother, daughter, mother-in-law, neighbour, friend etc.
→ Brainstorming, p. 140

2 Choose one person in any of the photos. Make up a complex sociogram (see photo F) which represents the social relationships this person might have. Use your imagination, but be as realistic as possible. Label the relationships using the words from task 1.

D

E

F

Ezra Pound

And the days are not full enough

And the days are not full enough
And the nights are not full enough
And life slips by like a field mouse
Not shaking the grass.

3 Work in pairs and interview each other to complete a sociogram for both of you.

4 Find words and expressions that describe the quality and closeness of relationships, e.g. an acquaintance, a friend, someone you know from school, etc. Order them from close to distant.

5 What idea of social relationships is created in the two poems?

6 Bring along a photo or a painting that expresses a special social relationship. Present your illustration in class.

Word bank

relatives • in-laws • colleagues • neighbourhood • leisure activities • to see sb. occasionally / from time to time • best friend • someone you know • partner • grandchildren • grandparents • to be related • to be popular with sb. • to be an outsider

A   Friends

 1   **Before you read**

a)   In a small group, agree on a short definition of the word "friend".

b)   In class, share your results and make a cluster with criteria of friendship.

A1.8

Friends ain't friends ...

How social media has changed the way young people form friendships

A friend is no longer necessarily a friend. The ongoing influence of social media has derailed the nature of the word's meaning, turned it into a verb, and is altering the
5   nature and the depth of our relationships with others.

In days long gone, the word friend was used to describe someone that you knew, liked and trusted. One joined to another in intimacy and affection. A person with whom you were allied to, a well-wisher who genuinely cared, a patron, a supporter, or a mate you could count on.
10   That was pre-facebook. Today, friends are more like attractive or quirky collectibles, and merely commodities to be accumulated and traded with the object of many young people being to 'friend' as many people as possible. Indeed, Wikipedia lists another meaning for friends, and that is people who are added to a list of contacts associated with a social networking website.
15   For the most part, the quality of friendships in the alternate reality that is the internet has been on the slide ever since 2004 when facebook hit the net. And the unfortunate reality is that far too many young people in particular have abandoned the traditional notion of what constitutes a friend and now immerse themselves in the currency of sheer numbers, to find an audience, boost their self-esteem, and prove
20   to others their appeal and importance.
Because many online friendships are distant affairs between people who in a lot of cases have never actually met face to face, it's easy to treat 'friends' in a much more abrupt way than you would in the offline world ... and unfriend, block and banish them at the click of a mouse.
25   In today's hyper-connected world, we know what our 'friends' are doing ... and often the exact place and time they're doing it ... if their updates and their location posts are to be fully believed.
Dr Damien Maher, a University of Technology Sydney lecturer specialising in social media, is one of many experts tracking the changing face of friendship.
30   "People have more friends and fewer deep friends. Some have more than a thousand friends and it's changed what it means to be a friend," he told Vanessa

---

³   **ongoing** – anhaltend

⁴   **to derail** – entgleisen lassen

⁸   **well-wisher** – jmd, der einem Gutes wünscht

⁸   **patron** – Gönner, Schirmherr

¹⁰   **quirky** – sonderbar

¹⁰   **collectible** – Sammlerstück

¹¹   **commodity** – Ware

¹¹   **to trade** – handeln mit

¹⁵   **alternate** – abwechselnd

¹⁶   **to be on the slide** – im Rutschen sein

¹⁷   **to abandon** – verlassen

¹⁸   **notion** – Idee

¹⁸   **to immerse oneself** – sich in etw. vertiefen

¹⁹   **sheer** – rein, lediglich

²³   **to banish** – verbannen

Stubbs of MX in May 2011. "It has a different meaning than it used to. Before the internet, a friend was a person you knew."

35 "What you put up, in photos, status updates and wall posts, can manipulate the way you represent yourself to people in the real world. So people can reveal what they choose to reveal and online is more accepting of face value," he observes. "But the connection to what is really going on in their lives can suffer."

The overwhelming trend among teenagers is that bigger is better. "Friend numbers confer status," says Dr Maher. "Having more friends is a good thing and somehow

40 means that you're a nicer person, and better to be with."

Leading social researcher Hugh Mackay made an exhaustive study on what makes us tick, investigated the 10 desires that drive us, and published the findings in a book of the same name in late 2010. He sees the key drivers in young people as the need for self-worth, self-respect, and belonging, and spoke on the topic at the

45 Young Life Australia annual Sydney banquet on 20 May 2011.

At the charity event Mr Mackay told the audience that the desire to be taken seriously was one of the big ones for young people. "Not to be seen as serious people ... that would often be frowned upon," he explained. "No, the desire to be taken seriously revolves around the desire to be noticed, to be appreciated, to be

50 acknowledged as the unique individual that we know ourselves to be."

"Generally speaking, this desire is at its most intense in teenagers," said Mr Mackay, "although it does stay with us to a diminished degree as we get older."

"But what happens if we are not taken seriously?" Mackay pondered. "What happens in young people is that if they are belittled, they are mocked, humiliated or

55 marginalised, then they can carry this as a burden, sometimes for life. So many over-compensate in other ways, to try and build themselves up."

This powerful yearning for acceptance, the quest to gain an appealing reputation, and a tribalistic sense of belonging in young people, certainly explains the ever-rising popularity of social media, where collecting as many like's as you can is the modern

60 measure of peer group status. [...]   (745 words)

35	**to reveal** – enthüllen
36	**face value** – Nennwert
39	**to confer** – gewähren
41	**what makes us tick** – was uns bewegt
48	**to be frowned upon** – Missbilligung erfahren
54	**to belittle** – herabsetzen, verniedlichen
54	**to mock sb.** – jmdn verspotten
54	**to humiliate sb.** – jmdn demütigen
55	**to marginalise sb.** – jmdn an den Rand drängen
57	**yearning** – Verlangen
58	**tribalistic** – Stammes-

2 **Comprehension**

a) In your own words, show how – according to the text – the understanding of friendship has changed since the arrival of social media.

b) Outline how the researchers Damien Maher and Hugh Mackay explain this change.

3 **Analysis** → Describing cartoons, p. 129
Describe and analyse the cartoon.

4 **Project** → see Hotspot 1, p. 35

"If you have any complaints, can you come to me before posting them on Myspace?"

B Family issues

1 Before you read

a) Work with a partner and agree on a list of ten characteristics of good parents.

b) Share your lists in class and agree on a ranking.

2 Comprehension
Summarise the passage in your own words.

The following text is a passage from "Slam", a novel by Nick Hornby. The story is about Sam, a sixteen-year-old with a passion for skateboarding. When he meets Alicia everything seems great until one moment changes their lives forever. Suddenly Sam is faced with new responsibilities he cannot escape from even though he tries to.

Nick Hornby
(English writer, born in 1957)

10 **dressing gown** – Bademantel

13 **guess** – Vermutung

17 **to be ashamed of sth.** – sich für etw. schämen

18 **kettle** – Wasserkocher

21 **to babble** – schwafeln

21 **to put sth. off** – etw. hinausschieben

27 **to screw sth. up** – *hier:* zusammenknüllen

27 **fold** – Falte

28 **crease** – Knitterfalte

30 **to smooth sth. out** – glätten

Slam

I'd told Mum I was going out after school, so I had no idea whether she was going to be in or not. I'd told her I was going round to a friend's for tea, and I'd be back around eight. If she knew I wasn't coming back straight after school, she sometimes went out for a drink with someone from work, or went round someone's house for a cup of tea.
5 I'd warned them, but Alicia's mum and dad said that seeing as it was a serious situation, they'd just come in and wait for her if she wasn't there.
Something made me ring on the doorbell, rather than just get out my key and let everybody in. I suppose I didn't think it was right to let Alicia's mum and dad in without warning Mum first. Anyway, there was no answer at first, but just as I'd got my keys out,
10 Mum came to the door in her dressing gown.
She knew something had happened straight away. I think she probably knew what that something was, as well. Alicia, her mum, her dad, four unhappy faces … Put it this way, she probably wouldn't have needed three guesses. It had to be sex or drugs, didn't it?
'Oh. Hi. I was just in the middle of …'
15 But she couldn't think what she was in the middle of, which I took to be a bad sign. I suddenly got worried about the dressing gown. Why couldn't she tell us she was having a bath? If that was what she was doing? Having a bath is nothing to be ashamed of, is it?
'Anyway. Come in. Sit down. I'll just go and put something on. Put the kettle on, Sam. Unless you'd like something stronger? We've got some wine open, I think. We don't
20 usually, but … And there might be some beer. Have we got beer, Sam?'
She was babbling. She wanted to put it off too.
'I think we're fine, thanks, Annie,' said Alicia's mum. 'Please, can we say something before you get dressed?'
'I'd rather …'
25 'Alicia's pregnant. It's Sam's, of course. And she wants to keep it.'
My mum didn't say anything. She just looked at me for a long time, and then it was like her face was a piece of paper that someone was screwing up. There were these folds and lines and creases everywhere, in places where there was never usually anything. You know how you can always tell when a piece of paper has been screwed up, no matter
30 how hard you try to smooth it out? Well, even as she was making that face, you could

3 Analysis

a) Characterise Sam and his mother as they appear in this passage.

b) Analyse the relationship between Sam and his mother.

c) Analyse the language the author uses to show the emotions Sam's mother goes through.

4 Text production → Writing an email, p. 118

a) Write an email to Sam's mother in which you comment on her behaviour in this scene.

b) Starting from line 25 ("Alicia's pregnant. It's Sam's, of course. And she wants to keep it.") write an alternative version of Sam's mother's reaction to the news of Alicia's pregnancy.

5 Projects → see Hotspots 2 and 3, p. 35

---

tell those creases would never go away, however happy she got. And then this terrible noise. I'd never see her if she ever found out I was dead, but I can't imagine the noise would be any different.

35 She stood there crying for a little while, and then Mark, her new boyfriend, came into the living room to see what was going on. So Mark explained the dressing gown. You didn't have to have any special powers to read the minds of Alicia's mum and dad. Their minds were easy to read, because they were written all over their faces and eyes. You people, I could hear her dad saying to me, even though he wasn't saying anything now, just looking. You people. Do you ever do anything else?

40 Apart from have sex? And I wanted to kill Mum, which was a coincidence, because she wanted to kill me.
'Of all the things, Sam,' Mum said after what seemed like ages and ages. 'Of all the things you could do. All the ways you could hurt me.'
'I wasn't trying to hurt you,' I said. 'Really. I didn't want to get Alicia pregnant. It was

45 the last thing I wanted to do.'
'Here's a good way of not getting someone pregnant,' said Mum. 'Don't have sex with them.'
I didn't say anything. I mean, you couldn't argue with that, could you? But her argument did mean that I could only have sex two or three times in my life, and not

50 even that many times if I decided I didn't want kids. That decision wasn't mine to make any more, though. I was having kids whether I liked it or not. One kid, anyway, unless Alicia was having twins.
'I'm going to be a grandmother,' said Mum. 'I'm four years younger than Jennifer Aniston and I'm going to be a grandmother. I'm the same age as Cameron Diaz and

55 I'm going to be a grandmother.'
Cameron Diaz was a new one. I hadn't heard her mention Cameron Diaz before.
'Yes,' said Alicia's father. 'Well. There is a great deal about this whole thing that is unfortunate. But at the moment we're more worried about Alicia's future.'
'Not Sam's?' said my mum. 'Because he had a future too.'

60 I looked at her. Had? I had a future? Where was it now? I wanted her to tell me that everything was going to be all right. I wanted her to say that she'd survived, so I could too. But she wasn't telling me that. She was telling me that I didn't have a future any more.

(880 words)

40 **coincidence** – Zufall

58 **unfortunate** – bedauernswert

C   Gender stereotypes

 **1 Stereotypes**

a) Work in groups and collect ten characteristics each for men and women. Try and leave out stereotypes and prejudices.

b) Share your lists with another group. Try to agree on ten characteristics each for men and women.

c) What then – if anything – is typical of a woman, and typical of a man? Discuss in class.

2 Before you read → Brainstorming, p. 140

a) The following text is entitled "Mütter im Berufsleben". Brainstorm ideas that you associate with this.

b) Share your ideas in class and cluster them.

p.103 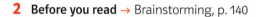 **3 Mediation** → Mediation, p. 132
Summarise the German article "Mütter im Berufsleben" in an English text.

DER TAGESSPIEGEL

RERUM · COGNOSCERE · CAUSAS

Search [   ] GO

| Home | Berlin | Politik | Sport | Kultur | Welt | Meinung |

Mütter im Berufsleben

Das bisherige Rollenmodell bleibt etabliert

Heute sind zwar mehr Mütter als früher berufstätig, dafür arbeiten aber deutlich weniger in Vollzeit. Das hat der jüngste Mikrozensus des Statistischen Bundesamts ergeben. Was bedeutet das?

5 Die Antwort lautet: Kommt ganz darauf an, was man erwartet. Wenn es etwa darum geht, eine ausgewogene Teilhabe von Frauen und Männern am Berufs- und Familienleben zu erreichen, sind die Zahlen nicht sehr ermutigend.
Zwar ist der Anteil der insgesamt erwerbstätigen Frauen von 1991 bis 2009 gestiegen, bei der Teilzeit in den vergangenen zwölf Jahren sogar um 20 Prozent.
10 Trotzdem kann man die Analysten des Statistischen Bundesamtes so verstehen, dass in Deutschland das bisherige Rollenmodell etabliert bleibt: Vater arbeitet, Mutter ist zu Hause oder arbeitet in Teilzeit.

Diese Aufteilung ist noch immer das mit Abstand häufigste Modell in diesem Land. Im Vergleich zu 1996 sind heute bei Ehepartnern und in Lebensgemein-

15 schaften Frauen viel seltener, minus 20 Prozent, in Vollzeit tätig.

Die Politik und manche Familienforscher konzentrieren sich deshalb gerne auf die Zahl der erwerbstätigen Mütter in Teilzeit, die 2009 auf ein Rekordniveau gestiegen ist. In den neuen Bundesländern hat sich die Zahl der in Teilzeit arbeitenden Mütter sogar verdoppelt. […]

20 Die größte Gruppe dieser Frauen, die in Teilzeit – oder Vollzeit – arbeitet, ist die der alleinerziehenden Mütter, danach folgen Mütter ab dem 55. Lebensjahr. Innerhalb der Teilzeitbeschäftigung steigen zudem atypische Beschäftigungsverhältnisse an: geringfügig Beschäftigte, Zeitarbeitsverhältnisse. Immer öfter wird die Frau aufgrund der ökonomischen Lage zum Arbeiten gezwungen,

25 beispielsweise weil der Mann arbeitslos wird. Arbeitsmarktforscher kommen in Studien zu dem Schluss: „In Bezug auf die Modernisierung der Geschlechterverhältnisse sind die Arbeitszeiten von Müttern und Vätern ernüchternd. Eine Umverteilung von bezahlter und unbezahlter Arbeit zwischen den Geschlechtern deutet sich bisher nicht an.“

(281 Wörter)

 4 **Listening comprehension: Miss World and women's rights go hand in hand**

3 → Listening, p. 108

Listen to the recording about Clara Belle, who as a student was strictly against beauty contests and then successfully took part in them. Draw up a table and complete it with information from the recording.

Why Clara Belle was against beauty contests in the past	Reasons that made her change her view	Beauty contests and feminism	Clara Belle's views on contests and pageants in general

5 **Analysis** → Describing cartoons, p. 129
Describe and analyse the cartoon.

6 **Giving a talk** → Presentation, p. 151
Prepare a three-minute talk on gender stereotypes in which you include the following aspects:
- male and female characteristics
- stereotypes and prejudices
- gender equality
- any other aspects you consider important

"No, this is not Mel's secretary, this is Mel."

D Volunteering

1 **Before you read** → Brainstorming, p. 140
"Ask not what your country can do for you – ask what you can do for your country."
What message was President John F. Kennedy (1917–1963; 35th President of the US)
trying to get across when he spoke these famous words?

Participate in the Tradition of Volunteering

⮑ Approximately 109 million American adults volunteer annually – that's 56 % of all adults.

⮑ Volunteers contribute an average of 3.5 hours per week – totalling 20 billion hours with an
    estimated dollar value of $225 billion.

5 ⮑ 59 % of teenagers volunteer an average of 3.5 hours per week – that's 13.3 million volunteers
    totalling 2.4 billion hours at a total value of $7.7 billion.

The nonprofit sector cannot take the place of government programs, nor can it single-handedly cure
the ills and disparities of society. But each of us can make a difference in a small way, in our own
sphere, and can find ways to help that will make our efforts worth the time and trouble we invest in them.

10 **Some of the Best Reasons to Volunteer**

Some of the best reasons to give are the ones you may not have considered – the ones that make it
worth your while to go that extra step. People who have spent time volunteering for a cause report
that they get back in satisfaction and joy more than they ever expend in inconvenience or effort –
what you get back is immeasurable. You'll also receive these benefits:

15 ⮑ Volunteering makes you feel needed.

⮑ Volunteering can lead to learning new skills.

⮑ Volunteering can help you deal with some of your personal problems.

⮑ Volunteering helps you meet new people and breaks down barriers of misunderstanding, mistrust
    and fear.

20 ⮑ Volunteering can create new contacts which may help your business or career.

It's What in the World You Can Do!

You might be thinking, "The little bit that I can do will never help much!" or "What in the world can I
do?" If you've ever spent ten minutes reading a book to a lonely child, you know that even that small
amount of compassion and attention can make a world of difference. No one person can solve the

25 world's problems, but what little you do can make your little corner of the world – or one far away from
yours – a happier, healthier, safer place to live for those who need your help. Each of us can right a
wrong, fill a plate, visit a shut-in or clean up a park – and that does make a difference for us all!

(375 words)

2 **Mediation** → Presentation, p. 151
Use the information of the Network for Good website to prepare a 3-minute talk
in German to convince young Germans to go to the US and spend time doing
voluntary work. Note down some keywords to structure your talk. Focus on what
the Network for Good can / cannot achieve and what personal advantages
volunteering offers.

---

2 **annually** – jährlich

3 **20 billion** – 20 Milliarden

4 **to estimate** – schätzen

7 **single-handedly** – im Alleingang

7 **to cure** – heilen, lindern

8 **disparity** – Ungleichheit

9 **to make sth. worth** – *hier:*
   etw. belohnen

11 **to make sth. worth one's
    while** – jmdn für etw.
    belohnen

12 **for a cause** – für eine Sache

13 **to expend in** – aufwenden
    für

13 **inconvenience** – Unannehm-
    lichkeit

14 **benefit** – Vorteil

24 **compassion** – Mitgefühl

27 **a shut-in** – jmd, der ans
    Haus gefesselt ist

Helping the elderly or disabled

Organising a game for inner-city kids

A 1.14

A poem

Compassion's heart

Compassion's ear is not too far
From us in darkest night;
It closely listens to the beat
Of hearts afraid with fright.
5 Compassion's mouth is not shut tight
When trouble hurts the soul;
Compassion speaks to souls that groan
Its purpose to console.
Compassion's head is never slow
10 To turn to meet our need;
It meets the foe that hurts us so
With urgency and speed.
Compassion's eye is never closed
To tears that stain the cheek;
15 Compassion sees the cause of tears
And gives the help we seek.
Compassion's heart is never cold
Or distant in our strife;
It beats from God's own pulse with might
20 To lift from death to life!

Taking part in political life

Clearing up after a natural disaster

5 **shut tight** – fest verschlossen
7 **to groan** – stöhnen
8 **to console** – trösten
11 **foe** – Feind
12 **urgency** – Dringlichkeit
14 **to stain** – Flecken machen
18 **strife** – Streit
19 **might** – Macht

3 What is the message of the poem? Write it down using your own words.

4 The poet uses lyrical devices such as "personification", "metaphor" and "contrasts". Try to identify them in the poem. → Dealing with poetry, p. 113

5 Together with a partner, think of ways besides volunteering in which individuals can contribute to the society in which they live. You can use the photos on this page as a starting point. Make a diagram showing how the individual and society interact in terms of rights and responsibilities.

E Generation Me?

1 **Before you read**

a) Look at the picture. Describe and analyse what you see.

b) With the help of the picture, try to predict what the text is about.

A 1.15

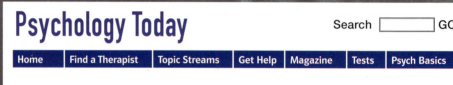

Psychology Today

Search [   ] GO

| Home | Find a Therapist | Topic Streams | Get Help | Magazine | Tests | Psych Basics |

Are today's youth even more self-absorbed (and less caring) than generations before?

Have kids today stopped caring about others?

Earlier this week, Sara Konrath, a researcher at the University of Michigan Institute for Social Research, released her results of a study analyzing and comparing empathy among college students over the last 30 years. The results? The "biggest drop in empathy" in recent history. She writes, "College kids today are about 40 percent lower in empathy than their counterparts of 20 or 30 years ago."

In related survey research, psychologist Jean Twenge has labeled the current generation of young people the "iGeneration," or "Generation Me". In her books she describes how young people today "take it for granted that the self comes first," and has labeled this time a "narcissism epidemic", stating that we are "living in the age of entitlement". Konrath and O'Brien link the self-absorption and lack of empathy together, calling the current generation "one of the most self-centered, narcissistic, competitive,

¹ **self-absorbed** – sehr mit sich selbst beschäftigt

⁵ **to release** – *hier:* veröffentlichen

⁶ **empathy** – Empathie, Mitgefühl

⁹ **counterpart** – Gegenstück

²² **narcissism epidemic** – *etwa:* Epidemie von Selbstverliebtheit

²⁴ **entitlement** – Anspruch

not surprising that this growing emphasis on the self is accompanied by a corresponding devaluing of others."

35 There are some who argue that this description fits most teens and young adults and is appropriate to some degree for everyone in this developmental phase of life. However, both researchers compare similarly aged kids from other generations and the difference is striking.

This difference raises the question of why? Researchers Konrath and
40 O'Brien hazard a few guesses, most related to the increase in exposure to and use of media. For example, many in this current generation have had repeated lifetime exposure to violent video games and films, and there is a growing body of research suggesting that violent video games (and perhaps films) are a cause of increased aggressive
45 behavior, thoughts, and feelings, and a decrease in empathy and prosocial behavior across both gender and culture. Additionally, the researchers surmise that the ease of having (and ignoring or dumping) online "friends" may make it easy to tune out when they don't feel like responding to the distress of others, and may carry over offline as
50 well. They also add that the inflated expectations of success fueled by "reality shows" create a social environment that encourages self-focus and works against slowing down and listening to someone who needs a bit of sympathy.

Obviously, any statements about an entire generation are not true
55 of every person in that generation. Clearly there are young people today who are deeply empathic and caring. But the general trends and statistics are alarming, and it would behoove those of us in a position to influence today's youth to pay attention and be proactive about it while we can. Paying attention to the forces that influence
60 children and young people so that they can grow up to be empathic is not only better for them, but ultimately better for us all.

(482 words)

---

34 **to devalue** – abwerten
36 **appropriate** – angemessen
41 **exposure to** – Ausgesetztsein
47 **gender** – Geschlecht
48 **to surmise** – mutmaßen
48 **ease** – Bequemlichkeit, Leichtigkeit
57 **empathic** – einfühlsam
58 **to behoove** (old) – erforderlich sein

---

2 Comprehension

a) In your own words, summarise what the studies mentioned in the article reveal about today's youth.

b) Outline the influence of the media on teenagers today as mentioned in the text.

3 Analysis → Text analysis, p. 115
Analyse the article in detail and point out where the author includes her personal opinion about today's youth as well.

4 Comment → Writing a comment, p. 116
Write a letter to the author commenting on the article and its findings. Add personal experience to support your ideas.

Reported speech

→ Grammar, p. 169

a) Your group publishes a school magazine and wants to print an interview with Peggy Olsen, an American family counsellor. Here are the questions you ask:
  1. How did you become a family counsellor?
  2. What do you like about your job?
  3. What kind of people do you work with?
  4. Do you mostly work from the office, or do you have to travel a lot?
  5. What are the most common problems you deal with?
  6. Have you ever visited a counsellor yourself?
  7. Why do so many families need to see a counsellor these days?
  8. Will you always work in this job?
  9. Can you give us some tips on how to lead a happy family life?
  10. What one piece of advice would you give to all families?

Later Ms Olsen tells her trainee about the interview for your magazine. Write down her exact words. Use different introductory verbs and start like this:
"Today some students from a German school magazine questioned me about being a family counsellor. They wanted to know how I became a family counsellor and asked me … "

b) The following statements are already in reported speech. Put them back into direct speech. Pay attention to whether it is a statement or a question.
  1. The woman's friend asked her where she had met her husband.
  2. The woman's friend wanted to know if they had liked each other straight away.
  3. The woman said that they had hit it off right away.
  4. My friend asked me whether or not he should open a Facebook account.
  5. I said that I was surprised he did not already have one.
  6. He answered that he had been anti-Facebook for a long time but now he realised that it was the only way to keep in touch with his friends in other parts of the country.
  7. My mother mentioned that she had been having problems with her neighbours.
  8. She told me that they had been playing loud music.
  9. I suggested that she try and talk to them before she called the police.
  10. My mother said she would discuss it with my father before she made a decision.

1 **Project: Parents and children** → Presentation, p. 151
Bring along photos or paintings that deal with the relationship of parents and children. Avoid choosing only photos / paintings from today; older ones can be telling, too. Write a short text for each photo / painting which describes what can be seen and why you have chosen this photo / painting. Arrange your photos / paintings
- either in a gallery walk and ask other students from your school to take this walk
- or in a slide show which you accompany with suitable music.

2 **Research project: Family types** → Internet research, p. 147

a) Search the web for information about family types and household organisations in an English-speaking country of your choice. Compare this information with facts about Germany. Prepare a presentation in which you outline similarities and differences between these two countries.

b) Search the web for information about family types in history in either of the following English-speaking countries: USA, England, Australia. Compare this information with facts about these countries today. Present the developments you have identified in diagrams to your class.

c) Analyse the diagram about household sizes in Germany in 2030. Draw up similar diagrams for either of the following English-speaking countries: USA, England, Australia.

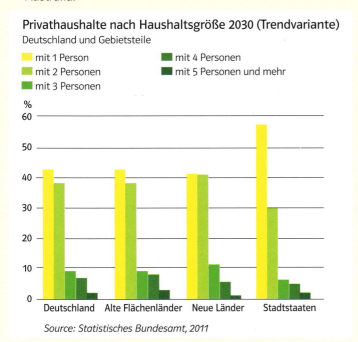

Source: Statistisches Bundesamt, 2011

3 **Project: Families in literature** → Projects and group work, p. 148
Make a list of a) father figures and b) mother figures in any of the novels or short stories you have read. In class, agree on a set of criteria which can be used to analyse the characters (i.e. loving, egoistic, cold, warm-hearted, tired, ambitious, etc.). Carry out an analysis of these characters. Do you find any gender specific results? Are there any clichés to be found? Do the results you have found out surprise you? Why (not)?

A 1.18

1	**homophobia** – Homophobie
2	**to stigmatise** – brand-marken
3	**peers** – Gleichaltrige
4	**stigma** – Makel
4	**to melt away** – (fig) weg-schmelzen
6	**prejudice** – Vorurteil
9	**to redefine** – neu definieren, neu festlegen
9	**masculinity** – Männlichkeit
9	**heterosexuality** – Hetero-sexualität
10	**to hold sth. in high esteem** – von etw. eine hohe Meinung haben
13	**to rubbish sth.** – runter-machen
14	**unrecognisable** – unerkenn-bar
20	**to come out** – sich outen
23	**to dispel** – verbannen
25	**LGBT (lesbian, gay, bisexual and transgender)** – Lesben, Schwule, Bisexuelle und Transsexuelle
26	**straight** – hier: hetero-sexuell
27	**peculiar** – eigenartig
32	**to ring true** – glaubhaft klingen
33	**charity** – Wohlfahrtseinrich-tung
34	**to bully** – mobben
38	**to eradicate** – beseitigen
38	**to be embedded** – tief verwurzelt sein
39	**bogus** – falsch
39	**hideous** – abscheulich

theguardian

News | Sport | Comment | Culture | Business | Money | Life&Style | Travel | Environment

Comment is free ❭ **Society** ❭   Search [   ] GO

Homophobia is declining in schools, study claims

Teenagers no longer stigmatise being gay, argues Brunel University sociologist Mark McCormack. Teenagers face far less homophobia among their peers than ever before because the stigma of being gay is melting away in secondary schools, according to a new
5 book.

The anti-gay prejudices of the 80s and early 90s are disappearing, claims Mark McCormack, a sociologist at Brunel University. McCormack spent six months in three schools in the same UK town to study attitudes of 16- to 18-year-olds. In his book, *The Declining Significance of Homophobia: How Teenage Boys are Redefining Masculinity and Heterosexuality*, he says
10 that, for this age group, pro-gay attitudes are held in high esteem and homophobia is as unacceptable as racism. He also suggests that the phrase "so gay", used to rubbish things, is unrecognisable to
15 teens as homophobic.

"A lot of prejudice is based on stigma," he added, "and actually the stigma around being gay has dropped off.
20 The coming-out narrative is changing too, with parents being OK." The internet had helped to dispel the isolation young gay people have felt in the past, he said. [...]

McCormack found teenagers to be open about their sexuality. "It's had a huge impact on
25 the LGBT kids: they are happy, out and proud at school. That's better for gay kids and better for straight kids, too."

But he says the change in attitude may well be peculiar to this age group: "I'm not saying the battle is over against homophobia, but it's getting better."

"These young people see homophobia as wrong. Guys used to prove they were straight by
30 being homophobic. Now, when young guys want to show they're straight, they do it in a more positive way by joking about being gay."

McCormack's findings do not ring true with everyone. "It's definitely not our experience, I'm afraid," said Jess Wood of youth support charity Allsorts. Its 2010 survey of Brighton schools found that 16% of bullied children in primary and 23% in secondary schools
35 reported that the bullying was homophobic in nature. Half of lesbian, bisexual, gay or transgender teens reported homophobic bullying at school or college.

"It remains the second-highest reason children give for bullying," said Allsorts' director, Jess Wood. "I do think to try and eradicate the word 'gay' is a waste of time; it's embedded in the language, but it's a bogus argument to suggest it's anything other than hideous for
40 gay people to hear the negative associations of the word."

Ruth Hunt of Stonewall UK also urged caution. "I think it matches what we know in that some schools which are good on this are very, very good. But plenty are not. Although we are seeing shifts in the way schools think about how boys should be seen to behave, we still see many schools with significant problems. We still have schools who tell us they
45 have no gay pupils."

"As for the abuse of the word 'gay', it's dangerous to be dismissive by using the argument, 'Oh the kids think it's fine and so it's fine'. That doesn't stand up. If the word is being used to mean stupid, then how does it make a young gay person feel? It makes them feel stupid. It's an inevitable connection in their minds."

50 ## ONE BOY'S STORY

Lee, 16, says that his life at school has improved since he came out as gay aged 14, but he still suffers homophobic bullying. "Sometimes it feels a bit weird because gay really means rubbish. I don't really like being called gay, I say 'That's so gay' myself. Yes, I get bullied. It's getting better. But I get called names every single day and I have done since
55 I was at primary school. I don't care anymore. Well, that's not true. I've cried about it a lot. I don't really like walking by myself anywhere. I've been kicked a few times and punched. I try to be myself at school and I've got friends who'll stick up for me, but I wish I could turn it off. I dropped out of one GCSE class because I couldn't take the abuse from one boy. The teacher couldn't see it, and I didn't see why I had to spell it out to him. They don't take
60 homophobia seriously. There's a poster up in our school, one of those 'Some people are gay, get over it' ones. It feels like it's me that's expected to get over it."   (744 words)

---

41 **to urge** – zur Vorsicht mahnen
41 **to match** – übereinstimmen
43 **shift** – Veränderung
46 **abuse** – Missbrauch
46 **to be dismissive** – *hier:* desinteressiert sein
49 **inevitable** – unvermeidlich
52 **weird** – eigenartig, sonderbar
56 **to punch** – schlagen
57 **to stick up for sb.** – für jemanden eintreten
58 **to drop out of sth.** – aus etw. aussteigen
59 **to spell sth. out** – etw. klarmachen

---

1 **Comprehension**

a) Outline how, according to Mark McCormack, attitudes towards homosexuality have changed over the last 30 years.

b) Explain why Jess Wood and Ruth Hunt believe there is still room for improvement.

2 **Analysis** → Describing diagrams, p. 130

a) Examine Lee's feelings about being a young homosexual male.

b) Analyse the statistic from the US and relate it to the text.

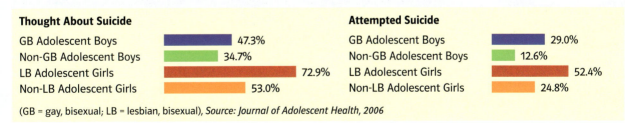

Thought About Suicide
GB Adolescent Boys — 47.3%
Non-GB Adolescent Boys — 34.7%
LB Adolescent Girls — 72.9%
Non-LB Adolescent Girls — 53.0%

Attempted Suicide
GB Adolescent Boys — 29.0%
Non-GB Adolescent Boys — 12.6%
LB Adolescent Girls — 52.4%
Non-LB Adolescent Girls — 24.8%

(GB = gay, bisexual; LB = lesbian, bisexual), *Source: Journal of Adolescent Health, 2006*

3 **Comment**

"I'm not saying the battle is over against homophobia, but it's getting better."
(ll. 27–28) Thinking about your own school, do you agree with the statement?

Topic 3
Progress and sustainability

Getting started

1 Look at the pictures and write down questions for each picture that relate to the concepts progress, sustainability and responsibility, e.g. "Which sources of alternative energy are there?" for picture C. Collect your questions on the board and try to answer as many as you can in class. Are there any questions which nobody can answer? → Describing pictures, p. 128

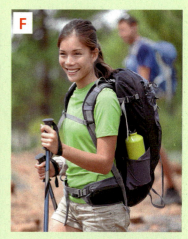

2 Magazine photos

a) Work with a partner and choose one picture you find most impressive. Imagine the picture has been chosen for the front page of a magazine. What type of magazine would it be?

b) Create a title for the picture and write a short caption. Present your results in class.

3 Research project → see Hotspot 1, p. 51

Word bank

wind energy • solar panel • renewable energies • nuclear power • nuclear waste • hazardous • recycling • GM food • data protection • hacking • privacy • free-range food • battery farm

A Climate change

1 Before you read → Brainstorming, p. 140

What do you know about climate change? Make a list of changes and their possible consequences. Present your list in class and discuss it.

2 Collect information from the text in note form under the following headings.

> Climate change • Geographical changes • Changes in temperature • Changes in atmosphere • Other predictions for the future

Vorhersagen

Certainties and uncertainties of climate change

The Earth's climate has varied in the past over many different timescales. Right now we are in an interglacial, a relatively mild period between ice ages. But humans are 5 changing the climate system.

The natural greenhouse effect
Some gases in our atmosphere, for example carbon dioxide, methane, nitrous oxide, and especially water vapour, trap heat emitted 10 from the Earth's surface, keeping the planet about 30 °C warmer than it would otherwise be. This is the 'natural greenhouse effect' and is well understood scientifically.
Human activities, especially burning fossil 15 fuels like coal and oil, have increased the level of these greenhouse gases in our atmosphere. This is throwing the climate system out of balance.
Climate change is the most important 20 environmental issue we face this century. Every one of the hottest 15 years on record has occurred since 1980 – the five hottest since 1997. [...]

Widely accepted facts
25 • Carbon dioxide and nitrous oxide levels are rising, primarily because of human activities connected with burning fossil fuels.
• Methane levels in the atmosphere more than doubled in the last century. Levels are 30 still rising, though the rise has slowed down.
• Carbon dioxide is responsible for 60 % of human-induced greenhouse warming, methane 20 %, and nitrous oxide and other gases 20 %.

35 • Carbon dioxide levels in the atmosphere have increased from about 280 parts per million (ppm) in the mid 18th century – the start of the industrial revolution – to around 379 ppm today. You would need to 40 go back millions of years to find another time when carbon dioxide was at such high levels in the atmosphere.
• Nitrous oxide levels are rising by about 0.25 % each year.
45 • Over the last century, the average global surface temperature rose by around 0.7 °C. Continents in the northern hemisphere have warmed the most.
• 1998 was the warmest year since 1860, 50 the earliest year for which a precise global estimate is possible. 2002 and 2003 tie for second place.
• The majority of the world's mountain glaciers are retreating and Arctic sea-ice 55 appears to be reducing in both extent and thickness.
• Global sea levels have risen 10 – 20 cm over the past 100 years. [...]

Global consequences
60 The IPCC has developed a number of scenarios for future greenhouse gas emissions, and has explored these with a range of climate models. They show that:

• Carbon dioxide levels are likely to at 65 least double from pre-industrial levels by the end of this century. When other factors are added, such as increased water vapour, the estimated average global temperature

8 **carbon dioxide** – Kohlendioxyd

8 **methane** – Methan

8 **nitrous oxide** – Stickoxid, Lachgas

9 **vapour** – Dampf

9 **to trap sth.** – etw. auffangen

9 **to emit** – ausstoßen

14 **fossil fuel** – fossiler Brennstoff

20 **issue** – Thema

32 **human-induced** – von Menschen erzeugt

51 **estimate** – Schätzung

51 **to tie for second place** – zusammen den 2. Platz belegen

54 **glacier** – Gletscher

54 **to retreat** – zurückgehen

55 **extent** – Ausmaß

60 **IPCC (International Panel on Climate Change)** – Internationaler Klimarat

65 **pre-industrial** – vorindustriell

occure = auftreten, vorkommen

3 **Paraphrasing** → Guessing new words, p. 142

With a partner, take turns to paraphrase one of the German terms below in English. See if your partner can guess the English term. (The English terms can be found in the text.)

> fossile Brennstoffe • Durchschnittstemperatur der Erdoberfläche • Treibhausgase • beispiellos, noch nie dagewesen • Eisschicht • Überschwemmungsgefahr • Klimawandel

4 **Research project** → see Hotspot 2, p. 51

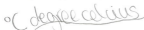
°C degree celsius

rise by 2100 is between 1.5 – 5.8 °C. Though
70 new evidence from climateprediction.net
suggests the increase could be as high as
11 °C.
• This rate of warming will be much higher
than experienced during the 20th century
75 and is probably unprecedented in the last
10,000 years.
• Global sea level is likely to rise by 10 – 90 cm
over this century. Low-lying coasts will flood,
affecting many human settlements, including
80 some major cities. Some habitats will be lost.
• If temperatures over Greenland increase
by more than about 3 °C – which appears
likely based on current model predictions –
the ice sheet there will eventually disappear
85 altogether, raising global sea level by several
metres over a period of 1,000 years or more.
• Some regions and seasons will become
wetter, others drier. Summer droughts
are likely to intensify in the interiors of
90 continents. Tropical cyclones may become
more severe. Intense cold weather will
become less frequent.
• Many areas will experience more extremely
hot weather, like the unprecedented heat
95 in Europe in 2003, and heavier rain, with an
increased risk of flooding.
• Food production in mid-latitudes could
benefit if climate change is not too severe.
However, in tropical and sub-tropical regions,
100 the risk of famine is likely to increase.
• Water availability will become even more
of a problem for people in regions where it is
already scarce, particularly in the sub-tropics.
• The world's vegetation zones will undergo
105 major changes. In particular, the boundaries

between grasslands, forests and scrublands
may shift.
• The temperature, flow and level in
freshwater systems will change, affecting
110 biodiversity, water supplies and water quality.
• Human and animal diseases, such as
malaria, will probably spread to new areas,
and deaths related to heat stress are
predicted to increase.
115 • 'Environmental migration' is predicted as
many people move from high flood risk areas
or arid regions. This could drive conflicts and
increase health problems.   (763 words)

75 **unprecedented** – beispiellos

80 **habitat** – natürlicher Lebensraum

88 **drought** – Dürre

97 **in mid-latitudes** – in mittleren Breitengraden gelegen

103 **scarce** – knapp

105 **boundary** – Grenze

106 **scrubland** – Buschland

107 **to shift** – sich verschieben

110 **biodiversity** – Artenvielfalt

117 **arid** – ausgedörrt

B Alternative energy

1 Before you read
→ Describing diagrams, p. 130
Describe and interpret the chart.

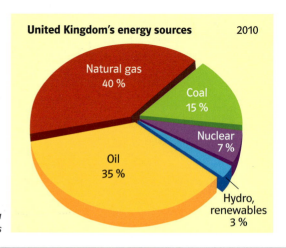

United Kingdom's energy sources 2010

Natural gas 40 %
Coal 15 %
Nuclear 7 %
Oil 35 %
Hydro, renewables 3 %

Source: Federal Coordinator, Alaska Natural Gas Transportation Projects

theguardian

Britain could be running on 100% renewable energy by 2050

It's ambitious but doable and we will need significant change to our energy systems, says Good Energy CEO

Last week the Committee on Climate Change
5 announced an ambitious target for the UK to reduce emissions by 60% by 2030 – which would require the complete transformation of the UK electricity market. This, it said, would ensure we meet our binding 2050 target of
10 reducing carbon emissions by 80% from a 1990 baseline figure.

Good Energy welcomes the scale of the CCC's ambition – we believe that by turning the energy market upside down the country
15 can exceed these targets, and become 100% renewable by 2050.

We'll need a new approach to how we heat our homes; how we travel; and how we fuel industry. Moving away from oil and gas to
20 increased electrification is the answer. This will push electricity demands to at least double current levels, and meeting this larger demand from renewable sources will be a necessity.

For many generations most of our energy has
25 come from large, centralised fossil-fuelled power stations – not just bad for climate change but for our energy security as we have to import increasingly more fuel. With more than one-third of our current generation capacity set
30 for retirement over the next two decades the UK energy of tomorrow needs to be drastically different from the energy of today – and we need to start making those changes now.

The answer is on our doorstep: renewable
35 energy. With our abundant natural resources the UK has the potential to lead a renewable energy revolution. As the windiest country in Europe, and with over 11,000 miles of coastline, we have instant access to an Aladdin's cave of
40 renewable resources. Renewable resources which are not only abundant, but free.

Good Energy has mapped out a pathway to a 100% renewable future which involves changes to UK energy at every stage of the
45 process, from grid management to investment, and from R&D to transport.

One of the fundamental changes required is managing output; supply must meet demand at all times. Because renewable electricity comes
50 from nature's abundant resources – wind, water and the sun – its generation isn't always predictable. The current systems require massive improvements in how to forecast, store and manage renewable power, and how

1 **ambitious** – ehrgeizig
1 **doable** – machbar
9 **binding** – bindend
11 **baseline figure** – Ausgangs-wert
12 **scale** – Ausmaß, Umfang
15 **to exceed** – übertreffen
35 **abundant** – reichlich
39 **Aladdin's cave** – Fundgrube
45 **grid** – Stromnetz
46 **R&D (Research and Development)** – Forschung und Entwicklung
48 **to meet demand** – die Nachfrage decken

55 to back it up. To secure this we will need a highly dynamic and interconnected European electricity grid.

In our model, wind will provide more than half of our electricity – with offshore turbines 60 generating most of our power from an army of over 20,000 turbines. This will require a total overhaul of our planning system so that Nimby's can no longer stand in the way of progress.

65 Despite the UK having one of the best tidal, wind and wave resources on Earth, a lack of investment has stunted the growth of an emerging technology which has the capability of becoming a world-leading one. Fixing it 70 either requires the government to underwrite the R&D risks or introducing such good incentives that the private sector will take them on board. […]

Transport will need to move away from 75 combustion; petrol and diesel-fuelled cars will be a thing of the past. Electric vehicles, charged by renewables, will need to act as

80 local capacitors through distributed energy systems; providing energy storage for the electricity network – with the potential to sell their excess stored energy back to the grid when demand outstrips local generation.

We will also require a much more intelligent approach to how we use electricity; through 85 encouraging a shift in demand to meet generation. A smarter grid will be needed – for example microchips controlling our fridges and washing machines so they switch on when the local wind farm is generating excess 90 energy.

We also need to change how energy is used in the UK – and individuals need to participate. For too long we have taken for granted that power is available at a low price whenever we 95 want it – at the flick of a switch! Changing our approach to how we use and when we use energy can not only reduce our overall energy consumption but also its carbon content. […]

It won't be easy, but a 100% renewable future 100 by 2050 is within our reach.   (723 words)

62 **overhaul** – Überarbeitung
63 **Nimby** (not in my backyard) – Person, die sich gegen umstrittene Bauvorhaben in der eigenen Nachbarschaft stellt, aber nichts dagegen hat, wenn diese woanders realisiert werden
67 **to stunt** – hemmen
72 **incentive** – Anreiz
75 **combustion** – (Treibstoff) Verbrennung
78 **capacitor** – Kondensator
81 **excess** – überschüssig
82 **to outstrip** – übersteigen
93 **to take for granted** – als selbstverständlich hinnehmen

2 Comprehension

a) What information can you find in the text about the following numbers:

> 60% • 80% • 100% • 1990 • 2030 • 2050 • 11,000 • 20,000

b) Summarise the new approaches and changes which are required by Britain to be able to run on renewable energy.

3 **Listening comprehension: Ten tips to prevent climate change** → Listening, p. 108
The earth's climate is changing and the effects are worrying. What can we do to stop this?

a) Before you listen, which 5 tips would you give to your friends and family to help prevent climate change?

b) Here are ten tips on small things that help to prevent climate change – every day! Listen to the tips and take notes.

c) Compare your tips with the ones you have just heard and discuss the similarities/ differences. Which of them do you find the most/least sensible and practical? Give reasons.

4 **Comment** → Writing a comment, p. 116
"We'll need a new approach to how we […] travel." (ll. 17–18) Write a newspaper article in which you outline arguments for and against mass tourism, which has become an important branch of industry in western consumer societies.

5 **Project** → see Hotspot 3, p. 51

C   Saving the planet

1   **Before you read**

Read the title of the novel extract. What could the novel be about? In your opinion, what makes someone a "friend of the earth"? Discuss with a partner.

2   **Comprehension** → Understanding fictional texts, p. 111

a)   In your own words outline Ty's environmental sins.

b)   Describe how Ty's attitude and behaviour change.

The story in the novel "A Friend of the Earth" by T. C. Boyle takes place in the 1990s and in 2025. The following extract is set in the future and told from the protagonist Ty's perspective.

T.C. Boyle
(American writer, born in 1948)

7   **to propose** – vorschlagen

8   **precious little** – reichlich wenig

9   **to preach** – predigen

15   **to commune** – kommunizieren

16   **squirrel** – Eichhörnchen

16   **muskrat** – Bisamratte

16   **fern bar** – schicke Bar

17   **dimly** – trübe

18   **periphery** – Randbereich

18   **consciousness** – Bewusstsein

18   **abused** – missbraucht

25   **fur** – Pelz

25   **to radiate** – ausstrahlen

25   **slavish** – sklavisch

26   **ancient** – antik

A Friend of the Earth

Mexico City, São Paolo, Shanghai, Buenos Aires, Seoul, Tokyo, Dhaka, Cairo, Calcutta, Reykjavik, Caracas, Lagos, Guadalajara, Greater Nome, Sakhalinsky, Nanking, Helsinki – all bigger than New York now. Forty-six million in Mexico City. Forty in São Paolo. New York doesn't even rank in the top twenty. And how does
5   that make me feel? Old. As if I've outlived my time – and everybody else's. Because the correction is under way – has been under way for some time now. Let's eat each other, that's what I propose – my arm tonight and yours tomorrow – because there's precious little of anything else left. Ecology. What a joke.

    I'm not preaching. I'm not going to preach. It's too late for that, and besides
10   which, preaching never did anybody any good anyway. Let me say this, though, for the record – for the better part of my life I was a criminal. Just like you. I lived in the suburbs in a three-thousand-square-foot house with redwood siding and oak floors and an oil burner the size of Texas, drove a classic 1966 Mustang for sport and a Jeep Laredo (red, black leather interior) to take me up to the Adirondacks so I could
15   heft my three-hundred-twenty-dollar Eddie Bauer backpack and commune with the squirrels, muskrats and fishers. I went to the gym. Drank in fern bars. Bought shoes, jackets, sweaters and hair-care products. I guess I was dimly aware – way out there on the periphery of my consciousness – of what I was doing to the poor abused corpus of old mother earth, and I did recycle (when I got around to it, which was
20   maybe twice a year), and I thought a lot about packaging. I wore a sweater in the house in winter to conserve energy and turn the flame down on global warming, and still burned fuel and more fuel, and the trash I generated plugged its own hole in the landfill like a permanent filling in a rotten tooth.

    Worse, I accumulated things. They seemed to stick to me, like filings to a magnet,
25   a whole polarized fur of objects radiating from my fingertips in slavish attraction. Paper clips, pins, plastic bags, ancient amplifiers, rusted-out cooking grills. Clothes, books, records, CDs. Cookware, Ginzu knives, food processors, popcorn poppers, coffeemakers, my dead father's overcoats and my dead mother's shoes. I kept a

)4 △ **3** **Analysis** → Text analysis, p. 115

a) Give examples of the author's use of direct address in the text and explain what effect it has on the reader.

b) Analyse the tone of the text. Point out examples of sarcasm, simile and word choice, and say how they influence the tone.

4 **Comment** → Writing a comment, p. 116
"Because to be a friend of the earth, you have to be an enemy of the people."
(ll. 57–58) Do you agree or disagree with this statement? Write a comment.

5 **Research project** → see Hotspot 4, p. 51

second Mustang, graffitied with rust, out behind the garage, on blocks. There were
30 chairs in the attic that hadn't been warmed by a pair of buttocks in fifty years, trunks of neatly folded shorts and polo shirts I hadn't worn since I was five.

I drove fast, always in a hurry, and stuffed the glove box so full of tickets it looked like a napkin dispenser in a restaurant. I dated (women, whole thundering herds of them, looking – in vain – for another Jane). I parented. Cooked. Cleaned.
35 Managed my dead father's crumbling empire – you've heard of him, Sy Tierwater, developer of tract homes in Westchester and Dutchess Counties? – and paid bills and collected rents and squeezed down the window of my car to add my share of Kleenex, ice-cream sticks and cigarette wrappers to the debris along the streaming sides of the blacktop roads.

40 Want more? I drank wine, spent money, spoiled my daughter and watched her accumulate things in her turn. And just like you – if you live in the Western world, and I have to assume you do, or how else would you be reading this? – I caused approximately two hundred fifty times the damage to the environment of this tattered, bleeding planet as a Bangladeshi or Balinese, and they do their share,
45 believe me. Or did. But I don't want to get into that.

Let's just say I saw the light – with the help of a good nudge from Andrea, Teo (may he rot in hell or interplanetary space or wherever) and all the other hard chargers down at Earth Forever! Forces were put in motion, gears began to grind. I sold the house, the cars, the decrepit shopping center my father left me, my wind
50 surfer and Adirondack chair and my complete set of bootleg Dylan tapes, all the detritus left behind by the slow-rolling glacier of my old life, my criminal life, the life I led before I became a friend of the earth. Friendship. That's what got me into movement and that's what pushed me way out there on the naked edge of nothing, beyond sense or reason, or even hope. Friendship for the earth. For the trees and
55 shrubs and the native grasses and the antelope on the plain and the kangaroo rats in the desert and everything else that lives and breathes under the sun.

Except people, that is. Because to be a friend of the earth, you have to be an enemy of the people. (800 words)

Line	Word	Translation
29	**rust**	– Rost
32	**glove box**	– Handschuhfach
33	**napkin dispenser**	– Serviettenhalter
34	**in vain**	– umsonst
34	**to parent**	– erziehen
36	**tract home**	– Reihenhaus
38	**debris**	– Trümmer
40	**to spoil**	– verwöhnen
43	**approximately**	– ungefähr
44	**tattered**	– zerfetzt
46	**nudge**	– Stoß, Stups
48	**gear**	– Zahnrad
49	**decrepit**	– baufällig
50	**bootleg**	– Raub-
51	**detritus**	– Müll
51	**glacier**	– Gletscher
55	**shrub**	– Busch
58	**enemy**	– Feind

D   GM and designer food

1   **Before you read**

a)   Do you read food labels that inform about a product's ingredients? Why (not)? Which information are you most interested in?

b)   Do you think food containing GM ingredients should be labeled? Why (not)?

2   **genetically modified (GM)** – gentechnisch verändert
3   **to insert** – einsetzen
6   **to breed** – vermehren
8   **desired** – gewünscht
8   **traits** – Eigenschaften
9   **breeding** – Züchtung
10   **fickle** – unbeständig
14   **attempt** – Versuch
16   **pronounced** – ausgeprägt
21   **vice versa** – andersherum
28   **purpose** – Zweck, Absicht

Facts on GM food

Genetically engineered or genetically modified (GM) foods have had foreign genes inserted into their genetic codes. For
5   thousands of years, farmers have bred plants as well as animals in order to select and pass on desired traits. Selective breeding, however, depends
10   on fickle nature to produce the desired gene. Only then could humans breed animals or produce plants containing that gene in an attempt to make
15   the related characteristics more common or more pronounced. Genetic engineering speeds up this process by moving desired genes from one plant
20   into another – or even from an animal to a plant or vice versa. A more general term is **genetically modified organism (GMO)**, which is applied to all genetically
25   engineered plants, animals or microbes. For example, bacteria were modified to produce insulin for medical purposes as soon as 1978.   (136 words)

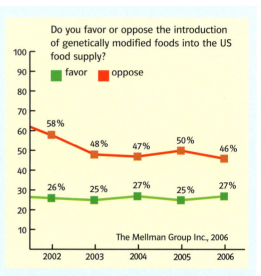

Do you favor or oppose the introduction of genetically modified foods into the US food supply?

- favor
- oppose

58%   48%   47%   50%   46%
26%   25%   27%   25%   27%

The Mellman Group Inc., 2006

Support for GM food across EU

%	1996	1999	2002	2005
Spain	80	70	74	74
United Kingdom	67	47	63	48
Germany	56	49	48	30
Greece	49	19	24	12

Eurobarometer survey on biotechnology, 2005

p.104   **2**   **Analysis** → Describing diagrams, p. 130
Look at the statistics above. Write a short text examining the attitudes towards GM food in Europe and comparing them to the attitudes of the US population.

Facts on Nanotechnology

Nanotechnology is a diverse branch of research and engineering working on the scale of atoms and molecules between 1 and 1000 nano-metres. (1 nano-metre (nm) is one billionth (10^{-9}) of a metre). Nanotechnology is employed to make ultra-small tools and then build powerful mini-machines smaller than a
5 pinhead. A fly could carry a camera on its back!

Nanoparticles are so small that they can pass boundaries within the body, which poses potential safety risks.

Programmable drinks

How could such a beverage be made?

10 **Step 1** Select a colourless, flavourless drink from the refrigerator. Press buttons to select chosen drink and any required additives.

Step 2 Microwaves activate the preprogrammed nanocapsules (milk, vitamin
15 C, caffeine). See the drink change visibly to whisky. Capsules containing unwanted flavour and additives remain inert.

Step 3 As the drink enters the mouth, the particles containing caffeine dissolve at the
20 back of the throat for an instant hit.

Step 4 Capsules containing vitamin C pass unharmed through the stomach and dissolve in the large intestine, passing straight into the bloodstream.

25 **Step 5** All remaining unused capsules pass harmlessly through the body and are excreted.

(191 words)

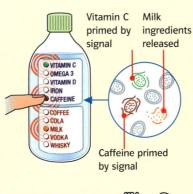

Vitamin C primed by signal

Milk ingredients released

Caffeine primed by signal

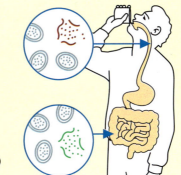

1 **diverse** – breitgefächert
1 **branch** – Sektor
5 **pinhead** – Nadelkopf
7 **to pose a risk** – ein Risiko darstellen
  ingredient – Zutat
  to release – entlassen
9 **beverage** – Getränk
12 **additive** – Zusatzstoff
17 **inert** – träge, inaktiv
19 **to dissolve** – auflösen
20 **throat** – Hals
20 **instant** – sofort
22 **unharmed** – unbeschädigt
23 **large intestine** – Dickdarm
26 **to excrete** – absondern, ausscheiden

3 Comprehension
Explain in your own words how programmable drinks might be produced, using the information and the pictures above.

4 Panel discussion → Discussions, p. 133

a) Prepare a panel discussion about the pros and cons of GM and designer food. Before you start, decide on roles which should be included in your discussion.

b) Collect arguments to prepare for the roles.

c) Make notes of the best arguments for both sides that come up in your discussion.

5 Project → see Hotspot 5, p. 51

E   Eco-tourism

1   **Before you read**

a) Look at the title of the text. What do you think it means to "travel green"? Make some notes.

b) Compare your ideas with a partner. What do you agree on?

c) Share your results with another pair and report back to the class.

d) In the same group, find an opposite for the term "green travel".

1   **to bandy sth. about** – mit etw. um sich werfen

3   **to compile** – zusammenstellen

3   **outstanding** – herausragend

12   **tad** – kleine Menge

23   **bracket** – *hier:* Klasse

23   **unimaginably** – unvorstellbar

26   **to demand** – verlangen

26   **to eschew** – unterlassen

28   **to assess** – beurteilen, bewerten

theguardian

News | Sport | Comment | Culture | Business | Money | Life&Style | Travel | Environment

Comment is free ⟩ Society   Search [   ] GO

What it means to travel green

The word "eco" is bandied about so much, it's difficult to tell what's authentic and what's not. So we've done the hard work for you, compiling a list of 75 outstanding green travel companies.

Nearly 40 years ago I took a three-day train ride from London to Istanbul,
5   a bus from there to Bodrum, and ended up walking to the village of Gumusluk because there was no road. I spent the summer picking and eating peaches and fishing with the locals. Net result: minimum
10   ecological damage, maximum cultural exchange, and a tad fewer octopuses in the Mediterranean.
15   In today's terms, this was as green as travel gets. Now you can get to Gumusluk in a few hours and spend a
20   month there without

Model village … Yachana Lodge in the Ecuadorian Amazon

hearing a word of Turkish. The fish may come from Singapore, the hotels are owned by the British, the villas by the Dutch, and the yachts that call in are in the million-dollar bracket. The place has changed unimaginably in a generation […]. Had I known then what I know now, should I have gone?
25   Yes. Green travel is not just what happens at the destination, or indeed how you get there. It does not demand that you eschew air travel altogether or hotels or comfort, or that your holiday is within 10 miles of your home. Rather, it asks you to pack your brain as well as your swimsuit, and to assess

and then act on the impact of your visit. At its best, it's kind to both place and
30 people, and rewards the host as much as the tourist. It is mostly small-scale, unique and personal. It certainly appeals to the intellectually curious, the ecologically and socially responsible, and to the politically aware. It seeks to add to the sum of knowledge and improve, or at least not harm, the natural world. It can be on the other side of the world or down your road, in a
35 forest or in the city. Even flying can be justifiable, if you take a plane only occasionally and are sensible about it. The golden rule must be that if our actions hurt in one way, then we should compensate in another.
Dave Martin, who helps run community-owned Bulungula Lodge in South Africa, argues that rather than cutting out flying, we should be selective
40 about where we visit. Africa is the least polluting continent on Earth but most needs the income, jobs and good development that inspired tourism brings. "Cancel your holidays to the rich world and save up for a worthwhile holiday to the developing world," he says. At its worst, green travel is a cynical lie, told by travel agents, tour operators, airlines and cruise
45 lines claiming to be green but actually peddling mass, crass tourism. It has been used to cover any encounter with indigenous peoples, any foray into a forest or trip by bicycle. Happily that is changing. Hotels used to call themselves green if they offered not to change the towels every day; these days, people demand evidence of real commitment to community, place and the
50 environment.
That is exactly what the 75 companies in Guardian Green Travel List do. Some cater for the adventurous, others for those who like their creature comforts. But they are phenomenally diverse; some are community-run, others are owned by international hotel chains. They range from the
55 English Midlands to the deepest jungle of Ecuador. [...]   (572 words)

30	**to reward** – belohnen
31	**to appeal** – ansprechen
32	**aware** – bewusst
33	**to harm** – schädigen, schaden
35	**justifiable** – gerechtfertigt
36	**sensible** – vernünftig
37	**to compensate** – entschädigen
39	**to cut out** – weglassen
39	**selective** – wählerisch
43	**worthwhile** – lohnend
44	**cruise line** – Kreuzfahrtgesellschaft
45	**to peddle** – feilbieten
46	**encounter** – Begegnung
46	**indigenous** – einheimisch
46	**foray** – Ausflug
48	**towel** – Handtuch
49	**commitment** – Bindung, Engagement
52	**to cater for** – sorgen für
52	**adventurous** – abenteuerlich
52	**creature comforts** – Annehmlichkeiten

2 Comprehension

a) Describe in your own words how the village Gumusluk has changed since the author of the article first visited.

b) Explain, in your own words, the author's idea of what green travel is and why it can be very attractive.

c) Interpret Dave Martin's statement: "Cancel your holidays to the rich world and save up for a worthwhile holiday to the developing world." (ll. 42–43)

3 Analysis → Describing cartoons, p. 129
Describe the cartoon and relate it to the text.

4 Comment
"The golden rule must be that if our actions hurt in one way, then we should compensate in another." (ll. 36–37) Give examples of how individuals can observe this rule when going on holiday.

5 Project → see Hotspot 6, p. 51

The passive

→ Grammar, p. 164

a) Rewrite the sentences below, adding one of the following nouns as a by-agent.

> Hurricane Andrew • European leaders • the Weather Office • researchers •
> the government • scientists

1. A record high temperature was recorded in London today.
2. Hundreds of homes were destroyed last night.
3. A nuclear power plant was closed down.
4. New alternative energy methods are being tested.
5. Further research on GM foods is being carried out.
6. New pollution laws will be voted on next month.

Example:
A record high temperature was recorded in London today *by the Weather Office*.

b) Now transform the following active sentences into the passive. Add the by-agent only where you think it's necessary.
1. European politicians have told large companies to lower their carbon emissions.
2. People consume more energy today than 10 years ago.
3. Experts warn travelers about their carbon footprints.
4. A team of researchers has created a new 'super food'.
5. A group of environmentalists stopped a cargo train carrying harmful waste into the country.
6. The government passed a new law on the sale of GM foods.

c) Transform the following statements and questions into the passive voice.
1. Should schools teach pupils how to recycle their waste properly?
2. Do you think travel agencies should do more to promote eco-tourism?
3. The government should impose large fines on companies that pollute the environment.
4. What can normal people do to help stop climate change?
5. Meteorologists have predicted that extreme weather conditions will become more common in Europe.
6. Should restaurants inform customers when they serve GM foods on the menu?

d) Translate the following sentences into English.
1. Jedes Jahr wird in Deutschland mehr erneuerbare Energie produziert.
2. Wieviel Natur ist bereits durch Massentourismus zerstört worden?
3. Viele Kleintiere werden ausschließlich für die Wissenschaft gezüchtet.
4. Verbraucher sollten über genmanipulierte Lebensmittel informiert werden.
5. Eine Fabrik wurde kürzlich wegen giftiger Gase geschlossen.
6. Werden Umweltverschmutzer in Zukunft härter bestraft werden?

1 **Research project: Energy sources** → Presentation, p. 151
Work in groups. Choose one of the following energy sources:

> fossil fuels • nuclear energy • wind energy • solar energy • hydroelectric energy •
> biomass • tidal energy • geothermal energy

Research how it is produced, its advantages and disadvantages, where in the world
it is mostly produced/used, and its prospects for the future. Present your results on
a poster or transparency and give a short presentation to the class. Include charts
or diagrams.

2 **Research project: Comparison between the US, the UK and Germany**
→ Internet research, p. 147
Write an article for a scientific youth magazine on the problem of global warming.
Compare how this problem is handled in the US, the UK and Germany and include
similarities and differences. Present your article in class.

3 **Project: Climate change** → Projects and group work, p. 148
Using the information from text A and the notes from the listening activity on
page 43 (Ten tips to prevent climate change), design a leaflet for an environmental
organisation on the causes and effects of climate change. Include tips on how to
prevent it. Display the leaflets in your classroom.

4 **Research project: Friends of the Earth** → Internet research, p. 147
Get together in groups and search the Internet to find information about the
organisation "Friends of the Earth". Watch several of the entries from the "Friends of
the Earth" short film competition. Then report on the ones you found most effective.
Say what you liked about them.

5 **Project: A survey on GM food** → Questionnaires and surveys, p. 149
Do a survey on genetically modified food. Develop a questionnaire with at least
ten questions concerning GM food and find out what students, your family and
friends know about the topic and what they think about it. When writing your
questionnaire, consider risks and advantages. Sum up your results in a graph and
present it to the class.

6 **Project: Working with words** → Working with a dictionary, p. 142
This topic deals with different aspects of the environment:

> nuclear power • alternative energy sources • climate change • GMF • eco-tourism

Write down important words on each aspect and arrange them in lists, word nets,
word families, etc. You can use a dictionary to look up more words and add them
to your collection.

Finding information

Look for information on
the Internet. Use a search
engine and try the following
search words:
global warming • GM food •
food labelling • Department
of Energy and Climate
Change • Bundesministe-
rium für Umwelt, Natur-
schutz und Reaktorsicher-
heit

A 1.24

The Telegraph

Search [   ] GO

Home | News | Sport | Finance | Comment | Culture | Travel | Lifestyle | Fashion

New film exposes unsavoury side of US food industry

For millions of Americans, a trip to the cinema involves loading up on popcorn and supersized drinks before the show.

5 But when the much-anticipated documentary Food, Inc. opens this week, many may find themselves unable to finish their snacks as the film exposes some unsavoury realities about how 10 food reaches the dinner table.

"There are no seasons in the American supermarket," a voice intones in the opening scene as a camera swept past supermarket shelves groaning 15 with plump-breasted chickens, perfect cuts of meat and bountiful fruit, vegetables and grains.

Major food producers would not agree to be interviewed for the movie 20 and they tried to ban the filmmakers from their stock yards, pig farms and chicken barns.

But the producers fought off law suits, grabbing headlines and impressive 25 reviews as they aim to do for the food industry what former Vice President Al Gore's controversial documentary An Inconvenient Truth did for debate about climate change.

30 The documentary was produced by the same company that made An Inconvenient Truth, which was widely criticised by global warming sceptics for its apocalyptic approach. Indeed,

---

0 **to expose sth.** – etw. enthüllen

0 **unsavoury** – unappetitlich

5 **anticipated** – erwarted

12 **to intone** – anstimmen

15 **plump** – mollig

16 **bountiful** – reichlich

17 **grain** – Getreide

20 **to ban** – verbieten

21 **stock yard** – Hühnerhof

23 **to fight off** – abwehren

23 **law suit** – Rechtsstreit

28 **inconvenient** – ungünstig

33 **sceptic** – Skeptiker(in)

34 **apocalyptic** – apokalyptisch

35 Food, Inc. has already been dismissed as one-sided propaganda by the food industry.

The documentary claims cows are fattened up on heavily subsidised
40 corn, even though they cannot digest the grain properly and their guts become breeding grounds for deadly E. coli strains as a result.

It also says chickens with oversized
45 breasts are grown to maturity and are ready to be slaughtered twice as quickly as they would be naturally, thanks to chemicals in their feed.

There is also stomach-churning
50 footage of conveyer belts packed with little yellow chicks being pushed around like mechanical parts; a cow, barely alive, being dragged around by a forklift; and herds of squealing
55 pigs being forced onto a factory "kill floor".

Knowing they would be cast as the villains of the documentary, food corporations refused to co-operate
60 with the producers. To counter what it says is "a one-sided, biased film"

that "demonises" American farmers and a system that feeds more than 300 million people, the agri-giant
65 *Monsanto* is fighting back with its own Web page.

The movie's director Robert Kenner compares the state of American food production to the current financial
70 crisis. "Stupid high risk decisions brought the financial system low," he told *The Daily Telegraph*. "Our food system is unrecognisable from 40 years ago and it could fall off a cliff
75 for the same reasons – unregulated greed and excessive risk-taking."

Eric Schlosser, the author of *Fast Food Nation* and one of the driving forces behind the movie, said: "There
80 is this deliberate veil, this curtain that's drawn between us and where our food is coming from."

"The industry doesn't want you to know the truth about what you're
85 eating because if you knew, you might not want to eat it. We've never had food companies this big and this powerful in our history."

(492 words)

35 **to dismiss sth.** – etw. abtun
39 **to fatten up** – mästen
39 **subsidised** – subventioniert
40 **to digest** – verdauen
41 **guts** – Gedärme
42 **breeding ground** – Brutstätte
43 **E.coli strain** – Kolibakterium
45 **maturity** – Reife
46 **to slaughter** – schlachten
48 **feed** – Futter
49 **stomach-churning** – widerlich
50 **conveyor belt** – Fließband
53 **barely** – kaum
53 **to drag** – ziehen
54 **forklift** – Gabelstapler
54 **herd** – Herde
54 **to squeal** – quieken
58 **villain** – Schurke
60 **to counter** – erwidern, dagegen sprechen
61 **biased** – voreingenommen
62 **to demonise** – verteufeln
74 **cliff** – Klippe
76 **excessive** – übermäßig
78 **driving force** – Antriebskraft
80 **deliberate** – absichtlich
80 **veil** – Verschleierung

1 Comprehension

a) Summarise the reasons the food companies give for forbidding filming on their premises.

b) Outline the different kinds of food production described in the film.

2 Analysis → Text analysis, p. 115

a) Analyse the film review. What is the author's attitude towards "Food, Inc."? Quote from the text to support your answer.

b) Analyse the stylistic devices the author uses and their effect on the reader.

3 Comment → Writing a comment, p. 116
"It is important to know where my food comes from and how it was produced." Do you agree with this statement?

Topic 4
Britain and the United States

🌐 86p4ig

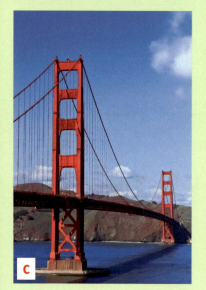

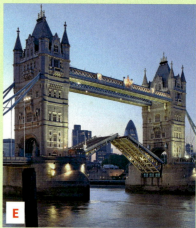

Getting started

1 Which regions of Britain or the United States do you know best and how did you learn about them (travel, movies, geography lessons, Internet, etc.)?

2 Look at the photos. Which parts of Britain or the United States do they show?

3 Look at the maps of the British Isles and of the United States of America. Match the pictures to the numbers on the maps.

F

G

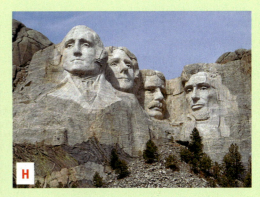

H

I

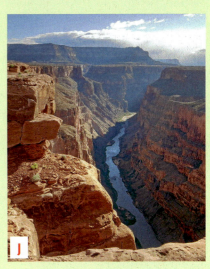

J

4 Use the phrases in the word bank to describe the locations of the places in the photos. If you need more information, consult the more detailed maps at the front and back of your book.

5 The British Isles consist of five separate countries: England, Scotland, Wales, Northern Ireland and the Republic of Ireland. Which of these countries belong to Great Britain, and which to the United Kingdom?

Word bank

it's located near the …
river / ocean / mountains •
on the east / west coast •
north / south / east / west of •
in the north / south / midwest •
to the north / south / east /
west of • mountainous •
flat • northern • eastern •
southern • western •
northerly • southerly •
easterly • westerly

A Britain and the US: A special relationship

1 Each of the boxes describes an important event in the relationship between Britain and the United States. Read the texts and match the events to the timeline. If you are correct, you will get the name of a US state.

2 Project → see Hotspot 1, p. 67

reluctantly – zögerlich
to found – gründen
persecution – Verfolgung
declaration – Erklärung
independence – Unabhängigkeit
to cut ties – Verbindungen lösen
United Nations Security Council – UN Sicherheitsrat
famine – Hungersnot
fungus – Pilz
harvest – Ernte
to emigrate – auswandern
immigration – Einwanderung

Timeline:
2003
1973
1949
1945
1941
1917
1845–1849
1776
1775–1783
1773
1620
1607
1492

A Unlike other European countries, England supports the USA in their war against Iraq.

N Britain reluctantly joins the European Community (now European Union), but still keeps up a "special relationship" with the US.

H Revolutionary War between the thirteen original American colonies and England.

O An English settlement is founded in Jamestown, Virginia, where the settlers begin to grow tobacco.

U The Mayflower – a ship of English Puritans fleeing from religious persecution in England – lands at Plymouth Bay on the coast of Massachusetts.

T The Boston Tea Party: the English settlers in America protest against the high taxes they have to pay to the English king by throwing a load of tea into the harbour of Boston.

O The USA enters World War II, fighting alongside England, France and the Soviet Union against Germany.

C The Declaration of Independence: the American colonies cut their political ties to England.

R The USA joins England and other countries in the war against Germany (World War I).

L The UK and the US become founding members of the United Nations and two of the five permanent members of the United Nations Security Council.

S Searching for a shorter sea route to India, Christopher Columbus discovers the New World.

I Britain and the US become members in the newly-founded North Atlantic Treaty Organization (NATO), a union of western states against the Soviet Union and its allies.

A The Irish potato famine: a fungus destroys the potato harvest in Ireland for a number of years in a row and causes millions of Irish citizens to emigrate to the US. This is one example of many waves of mass immigration from the British Isles to the USA.

B   Welcome to America

1 Look at these facts about the US. Write 1-16 onto a sheet of paper and match the numbers with the words and figures in the boxes. Compare your results with those of a partner.

Geography quiz

Location
North America is located between the North Atlantic Ocean and the North Pacific Ocean, with 1 to the north and 2 to the south.

Geographic coordinates
total area: 9,631,420 sq km
land: 9,161,923 sq km
water: 469,497 sq km

Area – comparative
approximately 3 of Russia; about half the size of 4 ; about three-tenths the size of 5 ; a little 6 than China; about 7 as big as the EU

Climate
mainly temperate, 8 in Florida and Hawaii, semiarid in the plains west of the 9 , and arid in the southwest; warm chinook winds in January and February from the eastern slopes of the 10 sometimes increase low winter temperatures in the northwest; 11 in Alaska

Environment – current issues
air pollution causes 12 in the US; the US is the largest single emitter of carbon dioxide from the burning of fossil fuels; water pollution from runoff of pesticides and fertilizers; natural fresh water resources are limited in the 13 part of the country; desertification

Population
314,809,000 (2012 estimate)

Ethnic groups
 14 79.6 %, black 12.9 %, Asian 4.6 %, Amerindian and Alaska native 1 %, Hawaiian and other Pacific islander 0.2 % (2010 estimate)

Languages
English 80.4 %, Spanish 15 , other Indo-European 3.7 %, Asian and Pacific island 16 , other 0.8 % (2010 estimate)

12.2 %
2.9 %
acid rain
Africa
arctic
bigger
Canada
half the size
Mexico
Mississippi River
Rocky Mountains
South America
tropical
two and a half times
white
western

acid rain – saurer Regen
approximately – ungefähr
temperate – gemäßigt
semiarid – Klima mit sehr wenig Niederschlag
arid – trocken, dürr
chinook wind – Fönwind
slope – Hang
emitter – Erzeuger
fossil fuel – fossiler Brennstoff
runoff – Sickerwasser
pesticide – Pestizid, Schädlingsbekämpfungsmittel
fertilizer – Dünger
resource – Vorrat
desertification – Versteppung
estimate – Schätzung
Amerindian – *kurz für:* American Indian

C City or suburb?

1 Translate the definition of "urban sprawl" with the help of a dictionary.
→ Working with a dictionary, p. 142

> **Urban sprawl** (*also:* suburban sprawl), a term which refers to the rapid and expansive growth of a greater metropolitan area, traditionally suburbs over a large area.
> (*From Wikipedia*)

2 **a)** List reasons why people often move – either from the city or the country – to the suburbs.

b) What problems might be caused if large numbers of people moved to the suburbs at one time?

3 Vocabulary → Guessing new words, p. 142
Find the three different uses of the verb "to rank" in the last paragraph of the text below. Translate the phrases in which the verb occurs.

---

2 **tax bill** – Steuerabrechnung

8 **subdivision** – *hier:* Wohngebiet

8 **strip mall** – Einkaufszentrum

10 **habitat** – Lebensraum

13 **relentless** – unablässig

14 **rural** – ländlich

20 **to preserve** – bewahren

21 **condo** (AE; short for **condominium**) – Eigentumswohnung

21 **town house** – Stadthaus; *meist:* Reihenhaus

25 **mass transit** – öffentliche Verkehrsmittel

30 **development** – Entwicklung

34 **to shell out** (*infml*) – bezahlen, „blechen"

36 **water and sewer lines** – Wasser- und Abwasserleitungen

39 **impact** – Auswirkung

40 **unchecked** – ungehindert, unkontrolliert

41 **foremost** – führend

42 **to predict** – vorhersagen

What urban sprawl costs you

You pay for it. Every time you get stuck in a traffic jam. Every time you get a tax bill. Every time you jump into the car just to go to a store for a loaf of bread. Urban sprawl
5 costs you time and money.
Sprawl defines life in Central Florida – one of the most spread-out regions in the country. Sprawl means one subdivision and strip mall after the next, spread across former farmlands
10 and natural habitat. It's marked by miles of pavement and annoying traffic jams. Sprawl separates homes from businesses. It serves cars rather than people. It is the relentless march of the city outward toward rural areas.
15 And little stands in its way.

There are some people, however, who think growth can be smarter and more compact with a stronger separation among urban, suburban and rural terrain. Smart growth means better
20 planning and more land preserved. It looks like condos and town houses mixed with single-family homes. Those homes are closer together, linked by walking paths that lead to stores, movie theaters and offices. There
25 may be mass transit. Smart growth in Central Florida is Baldwin Park in Orlando and Celebration by Disney. Across the nation, it's Boston and New York City.
It is hard to quantify, but according to many
30 experts, compact development costs less – in many ways.

TAXES
If Central Florida grows as it always has, Orlando-area taxpayers will shell out $44,955
35 each in taxes during the next 20 years to pay for roads, water and sewer lines and other services that governments provide as development stretches farther outward, according to a new book, *Sprawl Costs: Economic Impacts*
40 *of Unchecked Development*.
The authors – some of the nation's foremost experts on urban planning – predict the cost

"Your yard is starting to mess with my livingroom."

4 **Getting information from the text** → Word webs, p. 138
Complete the word web on the right using information given in the text.

5 **Preparing a short presentation** → Presentation, p. 151, Describing cartoons, p. 129
Look at the cartoon and describe what you see. Prepare a 5-minute presentation based on the cartoon in which you describe the cartoon, name the problem, and talk about the consequences and alternatives. You may use your word web but not the text itself.

6 **Composition**
Make notes on how you live in Germany (big city, small town, village or rural community, far away or close to shops, cinemas and other commodities, noisy or quiet, etc.).
Write a 200-word composition comparing life in an American suburb as it is described in the text with your own life in Germany.

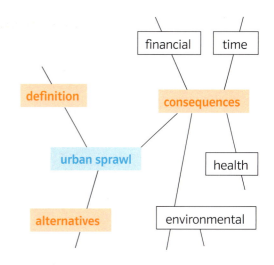

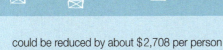

could be reduced by about $2,708 per person if 25 percent of new development doesn't
45 sprawl.
Such compact growth means more condos and town homes, filling vacant lots and rebuilding in already developed areas.
The savings could be greater if more new
50 development doesn't sprawl.

HEALTH
You could weigh up to 6 pounds more if you live in a sprawling area, and you may have a higher risk of obesity or high-blood pressure,
55 according to research paid for by the Robert Wood Johnson Foundation.
That's because sprawl makes people spend more time in their car and less time walking to the movie theater, corner store or tavern –
60 locations that are within easy reach in more compact communities that mix homes with businesses.

COMMUTING
Sprawl can get pricey when it comes to
65 roads – from auto expenses to time spent in traffic. In a more compact community, such as Boston, the costs are less.

FARMLAND
Sprawl eats up land. As property gets more
70 scarce, farmers find it more profitable to sell their land to developers. Many of Central Florida's old citrus groves are now residential neighborhoods.
Sprawl also destroys crucial habitat for
75 wildlife, including endangered animals, and interferes with their ability to travel from one natural area to another. Sprawling development also has destroyed many Florida wetlands that serve as breeding and
80 feeding grounds.

HOW OTHER CITIES STACK UP
On the scorecard of sprawl, Central Florida continually ranks among the worst regions in America. A 2005 national study by urban
85 planners, *Sprawl Costs: Economic Impacts of Unchecked Development*, ranked Orlando among the worst sprawling communities nationwide. It ranked 13th while two other Florida cities also joined the top
90 20: Miami at No. 8 and Jacksonville at No. 20.   (583 words)

47 **vacant** – leer stehend, frei
47 **lot** – Grundstück
54 **obesity** – Fettleibigkeit
59 **tavern** – Wirtshaus, Kneipe
60 **within easy reach** – leicht zu erreichen
69 **property** – Grundbesitz
70 **scarce** – knapp
72 **citrus grove** (AE) – Zitronen- oder Orangenhain
72 **residential neighborhood** – Wohngebiet
74 **crucial** – äußerst wichtig
75 **endangered** – gefährdet; *hier:* vom Aussterben bedroht
76 **to interfere with** – *hier:* verhindern
81 **to stack up** – sich mit jmdn/ etw. messen lassen
82 **scorecard** (*figurative*) – *hier:* Rangliste

D 9 / 11

 1 Before you read → Brainstorming, p. 140

Do you remember 11 September 2001? In small groups, put together everything you know about 9/11, from your own memory, from what other people have told you, and from the media.

4	**to strike, struck, struck** – treffen
6	**initial** – erste(r/s)
7	**stunned** – betäubt
8	**to chronicle** – aufzeichnen
12	**downing** – willentlich herbeigeführter Absturz
12	**to compound** – verschlimmern
13	**stark** – hart, *hier:* schockierend
14	**to hijack** – entführen
14	**magnitude** – Ausmaß, Größe
15	**overwhelming** – überwältigend
15	**to witness** – mitansehen
17	**to respond to** – *hier:* reagieren auf
18	**janitor** – Hausmeister
18	**executive** – Führungskraft
19	**to file in** – hineingehen (einer nach dem anderen)
19	**heap** – Haufen
20	**rubble** – Schutt
21	**to injure** – verletzen
21	**ultimately** – schließlich
21	**to determine** – *hier:* feststellen
22	**strike** – Schlag
22	**emblem** – Symbol
26	**to hail from** – kommen aus
26	**to gather** – zusammenkommen
27	**donation** – Spende
27	**to avalanche** – niederprasseln
28	**the bereft** – die Hinterbliebenen
28	**onsite** – vor Ort
29	**to boost** – stärken, erhöhen
29	**to vow** – schwören

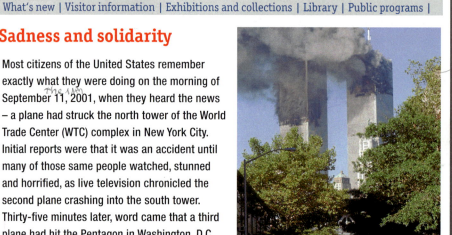

New York Historical Society | Making History Matter

Search [   ] GO

What's new | Visitor information | Exhibitions and collections | Library | Public programs |

Sadness and solidarity

Most citizens of the United States remember exactly what they were doing on the morning of September 11, 2001, when they heard the news – a plane had struck the north tower of the World
5 Trade Center (WTC) complex in New York City. Initial reports were that it was an accident until many of those same people watched, stunned and horrified, as live television chronicled the second plane crashing into the south tower.
10 Thirty-five minutes later, word came that a third plane had hit the Pentagon in Washington, D.C., followed by the downing of a fourth plane in a Pennsylvania field. Compounding the tragedy was the stark realization that the weapons used against the World Trade Center buildings and the Pentagon were hijacked U.S. commercial airliners, full of travelers. The magnitude of lost lives
15 was overwhelming, nowhere more than in the streets of New York where citizens witnessed the crashes with their own eyes. Within minutes, emergency personnel from across the massive city were mobilized to respond to the WTC crash sites.

At 9:59 a.m., as office workers, janitors, and executives fled the World Trade Center – while rescue workers filed in to help them to safety – the south tower suddenly collapsed into a heap
20 of rubble. The north tower followed a half-hour later. Hundreds of rescue workers and thousands of WTC workers and visitors were killed or injured. The U.S. Government ultimately determined that the four attacks on 9/11 were a symbolic strike at the financial and military emblems of the country and were coordinated through a Muslim terrorist group, al-Qaeda, under the leadership of a man named Osama bin Ladin.

25 In the days after 9/11, New Yorkers pulled together with a new appreciation for each other and their city. Thousands of volunteers hailing from the city and far beyond gathered to offer aid for rescue, recovery, and clean-up efforts, while donations avalanched in from across the country to support the injured and bereft. Mayor Giuliani was onsite at Ground Zero soon after the attacks, and he stayed onsite to boost the morale of workers and volunteers. The city as a whole vowed
30 that it couldn't be brought to its knees by fear-based tactics, and plans were almost immediately put into effect to prove just that.

While the smoke was still rising, New York Governor George Pataki and Mayor Giuliani created the Lower Manhattan Development Corporation to oversee the design and construction of a lasting memorial to the victims of 9/11, while also generating a plan to rebuild and revitalize the
35 area most profoundly affected by the horrific events.

After the smoke cleared, New York City remained the financial powerhouse of the world. The city won't forget the sacrifices made by its citizens on September 11th and on many previous occasions, and it's a city that realizes that the best memorial is to live on. The tourist trade rebounded with surprising speed, and New York City's gritty determination has pulled it through
40 tough economic times not necessarily related to the events of 9/11. The biggest city in the country was built on the diversity of its citizenry – Irish, Jewish, Palestinian, Russian, Italian, Muslim, African, Portuguese, and so many more – and it will continue to be the cultural, financial, and educational heart of the nation.

(546 words)

34 **memorial** – Denkmal
34 **to revitalize** – mit neuem Leben erfüllen
35 **profoundly** – stark
35 **to affect** – betreffen, beeinflussen
37 **sacrifice** – Opfer
37 **previous** – vorherig
39 **to rebound** – sich erholen
39 **gritty** – mutig, zäh
40 **tough** – *hier:* hart, schwer

2 **Comprehension: True or false?**
Read the statements below and decide whether they are true or false. Quote or paraphrase words from the text that confirm or disprove the ideas in the statements.

a) When people first heard about the attacks on the World Trade Center, they thought a plane had lost its way and crashed into the North Tower accidentally.

b) The US government came to the conclusion that what the terrorists really wanted to hurt in the attacks of 9/11 was the economic and military power of the country.

c) The citizens of New York lost all hope and courage after the attacks.

d) Shortly after the attacks the Governor of New York and the Mayor of New York City decided to rebuild the World Trade Center.

e) After 9/11, people soon started to visit the city again.

3 **Listening: This is too big to comprehend right now** → Listening, p. 108

a) As you listen, note down. → Taking notes, p. 141
   1. The number of subway stops from Brendan's home to Cortlandt Street.
   2. The distance from the subway station to the base of Tower 1.
   3. The time Brendan was sitting in his chair.
   4. The number of people on Brendan's side of the floor.
   5. The amount of time it took people to go down the stairs (sec. / floor).
   6. The floor where they met the firefighters.
   7. The number of firefighters walking up the stairs.
   8. The floor Brendan was at when he realized just how bad the situation was.
   9. The time Brendan was on the bridge and heard the sound of Tower 2 collapsing.

b) Complete the following sentences in German.
   1. Brendan hatte sehr großes Glück, denn …
   2. Eine überwältigende Erinnerung, die Brendan nie vergessen wird, ist, …

4 **Research project** → see Hotspot 2, p. 67

E   Talking about Britain

1   **Before you read**

    a)   When you think of Britain and the British, what do you think of?
Consider people, products, places, food, sports, music, etc.

    b)   Write down at least three clichés about Britain and the British.
Compare your ideas with those of others in your class.

    c)   Is your own view of Britain and the British based on clichés or on first-hand
knowledge? Explain your answer.

2   **Your opinion** → Brainstorming, p. 140

    a)   If you were asked to make a "German collage", what pictures would you choose?
Brainstorm ideas with a partner. Try to come up with a list of ten things that you
both agree on as being typically German.

    b)   Find out what other people in your class think and agree on ten ideas together.

    c)   Look up on the Internet what the British think about the Germans. Compare your
list with this information and give possible reasons for any differences you find.

3   **Finding information** → Internet research, p. 147

    a)   Find information about England, Scotland, Wales and Northern Ireland
(capital city, main industries, languages spoken, natural resources) and make
a table showing it.

"Sorry, where did you say
you were from again?"

Facts and figures

• • •

Britain is made
up of England,
Scotland, Wales
and Northern
Ireland. Each
country has its own
capital although
the government of
all four countries is
in London. Britain
is a member state
of the EU. Its full
name is the United
Kingdom of Great
Britain and
Northern Ireland.

Urban and rural population

Half of all Britain's
people live in just
seven super cities
such as Manchester,
Birmingham and
London, which were
formed from smaller
towns that grew
together. Many of
the cities grew up
as a result of industries
which began to develop
in the 19th century. At the beginning of the 19th century 8 out
of 10 people lived in the countryside – then Britain had a rural
population. Nowadays about 8 out of 10 people in Britain live
in a city or town – so Britain has a mainly urban population.

Scene in the centre of Manchester

Population

Britain covers a small area compared
with many other countries, but it
has a large number of people living
in it. The approximate population
(mid-2004) is 59,834,300 (England
50,093,100, Wales 2,952,500, Scotland
5,078,400, N. Ireland 1,710,300).
The population is spread unevenly
across Britain and the way it is
spread depends on things like
climate, resources, landscape and
past history. Population density in
England is higher than the rest of
Britain, with 375 people per square
km. The whole population is now
growing, but only very slowly.

b) Work with others in your class to compare your results. Make corrections and additions where necessary. Add two further categories to your table, e.g. famous people, sports, national dishes, etc. Fill in the relevant information in your table.

4 **Working with facts** → Understanding non-fictional texts, p. 109

a) Divide the class into six groups. Each group is allocated one of the short texts. Read your text carefully, and take notes of the most important information. If your text does not have a heading, find a suitable one. Now close your books.

b) Form new groups. Each group should have at least one student for each of the texts. Now exchange the most important information from the texts with the other group members. Do not open your books again. Use only your notes. Those listening may take notes while you speak.

c) Remaining in the new groups, discuss the following question: What are the most important factors which affect population distribution in Britain according to the information in the boxes? Find as many details as possible.

d) Return to your original groups, exchange and discuss your results.

5 **Vocabulary: Find the words in the text which mean . . .**

> 1 a country which belongs to a larger group of countries • 2 a weather condition that causes rain • 3 natural materials like oil, wood, minerals • 4 regions with high hills • 5 the land beside the sea

6 **Research project** → see Hotspot 3, p. 67

capital – Hauptstadt
urban – städtisch
rural – ländlich
population – Bevölkerung
approximate – ungefähr
population density – Bevölkerungsdichte
square km – Quadratkilometer
mountain range – Bergkette
densely – dicht
temperate – gemäßigt
depression – *hier:* Tiefdruckgebiet

• • •

Britain is made up of different landscapes from beautiful mountain ranges and flat open spaces, where few people live, to towns and cities which are densely populated. Not only are the areas of Britain different, they are always changing, for example, when factories close down and workers become unemployed, or when a new industry moves into an area and creates new jobs.

View from Mount Snowdon, Wales

Climate

Britain's climate is generally mild and temperate. There are frequent weather changes but few extremes of temperature. In general the daily weather is influenced by depressions moving eastward from the Atlantic. Winds are mostly south-westerly. There is more rainfall in the mountainous areas in the west and north than in central and eastern parts.

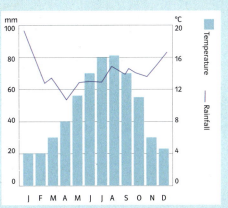

• • •

With an area of about 242,000 square km, Britain is just under 1,000 km from the south coast to the extreme north of Scotland and just under 500 km across at the widest point. The coastline of Britain is 14,549 km long including islands. The most northerly point on the mainland is Dunnet Head, north-east Scotland and the most southerly point is Lizard Point, Cornwall.

(413 words)

63

F   A journey around Great Britain

1 **Before you read**

The text you are about to read is an extract from the book *The Kingdom by the Sea*, an American writer's experience of travelling around Britain. If you were planning a month-long trip around Britain, what would your itinerary look like? Discuss with a partner and report back to the class.

p.104 **2** **Comprehension**

a) Sum up what Theroux says about the British and British travel writing.

b) Outline why Theroux has "a problem of itinerary" (l. 35).

c) Describe which route Theroux eventually decides to take when travelling in Britain and the reasons for his choice.

Paul Theroux
(American travel writer and novelist, born in 1941)

1 **blank** – leer
2 **fastidiously** – akribisch
16 **to simplify** – vereinfachen
16 **muffled** – gedämpft
16 **obliqueness** – Schrägheit
23 **discomfort** – Unannehm-
    lichkeit

The Kingdom by the Sea

There were no blank spaces on the map of Great Britain, the best-known, most fastidiously mapped, and most widely trampled piece of geography on earth. No country was easier to travel in – the British invented public transport. And yet I had
5 seen practically nothing of it. I felt ashamed and ignorant, but when I began to think about traveling around Britain, I became excited – because I knew so little. I wanted to write
10 about it.
Writing about a country in its own language was a great advantage, because
15 in other places one was

always interpreting and simplifying. Translation created a muffled obliqueness – one was always seeing the country sideways. But language grew out of the landscape – English out of England – and it seemed logical that the country could be accurately portrayed only in its own language. So what was I waiting for?
20 The problem was one of perspective: How and where to go to get the best view of the place? It was also a problem in tone; after all, I was an alien.
The British had invented their own solution to travel-writing. They went to places like Gabon and Paraguay and joked about the discomforts, the natives, the weather, the food, the entertainments. It was necessary to be an outsider, which was why

⁵ △ 3 Analysis

Analyse how Theroux felt about:

a) his upcoming journey around Britain.

b) writing about his travel experiences.

² ⊙ 4 Listening comprehension: A lonely island → Listening, p. 108

Listen to the extract from *Notes from a Small Island*, another travel book set in Britain, and decide whether the following statements are true or false.

a) The English Football team is better than the Norwegian one.

b) What is considered a short distance by many Americans can seem like a very long journey to the British.

c) In Britain, there is a sense that America is a lot closer, and that France and Germany and other countries are a lot further away than they really are.

d) After looking at the map, the author's colleagues still don't believe that Bournemouth is actually closer to Cherbourg than to London.

25 they had never written about Britain in this way. But it was a mystery to me why no one had ever come to Britain and written about its discomforts and natives and entertainments and unintelligible dialects. The British, who had devised a kind of envious mockery of other cultures, and who had virtually invented the concept of funny foreigners, had never regarded themselves as fair game for the
30 travel-writer. They did not encourage aliens to observe them closely. They were like a tribe that plundered abroad and were secretive and inhospitable at home. The British did not make me think of Shakespeare but rather of head-hunters – their travel-writing a literary version of headshrinking that had never been used on them. I was eager to try.
35 But it was also a problem of itinerary. In a place that was crisscrossed with ant trails, a kingdom of bottlenecks and private property and high fences, my route was a problem, because there were too many routes. To take all the trains would be no more than a mediocre stunt. The buses did not go to enough places. A bicycle was out – too dangerous, too difficult; another stunt. A car was too
40 simple, and anyway I had lived in London long enough to know that driving on English roads was no fun. My route was crucial. It was the most important aspect of travel. In choosing a route, one was choosing a subject. But every mile of Britain had a road through it; there was a track across every field, a footpath in every acre of woods. Perhaps this was why I had never traveled in Britain: I
45 had been unable to decide on the route.
And then I had my way: narrowly, around the entire coast.
It answered every need. There was only one coast, it was one undeviating route, and this way I would see the whole of Britain.   (536 words)

27 **unintelligible** – unverständlich
27 **to devise** – erfinden
28 **envious** – neidisch
28 **mockery** – Verhöhnung, Spott
28 **virtually** – praktisch
29 **to regard oneself as sth.** – sich für … halten
29 **fair game** – Freiwild
31 **tribe** – Volk
31 **to plunder** – plündern
31 **inhospitable** – ungastlich
35 **itinerary** – Reiseroute, Reiseplan
36 **bottleneck** – Nadelöhr
38 **mediocre** – mittelmäßig
41 **crucial** – entscheidend, ausschlaggebend
47 **undeviating** – unbeirrbar

Adjectives & Adverbs

→ Grammar, p. 165

a) Write down the missing forms on a separate piece of paper.

	adjective	comparative	superlative	adverb
1.	–	–	–	well
2.	–	more regular	–	–
3.	effective	–	–	–
4.	–	–	easiest	–
5.	recent	–	–	–
6.	–	–	–	efficiently
7.	–	slower	–	–
8.	–	–	fastest	–
9.	–	–	–	carefully
10.	bad	–	–	–

b) Comparisons

Make sentences comparing New York and London using the comparative and super-lative form of the adjectives in the box below.

> big • expensive • dangerous • interesting • cheap • multicultural • loud • dirty •
> famous • popular • warm • crowded • exciting • far away • clean • friendly

Example: New York is not as dirty as London. / New York is cleaner than London.

c) Adjective or adverb?

Complete the sentences below by choosing either the adjective or adverb.

1. In Manchester it often rains heavy / heavily.
2. Many people cannot afford to live in Manhattan because the rent is so expensive / expensively.
3. A lot of people in Miami come from Latin America, but they speak English good / well.
4. London is a large city but you can travel around easy / easily on the underground.
5. The weather in California varies greatly / great from the weather in the Rocky Mountains.
6. Despite its reputation, New York is a very safe / safely place to visit.

1 **Project: Timeline** → Projects and group work, p. 148
Form groups of 2–3 students each. Each group is allocated one of the events on the timeline. Collect information on your event and formulate a short text explaining it. Find pictures relating to your event. Draw the timeline on a long piece of packing paper and mark the given year. Glue your texts and pictures near the correct year and hang the poster on the wall in your classroom.

2 **Research project: The boroughs of New York City** → Internet research, p. 147
The events of 9/11 will always be remembered and talked about in connection with New York City. Also, the borough of Manhattan is often the place one has in mind when thinking of NYC. However, besides Manhattan, the city has four more boroughs and many more facets that should be known and talked about. The names of the other four boroughs are Queens, Brooklyn, The Bronx and Staten Island. In your class, form five groups and choose one of the five boroughs of New York City each. Go to the library and on the Internet and look for information on your borough. Make a poster on which you collect the most important information and some pictures, including a street map of NYC on which you indicate where your borough is located. Then prepare a short group presentation on your borough.

3 **Research project: Facets of Britain** → Presentation, p. 151

Work in groups and choose one of the following projects to present in class. Make sure that each member of your group is involved. To check that everybody has listened to your presentation carefully, prepare a short quiz for your listeners to answer and hand in after you have finished your talk.

A town or region in Britain
Your aim is to create a brochure a) for foreign tourists or b) for British tourists in Britain. First decide which city, town or region in Britain you would like to talk about. You may include geographical and socio-economic information, tourist attractions and famous sights, historical and cultural attractions. Don't forget to add pictures and maps, and use an attractive layout.

A famous British person
Decide which person you would like to introduce to your class. You could talk about a famous artist, e.g. a writer, playwright, musician, composer or actor, or you could choose a scientist, sportsman or a member of the royal family. It doesn't matter if the person is still alive or not. Create a poster with pictures as well as biographical information, and say what (has) made them famous.

National dishes from Britain
First brainstorm what you know about British food and decide which dishes you would like to present (no more than four!). Your aim is to create a little cookery book in which you include the ingredients, how the dishes are cooked and where and when they are eaten. Don't forget to add pictures!

Typical sports in Britain
Your aim is to create a poster about a sport that is popular in Britain. Your presentation should include information about the equipment, the rules, and either the national team or a successful club, or some famous players. Pictures or drawings will make your poster more appealing!

British customs and traditions
First brainstorm what you know about British customs and traditions. Think about occasions such as Christmas, Bonfire Night, April Fool's Day, Shrove Tuesday, birthdays, etc. Then select about three or four customs and create a leaflet in which you explain the traditions and their origins.

A1.33

London – love it and leave it

CityBlog

Search [ ] GO

2 **conclusion** – Schlussfolgerung

5 **genuinely** – echt, aufrichtig

10 **bloke** *(BE, coll.)* – Kerl

10 **swiftly** – schnell

12 **sardined** – eingequetscht
(wie eine Ölsardine)

12 **drenched** – durchnässt

12 **carriage** – Wagen (eines
Zuges usw.)

18 **grime** – Schmutz

19 **to grind sb. down** – jmdn
zermürben

21 **rudely** – unhöflich

23 **to bother** – *hier:* sich die
Mühe machen

23 **to extend** – verlängern,
ausdehnen

23 **licensing hours** – Öffnungs-
zeiten (einer Bar mit
Alkohollizenz)

26 **wee hours** – frühe Morgen-
stunden

26 **establishment** – Einrich-
tung

26 **pricy** – teuer

27 **pre-booking** – Vormerkung

28 **to kid** – Spaß machen

There are so many reasons to live in London … and at least as many to leave! That's the conclusion I came to a couple of months ago, talking to a friend who had just returned from a full year of city-hopping, as it were, around the globe. Tony, like me, had spent almost all his life in

5 London. That evening he had declared that he was genuinely glad to be back, which – to my own great surprise – surprised me. Since then I haven't stopped thinking about why, and have begun to open my eyes and look around me.

Well, take the daily journey to and from work on the Tube. I bet that's an

10 aspect of London the bloke had swiftly wiped out of his memory. I would too if I could. There's litter everywhere and overcrowded isn't the word for it: You're more like "sardined" into sweat-drenched carriages, though unlike the tinned fish, you're not quite dead to the world. And why is it that just when you're hurrying to get to an airport or an important

15 interview, trains aren't operating on the line you need? Most Londoners I know also complain that the Tube stops too early, making it difficult to have a good night out.

Overground it's not much better, I notice. The crowds, the grime, the high prices – they all do their bit to grind you down. So you go for a

20 drink with your friends, but before you know it, the pub is closing and you'll be rudely reminded to "drink up". Yes, the law dictating that all pubs must close at eleven was relaxed back in 2005. Yet I find that the pubs around where I live haven't bothered to extend their licensing hours. Of course there are places elsewhere that do business till twelve

25 or one o'clock, not to mention bars and clubs up in town which often stay open till the wee hours – but these establishments are pricier, may require pre-booking, often turn away male-only groups (three blokes make up a group, I'm not kidding), and there's still the problem of how to get home.

30 Then, walking towards Regent's Park one evening, I suddenly catch the rosy light of sunset on the creamy facades of the stylish buildings on one side of the street. The park, I notice, is vast and green and tranquil and I am struck by the beauty of the moment. That's when it comes back to me: London is, of course, full of parks, heaths and commons, my favourite

35 being the more unruly Hampstead Heath, the park of my childhood. It's a fact I'd simply taken for granted. I wonder if there's any other city of this size elsewhere as green …

I realise that the best way to find out is to leave London for a while in order to explore cities abroad. And who knows how I'll feel about this place

40 when (or if) I return.   (498 words)

31 **facade** – Fassade
32 **tranquil** – ruhig, friedlich
33 **to be struck by sth.** – von etw. beeindruckt sein
34 **heath** – Heide
34 **common** – öffentliche Grünfläche
35 **unruly** – wild, ungebändigt
36 **to take sth. for granted** – etw. als gegeben hinnehmen

1 **Comprehension**
Summarise the text in your own words, outlining the positive and negative aspects of living in London.

2 **Analysis**
Look at the two pictures of New York and London. Describe what you can see and analyse the differences and similarities, e.g. architecture, size of buildings, streets, layout, surroundings, etc.

3 **Comment: Choose one of the following tasks.**

a) "Well, take the daily journey to and from work on the Tube." (l. 9)
Discuss the pros and cons of using public transport.

b) Big city life is said to make a big contribution to environmental pollution. Come up with examples to support the statement and make suggestions how to solve the problem.

Topic 5
Private and professional communication

I don't believe in email. I'm an old-fashioned girl. I prefer calling and hanging up.
1 Sarah Jessica Parker, American actress

What a lot we lost when we stopped writing letters. You can't reread a phone call.
3 Liz Carpenter, American writer and feminist (1920–2010)

Suddenly, it seems as though all the world's a-twitter.
4 Newsweek, weekly American news magazine

The more elaborate our means of communication, the less we communicate.
2 Joseph Priestley, English clergyman (1734–1804)

Getting started

1 Look at the pictures A–F. Explain what they show. → Describing pictures, p. 128

2 Read the quotes. Choose one for each picture.

D

Electric communication will never be a substitute for the face of someone who with their soul encourages another person to be brave and true.
Charles Dickens, English novelist (1812 – 1817)

5

elaborate – kompliziert

means of communication – Kommunikationsmittel

clergyman – Geistlicher

substitute – Ersatz

to encourage – ermutigen, ermuntern

philanthropist – Wohl-täter(in)

accessible – zugänglich

to found – gründen

to foster – fördern

Communication – the human connection – is the key to personal and career success.
Paul J. Meyer, American businessman and philanthropist (1928 – 2009)

6

E

F

Talk is by far the most accessible of pleasures. It costs nothing in money, it is all profit, it completes our education, founds and fosters our friendships, and can be enjoyed at any age and in almost any state of health.
Robert Louis Stevenson, Scottish novelist (1850 – 1894)

7

3 Share your ideas with your partner and give reasons for your choice.

4 In pairs, come up with your own quotation about communication and report back to the class.

5 Research project → see Hotspot 1, p. 83

Word bank

Giving opinions
I think that … • In my opinion … • I believe that … • It seems to me … • I agree / disagree because … • What do you think? • What is your opinion on this?

A   Communicating online

1   **Before you read** → Brainstorming, p. 140

a) How much time do you spend online every day? What do you do? What do you think is a "healthy" amount of time to spend online per day?

b) Interview your partner on the same questions. Does he / she spend more or less time online than you? What does he / she do online? Share your findings with the class.

FAMILY MATTERS *is a weekly column which appears on the US online news site mywesttexas.com. In the column, qualified marriage and family therapist Dr. Jim May offers advice and support on personal issues.*

FAMILY MATTERS:
Time spent chatting online is time lost with family

DEAR FAMILY: My husband somehow started "chatting" with some people on the Internet and has wound up talking to them
5   more now than he does to me. He's not secretive or anything about it; he's just obsessed about having to be on the computer at 9 p.m. so they can all talk. I can
10   come and see what he's doing and it's all very innocent mostly about politics and hunting. I think that is all pretty strange to spend that much time (usually from 9 to 11 p.m.) on the computer talking to people he's
15   never met. When I tell him those people aren't real and that he's ignoring his real family for them, he gets mad at me and clams up.

At any rate, the problem is that we have no time for us anymore. He's a really good father and is involved with our kids, helps them with homework, baths and bedtime stories. But then he's off to the computer until bedtime. I usually am already
20   in bed and sometimes asleep when he comes to bed, so we usually don't talk then. We had had a good sex life but now I'm not willing for him to come to bed and just have

4   **to wind up doing sth.** – schließlich etw. tun

6   **secretive** – geheimnisvoll

7   **obsessed** – besessen

11   **innocent** – harmlos

16   **to clam up** – still werden

sex without any connecting time at all. So he's mad at me about that and I'm mad at him because he's choosing his "friends" over me. Am I just being selfish? We never did a lot together or talk a lot before, but this is ridiculous. Does he have some kind of Internet
25 addiction problem? – LEFT OUT WIFE

DEAR LEFT OUT: You and your husband need to address this problem directly and calmly. I would not characterize your husband as having any kind of addiction problem but he would want to consider re-balancing his life with you and his online activities. Given all of the demands and pressures that are placed on marriage and the family these
30 days, it is even more important that time is set aside exactly for what your husband is doing on the Internet – talking and sharing. This getting-to-know effort is critical in establishing and maintaining healthy family and marital relations.
The main problem with your husband spending so much time on the Internet is that it replaces direct face-to-face interactions and takes away from them. The parts of one's
35 life that should be shared with family and spouse are being shared with others. Strangely enough, those chat-room relationships are real to those involved. They are not real in the face-to-face sense but they are real in terms of real communications. Such communicating does in fact build relationships. The time and energy that should be going to the marriage and family are going to another relationship.
40 I think at this point you could set aside time to share this column with your husband and reach an agreement on how long he can chat that works for him, you and the family. It is a real compliment to him that you do want to spend time with him.   (599 words)

23 **selfish** – egoistisch
24 **ridiculous** – lächerlich
29 **demand** – *hier:* Anforderung
29 **pressure** – *hier:* Zwang, Druck
30 **to set aside** – reservieren
32 **to establish** – aufbauen
32 **to maintain** – aufrechterhalten
32 **marital relations** – eheliche Beziehungen
35 **spouse** – Ehegatte / -gattin

2   Comprehension
Summarise "LEFT OUT WIFE's" problem and "FAMILY's" answer in your own words.

3   Text production: Writing an email → Writing an email, p. 118
"[...] chat-room relationships are real to those involved. They are not real in the face-to-face sense but they are real in terms of real communications. Such communicating does in fact build relationships." (ll. 36 – 38)
Do you agree? Can people form relationships without ever meeting face-to-face? Write an email to Dr. May in which you give your opinion on the statement above.

4   Analysis → Describing cartoons, p. 129
Describe and analyse the cartoon and relate it to the text.

Technology continues to improve communication.

B   Letter writing – a lost art?

1   **Before you read**

a) Think about the following questions:
- When was the last time you sent or received a letter?
- What kind of letter was it – handwritten or typed?
- What was the letter about?
- Do people nowadays write more or fewer letters than ten years ago? Why?

b) Discuss these questions with a partner and report back to the class.

News | Sport | Comment | Culture | Business | Money | Life&Style | Travel | Environment

Comment is free › Society   Search [   ] GO

A fifth of children have never received a letter

Young people who rely on email and text are missing out on the pleasures and benefits of letter writing, say experts

5   One in five children in the UK has never received a handwritten letter, according to a survey published today. With young people increasingly relying on email and social networking 10 sites to communicate, a tenth had never written a letter themselves, the research found. Teachers and experts said they feared young people were missing out on the pleasures and developmental benefits of letter writing.

15   The survey of 1,200 seven- to 14-year-olds, commissioned for children's charity World Vision, found that more than a quarter had not written a letter in the last year and 43% had not been sent one. But in the previous week alone, almost half had either sent or received an email, or a message on a social networking site. Boys were twice as likely as girls never to have written a letter.

Child education expert Sue Palmer, the author of *Toxic Childhood,* said: "If children do not write or 20 receive letters, they miss out on key developmental benefits. Handwritten letters are much more personal than electronic communication. By going to the trouble of physically committing words to paper, the writer shows their investment of time and effort in a relationship. That's why we tend to hang on to personal letters as keepsakes. The effort of writing is a very real one for a child. Painstakingly manoeuvring the pencil across the page, thinking of the best words to convey a message, struggling 25 with spelling and punctuation. It is, however, an effort worth making, because it's only through practice that we become truly literate – and literacy is the hallmark of human civilisation. If we care about real relationships, we should invest in real communication, not just the quick fix of a greetings card, text or email. What's more, if we care about civilised human thought, we should encourage our children to invest time and energy in sitting down to write."

---

13   **to miss out on sth.** – etw. verpassen

13   **developmental** – Entwicklungs-

15   **to commission** – in Auftrag geben

21   **to commit** – *hier:* niederschreiben

22   **to hang on to sth.** – etw. behalten

23   **keepsake** – Andenken, Erinnerung

23   **painstakingly** – gewissenhaft, sorgfältig

24   **to manoeuvre** – manövrieren

24   **to convey** – vermitteln

25   **punctuation** – Interpunktion

26   **literate** – lese- und schreibkundig

26   **literacy** – Lese- und Schreibfähigkeit

26   **hallmark** – Kennzeichen

30 Half of 11-year olds were not sure how to lay out a letter and a third of 14-year olds weren't either. The traditional thank you letter was the most common reason for putting pen to paper, making up 70% of children's efforts. Only one in five wrote letters to friends. World Vision carried out the survey for today's National Letter Writing Day. Writing letters to children in developing countries is a key part of its child sponsorship programme. Helen Smith, the headteacher at Lum Head primary school in

35 Manchester, said: "Schools play a central role in child development, and we should always be thinking of new ways to get children writing. This is a great way to help enhance their literacy development."

(575 words)

34 **sponsorship** – Förderung
36 **to enhance** – verbessern

2 **Comprehension: True or false?** → Comprehension questions, p. 115
Read the statements below and decide whether they are true or false.
Quote or paraphrase words from the text that confirm or disprove the ideas in the statements.

a) 25% of children in Great Britain have never been sent a letter.

b) Teachers argue that writing letters is not only fun, but also teaches valuable skills.

c) The survey found out that girls tend to write significantly more letters than boys.

d) For a child, writing a handwritten letter is as easy as writing an email.

e) According to the author, texting, emailing or sending greeting cards to somebody show that this person is important to you.

f) Seven in ten children write a letter after they have received a gift.

g) Helen Smith thinks that teachers are responsible for encouraging children to write.

3 **Classroom discussion** → Discussions, p. 133
Currently, only primary school children are required to practice handwriting in class. However, as the standard of handwriting of older students has deteriorated, some experts argue that secondary schools should introduce special handwriting lessons. This subject would be tested and would contribute to the students' final grades. Would you be in favour of handwriting lessons at your school? What would be the advantages and disadvantages? Think about it from the students' and teachers' points of view.

4 **Analysis** → Describing cartoons, p. 129
Describe and analyse the cartoon and relate it to the text.

5 **Project** → see Hotspot 2, p. 83

© John McPherson/Distributed by Universal Uclick via CartoonStock.com

"See kids? This is a LETTER. A LETTER. Back when I was a kid, people would send these all the time. There was no such thing as e-mail."

C Communicating at work

Business communication

8	**majority** – Mehrzahl, Mehrheit
15	**privacy** – Privatsphäre
24	**to remain** – bleiben
35	**progress** – Fortschritt
38	**destination** – Ziel
41	**intended** – *hier:* bestimmt
46	**enquiry** – Anfrage
46	**offer** – Angebot
46	**order** – Bestellung, Auftrag
48	**brochure** – Prospekt, Broschüre
48	**delivery times** – Lieferzeiten
50	**quotation** – *hier:* Angebot, Kostenvoranschlag
54	**wherein** – worin
59	**to proceed** – fortfahren

Communication plays an essential role in any company, and over the years the business world has seen many developments in this area. From the early days of the hand-written letter, to the
5 telephone, computers and the internet, the speed and possibilities of professional communication have increased greatly.

In the majority of professional situations, emails have replaced traditional letters. The advantages
10 are clear: they are fast, can be stored easily, and sent to anywhere in the world, and – thanks to smart phones – at anytime. However, there are also disadvantages. For instance, around 95% of all emails sent worldwide are spam. Then there are the
15 more serious issues of security and privacy – both of which are very important to any business. Emails and attachments may be used to transfer viruses or spyware. And, in terms of privacy, how can you be sure that nobody else is reading your emails?

20 One thing that has stood the test of time is the telephone. Although it has seen many developments in technology and design over the years, the telephone still has a place on most office desks in the world. It has remained popular for a number of
25 reasons: it is fast, allows you to be spontaneous and make quick decisions, it is relatively inexpensive and simple to use. The major downsides, however, are that it is dependent on the other person being available. For example, if you suddenly have a great
30 idea to put to your partner in Tokyo, you may have to wait six hours for them to wake up before you can tell them. Phone conversations can also lead to misunderstandings, whether due to language difficulties, bad connections, or other factors.

35 Despite constant technological progress and innovations, the simple written letter (rather cruelly named 'snail mail' as it can take days to reach its destination) still has a key role to play. It offers a level of security missing in emails, i.e. the letter is
40 (ideally) only opened and read by the person it was intended for. Furthermore, a written document with a signature is more formal and may still be required in legal situations.

In the majority of companies, local or international,
45 three types of business letters keep the wheels turning: enquiry, offer and order. An enquiry letter may be general – such as requests for price lists, brochures, or delivery times – or more specific. Such enquiries are often requests for more
50 thorough information, such as detailed quotations.

Once an enquiry has been received the next step is often for the buyer and the seller to agree on a contract. This is generally initiated by an offer letter wherein the seller quotes a price for their
55 goods or services and outlines terms of payments, delivery times and other conditions. After a buyer has received an offer letter from a potential business partner they must decide whether or not to proceed. If the buyer finds the offer satisfactory
60 they will place an order.

The fact that these written documents, and a number of others, still form the backbone of business relations shows that companies still place a great deal of value on having things on paper –
65 not just in the inbox or the answering machine.

(654 words)

1 Comprehension

a) Work with a partner. Make a grid for yourself like the one below. Then read the text again and complete the grid.

	Advantages	Disadvantages
Email Telephone Letter		

b) Enquiry, offer or order? Match the following phrases with the corresponding type of business letter.
1. "Please supply the following items on the terms stated below."
2. "Please state your earliest delivery date."
3. "We saw your advertisements for laser printers in the October edition of *What PC?* magazine."
4. "We look forward to welcoming you as our customer."
5. "As agreed, payment will be made 30 days from date of invoice."
6. "We can offer a 10% discount on orders over €5,000."
7. "Please send us a quotation for 24 black leather office chairs, article number OCB22."
8. "Please make sure that any glass articles are packed with great care."
9. "We were pleased to hear that you are interested in our products."

2 Listening comprehension: Taking phone calls → Listening, p. 108
In her first week at Herkules AG, the new apprentice Sandra Kohl finds herself alone in the office and the telephone rings.

a) Listen to the telephone conversation twice and list as many telephoning phrases as possible.

b) Compare your list with a partner and complete it.

3 Listening comprehension: Taking messages → Taking notes, p. 141
Listen to the telephone conversation and take the message in German.
Use the following message form:

4 Role play: Taking messages → Making phone calls, p. 136
Work in pairs and sit back to back. Partner A "rings" partner B and leaves a short message, e.g. when and where to meet a customer, a response to an enquiry, a telephone order, etc. Partner B takes down the message. Then change roles.
Use the phrases from task 2.

5 Project → see Hotspot 3, p. 83

Telefonnotiz
Nachricht für: _____
Aufgenommen von: _____
Anrufer: _____
Betreff: _____
_____
_____

D Office life

The new job

From the novel
Martin Lukes: Who moved my BlackBerry?
by Lucy Kellaway

⁹ **pager** – Funkrufempfänger

⁹ **BlackBerry** – Smartphone

¹⁷ **to make amends** – etw. wiedergutmachen

⁴⁰ **FTSE 100** – die 100 umsatzstärksten Firmen der Londoner Börse

⁴¹ **hush hush** – geheimnisvoll

⁶⁰ **Sainsbury's** – britische Supermarktkette

⁶¹ **yours truly** – mit freundlichen Grüßen

December 2
From: Martin Lukes
To: Sylvia Woods

Hi Sylvia
5 What's this message to call
Sebastian Fforbes Hever? Did he say
what it was about? I'm going out now
for a spot of lunch. If he calls back, I've
got my mobile, pager and BlackBerry
10 with me.
Martin

From: Martin Lukes
To: Jenny Lukes

Darling –
15 Sorry about last night … had a few too
many. Will try to get back early tonite to
make amends.
 btw one of the top headhunters at
Heidrick Ferry has been trying to get
20 hold of me (!) … dunno what it's about
Love you, M xx

From: Martin Lukes
To: SebastianFforbesHever@
HeidrickFerry

25 Hi Sebastian
Thanks for your intriguing email. Yes,
indeed, I could find a window to meet
up with you tomorrow. I'll have to juggle
a couple of meetings, but should be do-
30 able – could see you at your offices in
Buckingham Palace Road at around 3ish.
Bestest
Martin Lukes
Marketing Director, A&B (UK)

---

35 From: Martin Lukes
To: Jenny Lukes

Darling –
Guess what?? I've been approached to
be director of marketing and strategy
40 at a major FTSE 100 company!! All very
hush hush … the headhunter wouldn't
say which one over the phone, but I'm
going to meet him tomorrow.
I know you're really up against it this pm
45 but wld be v grateful if you'd pick up my
grey Hugo Boss suit from the cleaners.
Love you M xx

December 3
From: Martin Lukes
50 To: Sylvia Woods

Hi Sylvia, I'm popping out now. If anyone
wants to know where I am, say I'm at a
forward planning meeting with Tim at
BGF. Will be back 5ish.
55 Martin

From: Martin Lukes
To: Jenny Lukes

Darling – FANTASTIC meeting with
Sebastian just now. The job is marketing
60 director of Sainsbury's!! The role's
heaven made for yours truly – I'd be
in charge of 350 people globally, $1bn
annual budget. Very high profile.

Sebastian didn't mention the
65 package at this stage, but said it
wouldn't be an obstacle to finding the
right person. I assume at least twice
what I'm on now … It's got my name all
over it – what they want are unrivalled
70 communications skills, results-driven
mentality and an outstanding track
record in driving performance … I've
got ticks in all the boxes. Coming
straight home now.
75 Love you M xx
*Sent from my BlackBerry Wireless
Handheld*

December 4
From: Martin Lukes
80 To: Sebastian FforbesHever@
HeidrickFerry

Hi Sebastian
Great to meet with you yesterday –
I felt we were very much singing from
85 the same hymn sheet. I just wanted to
reiterate how positive I am about this
position, and how much I have to bring
to the party.
    Just to re-cap: I'm very can-do, very
90 get-up-and-go – I operate very well
within a large company – but have a
pronounced entrepreneurial streak that
keeps me thinking outside the box.
Look forward to hearing from you.
95 All my very bestest
Martin

From: Martin Lukes
To: Jenny Lukes

Darling –
100 I'm on the shortlist!!! I'm going to
meet all the top bods at Sainsbury's
on Monday. I've got to prepare a
presentation on how I would transition
the marketing strategy onto a higher
105 plane. As a shopper, have you got any
pointers on supermarkets – from the

consumer's perspective? Debrief tonite?
Love you, M xx

PS I'll be working flat out all weekend
110 … so don't think I'll be able to make it
to your parents on Sunday.

From: Martin Lukes
To: Jenny Lukes

Darling – don't think you understand
115 this is the biggest point in my career to
date. I'm sure your parents won't mind –
they don't like me anyway …

December 9
From: Martin Lukes
120 To: Jenny Lukes

Darling – total triumph!! The chief
executive of Sainsbury's has the
IDENTICAL take on the future of
marketing to yours truly. The interview
125 was meant to last an hour, but I got the
feeling they had made up their mind
after 15 minutes.
    My presentation on their marketing
strategy was 110 per cent on the button.
130 I was pretty critical – though obviously
in a positive sort of way. Basically I
said that in the past they've relied too
heavily on Jamie Oliver – they need
a more flexible approach to winning
135 hearts and minds of today's shoppers.
See you later.
M xx

From: Martin Lukes
To: Jenny Lukes

140 Darling – Just had a brief chat with
Sebastian – and he says they are 'very
interested' in me. Re package, we're
talking of something in the region of
350k, plus bonuses which could be
145 same again. Obviously share options,
pension, health insurance, gym club
membership. Car allowance would be

65 **package** – *hier:* Gehalt plus
Bonuszahlungen
71 **track record** – Erfolgsgeschichte
89 **to re-cap** – die wesentlichen Punkte wiederholen
92 **streak** – Charakterzug
101 **bods** *(infml)* – Leute
107 **to debrief** – einen Einsatzbericht abgeben
133 **Jamie Oliver** – britischer
Starkoch
142 **Re(ferring to)** – Betr(eff)
144 **350k** – 350 Tausend
145 **share options** – Aktien-
bezugsrecht

double so that we could trade in the Mitsubishi Shogun and get a Porsche
150 Cayenne V8 Turbo S.
Love you M xx

From: Martin Lukes
To: Jenny Lukes

Darling – Yes, I know I shouldn't count
155 my chickens. And I'm not. I'm simply repeating what I've been told.
M

December 10
From: Martin Lukes
160 To: Graham Wallace

Hi Graham
Did you notice that I wasn't firing on all cylinders in the board meeting just now? Between you and me and the gatepost,
165 that could be the last one I'm ever going to attend. I'm up for a big job. It's as good as in the bag, though can't tell you what at this juncture. But put it this way. Think supermarket. Think Jamie Oliver.
170 Think Chief Marketing Officer …
Mart

From: Martin Lukes
To: Graham Wallace

Cheers, Graham. Yes obviously I am
175 totally over the moon. At the end of the day, being marketing director has been a load of fun, but I've outgrown it.
Mart

PS Keep this under your hat till it's
180 greenlighted. Then monster drinks in order.

From: Martin Lukes
To: Sylvia Woods

Hi Sylvia
185 I think I should let you into a little secret. I'm afraid our ways are about to part.

I've been headhunted for a very senior job, so looks like this might be my last week here. If anyone from Sainsbury's or
190 Heidrick Ferry calls in the next hour when I'm in the budget meeting come and get me out.
M

From: Martin Lukes
195 To: Sylvia Woods

Anyone called?

December 11
From: Martin Lukes
To: Sebastian FforbesHever@
200 HeidrickFerry

Hi Sebastian
I don't want to hassle you, but I just wondered if there was any news?
Bestest, Martin

---

205 From: Martin Lukes
To: Sebastian FforbesHever@
HeidrickFerry

I don't understand. That wasn't what you implied earlier. I thought the Sainsbury's
210 board loved me.
Is this a joke, or what?

From: Martin Lukes
To: Jenny Lukes

I don't fucking believe it. They've gone
215 and fucking given it to someone fucking else. Sebastian is a fucking lying sod. He said they LOVED my presentation – practically said the job was in the bag. And now he's saying I didn't have the
220 right skillsets, fit not quite right blah, better qualified candidates … blah blah. I still just can't fucking believe it. It's so unfair. My dream job.
M

225 From: Martin Lukes
To: Sylvia Woods

Sylvia I'm feeling very unwell. I think I'm coming down with the flu. I'm going home now.

----

230 **December 15**
From: Martin Lukes
To: Graham Wallace

Just to check – you haven't told anyone about that job, have you? As it happens
235 I've decided against. Basically, I've

always believed that work is all about the people. And although it was very flattering to be offered such a mega job at Sainsbury's, at the end of the day, I
240 didn't want to work with them. Feeling a bit rough this am. Hair of the dog later?
M

(1249 words)

241 **hair of the dog** (*infml*) – einen Kater mit Alkohol bekämpfen

---

1 Comprehension
Summarise what happens in this extract.

2 Vocabulary → Guessing new words, p. 142
Check these expressions in their context and explain what they mean in your own words.

• find a window (l. 27)	• thinking outside the box (l. 93)
• up against it (l. 44)	• the identical take (l. 123)
• I'm popping out (l. 51)	• on the button (l. 129)
• what I'm on now (l. 68)	• firing on all cylinders (l. 162)
• It's got my name all over it (l. 68)	• in the bag (l. 167)
• singing from the same hymn sheet (l. 84)	• Keep this under your hat (l. 179)

3 Analysis → Understanding fictional texts, p. 111

a) Characterise Martin Lukes by showing what his communications with the other characters reveal about him.

b) Compare the content and style of the last three emails.

4 Text production: Writing an email → Writing an email, p. 118
Imagine you are Martin's long-serving secretary Sylvia Woods. You have access to all of the emails above and have decided to write to Martin, who is currently on sick leave. Explain to him why – in your opinion – he probably didn't get the job, and how he can improve his behaviour in the future.

5 Research project → see Hotspot 4, p. 83

If-clauses

→ Grammar, p. 162

a) Complete the sentences by using the correct if-clause. Write your answers on a separate piece of paper.
1. If Laura had to, she … (move) to another city for a job; but she would rather stay where she is.
2. Achim will take a job if the company … (offer) him one.
3. If Irene gets the chance to attend the job fair next week in Munich, she … (meet) a lot of prospective employers.
4. If Michael had paid more attention in school, he … (get) better grades.
5. Volunteering … (be) an option for Lena if she doesn't find an internship over the summer.
6. I would drive to work if I … (have) my own car.
7. If you write your application letter too quickly it … (not be) very good.
8. If I had known that you were interested in graphic design, I … (send) you the link to the job advertisement.
9. Lena would have written the application letter by hand if Tim … (not repair) her printer at the last minute.
10. If I … (be) you, I would write more about my hobbies in my CV.

b) Decide which means of communication (telephone, email, letter) is best in the following situations and why. Use the text on page 76 to help you.
1. What will you do if …
   a) … it is 10 am local time and you need some figures from a sales representative in the US?
   b) … you want to meet up with a colleague on the second floor for lunch later?
2. What would you do if …
   a) … you were school headmaster and wanted to inform the parents about a school event?
   b) … you were a fashion designer and had to order some fabric from a supplier in India?
3. What would you have done if …
   … you had injured yourself while working on a machine, and needed medical assistance?

c) Rewrite the following sentences using the appropriate if-clause.
Example:
Michael has a lot of experience doing presentations. He doesn't get nervous.
If Michael didn't have a lot experience doing presentations, he would get nervous.
1. Sally's letter was well written. She has a good chance of getting an interview.
2. Matthew speaks three languages. He was chosen to represent his company at international events.
3. Ruben didn't ask somebody to read through his application letter. His letter was full of mistakes.
4. Teenagers 20 years ago didn't have mobile phones. They had to use payphones.
5. My boyfriend spends a lot of time chatting online. We don't have time to talk to each other.

1 **Research project: A timeline** → Internet research, p. 147
Search for information on the "history of communication". Create a timeline that shows how communication between people has developed over time. Include predictions for the future in your timeline.

2 **Project: Letter writing** → Writing a personal letter, p. 120
Draw the name of a classmate at random and keep the name secret. At home, write a short handwritten personal letter to this person. Pay attention to your hand-writing, the layout of the letter, spelling and punctuation. Make sure you also include some questions. Here are some things you can write about:

> school • family • hobbies • hopes and ambitions for the future • your last / next holiday • …

Find an envelope and address your letter to this person, and give it to your teacher, who will hand the letters out to the recipients. When you receive your letter, write a reply at home and "send" it the same way.

3 **Project: Telephone etiquette** → Mediation, p. 132, Presentation, p. 151
Work in groups. Go online and search for English video clips about how to behave correctly on the telephone. In German, create a list of the ten most important tips and copy them onto a transparency. In German, present your results to the class.

4 **Research project: German job advertisements**
→ Mediation, p. 132, Writing a formal letter, p. 121

a) Work in groups. Go online to find a German job advertisement (*Stellenangebot / Stellenanzeige*) for a job that interests you. You can find ads on the website of every major newspaper. Create a poster that shows the most important information of the job ad in English. Present your poster to the class.

b) In pairs, choose one of your classmates' posters and write a letter of application.

A1.40

THE UNIVERSITY OF ALABAMA

Search [   ] GO

| About UA | Academics | Admissions | Athletics | Giving | Libraries | Life of UA |

Text messaging and its effects on teens' grammar

"IYO TXTng = Gd 4 or NME of GMR?" If you cannot understand the previous statement, then you most likely have not been exposed to the language of text messaging. Who are the creators of this language? The answer is today's teenagers. The translation for the opening sentence is, "In your opinion, is
5 texting good for or the enemy of grammar?" Text messaging has surely given our society a quick means through which to communicate, taking out the need for capitalization, punctuation, the use and knowledge of sentence structure and the detail that make good statements great. Some educators suggest that this
10 new age form of messaging may be hindering today's teens' abilities to apply grammar
15 correctly in their writing and social skills. Others, however, take pride in the notion that
20 teenagers are essentially creating their own language of the twenty-first century

and see no effect on their students' writing skills. Edutopia, an educational
25 website, conducted an online poll regarding this issue of text messaging vs. grammar. Out of 293 votes, 137 votes (47%) chose "Yes, I believe students are carrying over the writing habits they pick up through text messaging into school assignments." 98 votes (33%) chose "No. I believe students can write one way to their friends and another way in class. They can keep the two methods
30 separate." 55 votes (19%) chose "Maybe. Although text messaging may have some impact on how students write, I don't think it's a significant problem." […]
Wat do u tnk? (What do you think?) The Sacramento News published an article in April of 2008 about a study conducted by the Pew Internet and American
35 Life Project and the National Commission on Writing regarding text messaging and its effect on teens' schoolwork. The study concludes, "A national telephone poll of 700 youths ages 12 to 17 and their parents found that 64 percent of teens admit that the breezy shortcuts and symbols

commonly used in text messaging have appeared in their school assignments."

40 One teacher in the article states, "'When informal language does pop up in papers, I definitely am going to correct it,' she said. 'But it's part of our job as teachers to help students move in and out of formal and informal language.'" This teacher is very correct; in Alabama as well as other states across the United States, one of the standards for teachers of English Language

45 Arts is to educate students on the difference of and appropriate use of formal and informal language. [...]

Overall, it really is no surprise that text messaging is leaking into students' schoolwork because teenagers are generally known in our society as constant texters. In fact, teens in the United States (ages 13 to 17) statistically,

50 according to phone bills, have the highest levels of text messaging, sending and receiving an average of about 1800 text messages per month. [...]

Many teens, though, go above and beyond the average of text messaging among our youth today. One online article featured a thirteen-year-old girl who text messaged 14,528 text messages in a single month. Her father noted

55 that the online AT&T statement ran 440 pages long. [...] When calculating the amount of hours in a single month, just think about the astronomical amount that this girl is texting per minute. Imagine what this California girl's teachers are probably seeing in her schoolwork. (567 words)

47 **to leak into** – *hier:* sich einschleichen

1 Comprehension

a) In your own words outline the benefits and disadvantages of texting abbreviations according to the text.

b) Briefly outline the results of the online poll and the study mentioned in the article.

2 Analysis → Understanding non-fictional texts, p. 109

a) Analyse the structure of the article and explain its effect on the reader.

b) Analyse the cartoon and relate it to the text.

3 Comment

"[…] this new age form of messaging may be hindering today's teens' abilities to apply grammar correctly in their writing and social skills." (ll. 9-17)
Do you agree with this statement?

"Possessive pronouns? Um, iPod, yourPod, theirPod?" *TidePod*

1 Binge drinking

 Topic 1

 BBC Motion Gallery

Before watching

a) According to the dictionary, binge drinking is *"the activity of drinking a large amount of alcohol in a short period of time, usually in order to become drunk"*. What is your personal opinion on binge drinking? Have you experienced it in one way or the other?

b) Why do you think people binge drink?

c) Share your ideas with a partner. Decide on three final reasons.

d) Discuss your ideas with the class.

While watching

Watch the video and take notes on the following questions.
Short answers will do.

a) The report states "Nearly half of all men and a quarter of all women have become binge drinkers." How does the report define binge drinking?

b) How much does binge drinking cost the UK economy? How is this figure calculated?

c) In what age group has there been the largest increase in binge drinking numbers?

d) What does the report say about the effect of binge drinking on the nation's health? What figures are mentioned to support this assessment?

e) What does the government want to do about the problem?

f) What do charities think needs to be done to stop binge drinking?

After watching

a) Write a German summary of the video using your notes.

b) Why do you think approximately twice as many males than females are binge drinkers? Share your ideas with a partner.

c) Work in groups of 3–4 and design an anti-drinking poster to be put up around high schools to stop young people from binge drinking.

2 Kid's Company

 Topic 2

BBC Motion Gallery

This video is about *Kid's Company*, a London-based charity that works for neglected and abused children. It is run by Camila Batmanghelidjh.

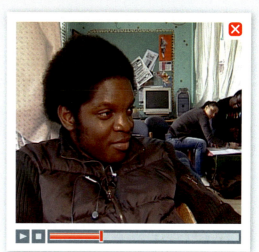

 Before watching

a) Discuss in groups what kind of help neglected and abused children need.

b) Here are some quotes from the video. What do you think the film is about?

> Every single one of these children is worth every minute of my time.

> Here in London, a brave experiment is changing lives.

> A boy who might end up in gangs is studying to be a fashion designer.

> There are only two places you can end up: dead or in jail.

> Trouble is that kind of thing that just naturally folllows me, unfortunately.

> It's the everyday one-on-one help which is key to turning troubled lives around.

While watching

a) Watch the video for the first time. What are its main parts?

b) Watch the video again, concentrating on the following aspects. What is Batmanghelidjh's approach to neglected and abused children? What role do former gang members play in *Kid's Company*?

 After watching

a) Write a short report about the activities and the success of *Kid's Company*.

b) Go online and search for further information about *Kid's company*. Summarise the main aspects of this charity in a short German text for your school newspaper.

c) Discuss whether the following statement by Camila Batmanghelidjh is true for any kind of care for neglected and abused children: "It's the everyday one-on-one help which is key to turning troubled lives around."

d) You work in the personnel department of a company that is looking for trainees. You receive an application from a young man who offers the qualifications and work experience your company is asking for. All this experience was gained in a project similar to *Kid's Company*. Do you think you should invite him to a job interview? Discuss in groups and agree on one opinion. Present your opinion to the class and exchange your views.

3 Green Fuel from Pond Scum   Topic 3   BBC Motion Gallery

The film introduces the idea of hydrogen-fuelled cars and explains different ways of producing the hydrogen needed.

Before watching

a) Make a list of fossil fuels and a list of renewable energy resources.

b) Which of these resources are currently used to power cars? Which ones do you consider green?

c) Copy and complete the word web about green technologies in cars.

- disadvantages of using green fuels in cars
- advantages of using green fuels in cars
- green technologies in cars
- types of green fuels available
- anything else you know

d) Agree on one statement which expresses your opinion about green technologies in cars, e.g. "We believe that more has to be done to develop alternative technologies because at the moment green technologies are so expensive that not everyone can afford to drive a green car." Collect these statements in class.

While watching

a) Complete the sentences with suitable information from the box.

1. The real trick would be to get hydrogen …
2. The car prototypes shown are powered by … that make electricity.
3. The only exhaust is …
4. Politicians in California believe the hydrogen revolution will …
5. The only problem about using hydrogen to power cars is that much of the hydrogen …
6. California law says that greenhouse gas emissions from cars must be reduced …
7. California leads the world with its …

> span the US • is produced from natural gas • clean car laws • hydrogen fuel cells • by a third by 2014 • from renewable sources of energy • harmless water vapour

b) Apart from the traditional use of natural gas, the film shows two new ways of producing hydrogen. Copy and complete the table with information from the film.

solar foil	pond scum

After watching

a) In groups, agree on one statement which expresses your opinion about green technologies in cars. Compare these statements with the ones you made before you watched the film. Has your attitude changed?

b) Summarise the information shown in the film about hydrogen-fuelled cars in a short German text.

c) Find out about hydrogen-fuelled cars on the German market. Inform your classmates about technical details, prices, etc. Based on the information in the film, make a poster to advertise the idea of buying cars powered by renewable energy sources.

4   The Interview

▶ Topic 5   **BBC** Motion Gallery

Before watching

a) What three tips would you give somebody going to a job interview?

b) Discuss your ideas with a partner and decide on a final list of three.

c) Share your tips with the class and be prepared to explain your choices.

While watching

a) Why has working in a café become more attractive?

b) What qualities is the HR & Training Director looking for in the applicants?

c) What criticism does the expert have of the first applicant (two things)?

d) What question does the interviewer ask the second applicant?

e) According to the expert, what is the worst question you can ask as an applicant and why?

f) Watch the film again and find out the following information:
  1. What are the applicants' names?
  2. What position are they applying for?
  3. What countries do the applicants come from?
  4. Which applicant is successful?

After watching

a) Imagine you are the interviewer. Work together with a partner and come up with a list of positives and negatives about each applicant based on what you have seen in the video.

b) In groups of 3–4, discuss which applicant you would choose for the job and why.

c) Share your thoughts with the class and see if you have chosen the same person.

Self-assessment – Selbsteinschätzung

Nachdem Sie die Aufgaben (Seite 94 – 99) bearbeitet haben, können Sie die Ergebnisse mit den Lösungen vergleichen. Schätzen Sie dann bitte Ihre Leistung in den folgenden Kategorien selbst ein: Leseverstehen, Hörverstehen, Schreibfertigkeit und Sprechfertigkeit. Bitte beurteilen Sie für jede Kategorie, ob Sie die einzelnen Stufen „überhaupt nicht erreicht", „voll erreicht" oder Ihrer Meinung nach „deutlich überschritten" haben.

In den danach folgenden Kategorien Wortschatz, grammatische Strukturen, Aussprache und Flüssigkeit sowie Aufbau und Gedankenführung wählen Sie die Kategorie, die Ihre Leistung am besten beschreibt.

Leseverstehen

Stufe 1
Wenn ich einen unbekannten englischen Text lese, kann ich oft die wesentlichen Punkte erfassen. Die Texte sollten nicht zu kompliziert und nicht zu lang sein, es ist leichter, wenn sie ein Thema behandeln, bei dem ich mich gut auskenne. Die Informationen, die ich benötige, finde ich dann schnell. Mit dem vorliegenden Text hatte ich nach wiederholtem Lesen keine großen Schwierigkeiten, ich habe alle gesuchten Informationen ohne sehr große Probleme gefunden.

Stufe 2
Ich lese englische Texte insgesamt sehr selbstständig und verstehe auch dann vieles, wenn ich Fachartikel lese. Längere Texte machen mir meistens keine Schwierigkeiten, Zeitungsartikel zu aktuellen Fragen verstehe ich zum größten Teil. Den vorliegenden Text habe ich schnell auch im Detail verstanden, nur wenige Sätze musste ich mehrfach lesen.

Stufe 3
Ich verstehe fast alle englischen Texte. Ich kann lange, komplexe Texte im Detail verstehen, auch wenn sie ein Thema behandeln, mit dem ich mich nicht gut auskenne. Manchmal lese ich komplizierte Passagen mehrmals, aber ich fühle mich im Lesen von englischen Texten insgesamt sehr sicher. Den vorliegenden Text fand ich insgesamt leicht, er hat mir keine Probleme bereitet. Alle Details habe ich sehr schnell gefunden.

Hörverstehen

Stufe 1
Ich verstehe die Hauptaspekte in Redebeiträgen zu alltäglichen oder vertrauten Themen. Das Hörverstehen fällt mir leichter, wenn die Sprecher(innen) deutlich artikulieren. Die Beiträge sollten aber nicht sehr lang sein.

Stufe 2
Ich verstehe die Hauptaussagen in Redebeiträgen auch zu komplexeren Themen. Wenn der Akzent vertraut ist und deutlich gesprochen wird, verstehe ich auch Fachdiskussionen zu weniger vertrauten Themen. Das Hörverstehen fällt mir leicht, wenn die Sprecher(innen) deutlich artikulieren.

Stufe 3
Wenn ich einen längeren englischen Redebeitrag höre, kann ich meist die wesentlichen Punkte erfassen. Die Texte können auch fremde und komplexe Themen behandeln. Ich verstehe auch Unterhaltungen mit zwei oder mehr Sprecher(inne)n ohne Probleme, leichte Probleme habe ich eigentlich nur bei fremdem Akzent.

Texte verfassen

Stufe 1
Ich kann zu bekannten oder alltäglichen Themen zusammenhängende Texte verfassen, in denen eine klare Struktur zu finden ist.

Stufe 2
Ich kann in strukturierten, zusammenhängenden Texten Vor- und Nachteile von bestimmten Standpunkten darlegen und meine Meinung besonders zu vertrauten Themen aus meinem Interessengebiet darlegen. Hier kann ich auch Detailinformationen klar und überzeugend präsentieren.

Stufe 3
Ich kann klar, flüssig und gut strukturiert über komplexe Themen schreiben, es fällt mir nicht schwer, bestimmte Punkte besonders hervorzuheben. Mein gedanklicher Aufbau ist mit Standpunkt(en), Beispielen und klarem Ende gut nachzuvollziehen.

An Gesprächen teilnehmen

Stufe 1
Die meisten vorhersehbaren Situationen kann ich in Gesprächen so lösen, dass mein(e) Gesprächspartner(in) versteht, was ich sagen möchte. Ich kann Informationen austauschen, meine Meinung darlegen und Argumente für vertraute Sachverhalte vorbringen.

Stufe 2
Ich kann mich soweit fließend und spontan verständigen, dass ein normales Gespräch über verschiedene Freizeit-, aber auch berufliche Themen möglich ist, ohne dass mein(e) Gesprächspartner(in) sich anstrengen muss, mich zu verstehen. Ich kann mich auch über einen längeren Zeitraum an Gesprächen beteiligen und habe keine Mühe, ein Gespräch durch meine Initiative aufrechtzuerhalten.

Stufe 3
Ich kann mich fast mühelos spontan und fließend ausdrücken. Mein Wortschatz ist groß genug, um immer auch Umschreibungen für das zu finden, was ich sagen möchte. Schwierigkeiten habe ich nur bei Fachthemen, bei denen mir zum Teil Begriffe unbekannt sind. Ich kann flexibel auf Gesprächspartner(innen) eingehen und eigentlich immer alles ausdrücken, was ich sagen möchte, dies schließt auch z. B. Scherze, Emotionen usw. ein.

Wortschatz

Ich denke, mein Allgemein- und Fachwortschatz ist …	… sehr differenziert, d. h. ich kann fast alles sagen, was ich möchte, bei vielen Wörter kenne ich auch andere Wörter mit gleicher oder ähnlicher Bedeutung oder die jeweiligen Gegenteile; die Wörter kann ich auch alle korrekt schreiben.
	… differenziert, ich kann vieles sagen, was ich möchte, manchmal kenne ich Wörter mit gleicher oder ähnlicher Bedeutung; ich mache sehr wenige Rechtschreibfehler.
	… weniger differenziert, d. h. manchmal fehlen mir auch alltägliche Wörter; für viele Aspekte kenne ich nur jeweils ein Wort. Insgesamt kann ich aber vieles sagen, was ich sagen möchte, auch wenn ich ab und zu Rechtschreibfehler mache.
	… begrenzt, d. h. häufig fehlen mir auch alltägliche Wörter; nicht immer kann ich sagen, was ich sagen möchte; die Zahl der Rechtschreibfehler ist insgesamt hoch.
	… deutlich begrenzt, ich weiß viele Wörter nicht, die ich schon vor Jahren gelernt habe; häufig muss ich im Wörterbuch nachsehen, ich mache auch bei einfachen Wörtern sehr viele Rechtschreibfehler.
	… stark begrenzt; ich kann sehr vieles (auch Alltägliches) nicht sagen; die Wörter, die ich dann im Wörterbuch finde, habe ich häufig noch nie gehört; die Grundregeln der englischen Rechtschreibung kenne ich nicht.

Grammatische Strukturen

Ich denke, die von mir benutzten grammatischen Strukturen …	… haben einen sehr hohen Grad an Korrektheit, ich weiß, dass ich kaum Grammatikfehler mache; gelegentliche Fehler kann ich als Fehler erkennen und entsprechend schnell korrigieren.
	… haben einen hohen Grad an Korrektheit, ich mache nur gelegentlich Grammatikfehler, diese kann ich selbst erkennen und korrigieren, wenn ich in einer Grammatik nachschlage.
	… zeigen, dass ich eigentlich die englische Grammatik beherrsche, obwohl ich vermehrt Fehler mache; ich kenne die wichtigsten grammatischen Regeln, sie sind nur im Sprachgebrauch nicht immer selbstverständlich für mich.
	… sind bei einer ziemlich hohen Fehlerzahl noch im Rahmen; ich weiß, dass ich einige Regeln im Detail wiederholen müsste, aber ich habe von den wichtigsten Regeln schon gehört und kann sie eigentlich auch anwenden, wenn ich sie wiederholt habe.
	… zeigen, dass ich im Bereich Grammatik ziemliche Lücken habe; ich mache sehr viele Fehler und weiß auch oft nicht, was an meinen Sätzen von der Grammatik her falsch ist.
	… zeigen, dass ich die englische Grammatik kaum beherrsche; ich kenne auch sehr elementare Regeln nicht und bin auch nicht in der Lage, meine Fehler ohne Hilfe zu korrigieren.

Aussprache und Flüssigkeit

Ich denke, meine Aussprache ist …	… klar, korrekt, flüssig; die Zuhörer(innen) können immer sofort verstehen, was ich sagen möchte, meine Sprechgeschwindigkeit ist recht hoch.
	… weitgehend klar, korrekt, flüssig; manchmal zögere ich kurz, wenn ich ein Wort nicht sofort weiß, aber das bedeutet keine langen Pausen.
	… so, dass die Zuhörer(innen) mich eigentlich schon verstehen, auch wenn ich manchmal recht langsam spreche; die Aussprache bei einigen Wörtern fällt mir manchmal schwer und ich weiß nicht alle Wörter sofort.
	… ist bei einer ziemlich hohen Fehlerzahl noch im Rahmen; ich weiß, dass ich Wörter falsch ausspreche, aber meine Beiträge sind weitgehend zu verstehen, auch wenn ich manchmal Pausen mache.
	… geprägt von einigen Aussprachefehlern, ich zögere vielfach, manchmal sind die Pausen auch länger.
	… geprägt von vermehrten Aussprachefehlern, das Verständnis ist nicht gesichert, für die Zuhörer(innen) ist eine Unterhaltung mit mir insgesamt anstrengend.

Aufbau und Gedankenführung

Meine Gedankenführung halte ich für …	… stringent, komplex und differenziert; ich kann einzelne Aspekte und die gedanklichen Verbindungen zwischen Aspekten sehr gut darstellen.
	… klar, stringent und nachvollziehbar.
	… angemessen, da ich immer eine Gliederung habe und meine Ausführungen nachvollziehbar sind.
	… verbesserungswürdig, da ich oft Schwächen im logischen Aufbau habe; ich schaffe es trotzdem, eine grundsätzliche Gliederung zu erstellen.
	… häufig zusammenhanglos; ich weiß, dass ich mir oft widerspreche und dass man eine Gliederung kaum erkennen kann.
	… sehr unzureichend, da mir eine Strukturierung und Gliederung dessen, was ich sagen möchte, fast nie gelingt.

Assessment test 1 – Diagnose

A1.42  **1** **Listening comprehension: Teenagers and social networking sites** → Listening, p. 108
Listen to the recording about social networking sites and say whether each
statement is true, false or not in the text.

a) More than 500 million teenagers worldwide use Facebook.

b) Facebook is more popular than MySpace.

c) Social networking sites have become integrated into the everyday social lives
of teens.

d) These online platforms can only be accessed by personal computers.

e) Teenagers use these sites to stay in touch or make new friends.

f) Flirting with somebody online is not very common.

g) The majority of teenagers do not like posting photographs.

h) A large number of teenagers do not see a risk when posting confidential
information such as telephone numbers or postal addresses.

i) These confidential pieces of information may be passed on for advertising
reasons or can even be misused for identity theft.

j) Parents warn teenagers not to post photos.

---

³ **glued to the screen** – vor
dem Fernseher kleben

³ **to engage in sth.** – sich an
etw. beteiligen

⁴ **likelihood** – Wahrschein-
lichkeit

⁵ **to claim** – *hier:* behaupten

⁵ **to reveal** – *hier:* veröffent-
lichen, zeigen

⁶ **peer** – Gleichaltrige(r)

¹¹ **social cognitive theory** –
Kognitions- und Lern-
theorie, die u. a. besagt,
dass man lernt, indem man
andere beobachtet

¹⁵ **to adopt** – anpassen

MailOnline   Search [   ] GO

| Home | News | U. S. | Sport | TV & Showbiz | Femail | Health |

How spending too much time online 'can increase the chances of your teenager taking drugs'

Those regularly glued to screens are 'far more likely to engage in risky behaviour'

Spending time online increases the likelihood of a teenager taking drugs or having
5 unprotected sex, it has been claimed. Research revealed those who are regularly glued
to their screens are far more likely to engage in risky behaviour than their peers. The
researchers from the Queen's University in Canada found that young adults who logged
the most hours on their computers were 50 per cent more likely to engage in a cluster of
six 'multi-risk behaviours'. These included smoking, drunkenness, cannabis and illegal
10 drug use, having unprotected sex and not using seat belts.

Research author Valerie Carson, said: 'This research is based on social cognitive theory,
which suggests that seeing people engaged in a behaviour is a way of learning that
behaviour. Since adolescents are exposed to considerable screen time – over 4.5 hours
on average each day – they're constantly seeing images of behaviours they can then
15 potentially adopt.'

One explanation behind the findings is that a considerable amount of advertising that used to be shown on TV is now being shown on the internet. In addition, computer usage by adolescents has increased considerably in recent years. 'TV and video games have more established protocols in terms of censorship, but Internet protocols aren't

20 as established,' Ms Carson said. 'Parents can make use of programs that control access to the Internet, but adolescents in this age group are quite savvy about technology and the Internet. It's possible that these types of controls aren't effective in blocking all undesirable websites.'

The research, recently published in the Journal of Preventative Medicine, suggests that

25 future studies should examine the specific content adolescents are being exposed to in order to help strengthen current screen time guidelines for youth.   (314 words)

19 **protocol** – *hier:* Ordnung, Vorgabe
20 **access** – Zugang
24 **preventative** – vorbeugend
26 **to strengthen** – verstärken

2 Comprehension → Word webs, p. 138
Copy and complete the word web with relevant information from the text.

censorship and control

facts about the research

How spending too much time online 'can increase the chances of your teenager taking drugs'

reasons for risky behaviour

risky behaviour

3 Comment → Writing a comment, p. 116
"Teenagers' access to the Internet should be limited to a maximum of 2 hours a day." Comment on this statement, also with reference to the findings presented in the text. Make sure that you include pros and cons!

4 Role play: Teenagers and the Internet → Discussions, p. 133
Now prepare for a role play. There are four roles. Work on your own and collect arguments to prepare for the discussion.

a) You are a teenager and are strictly against limiting Internet access for teenagers.

b) You are a parent and are concerned about your children spending too much time on the Internet. However, you do not know if a limit would really help.

c) You are a parent and are strongly in favour of limiting your teenage child's Internet access to a maximum of two hours a day.

d) You are a teacher. You believe that for many teenagers the Internet has replaced all other communication media, but you are also concerned that the contents children and teenagers are consuming can no longer be controlled.

Assessment test 2 – Diagnose

A1.43

1 Listening comprehension: Globetrotters – a radio documentary → Listening, p. 108
Listen to the interview with Max Ranter, a popular musician who travels all over the world with his band. Copy and complete the word web with information from the interview.

2 Comprehension: Teenagers and music
Work through the table of facts about teenagers and music and choose the correct answer. Be careful! Sometimes more than one answer is correct.

3 **destructive** – zerstörerisch

5 **drug abuse** – Drogen-missbrauch

11 **to estimate** – schätzen

14 **to enhance** – verbessern

16 **motor control** – Motorik

21 **guidance** – Führung, Orientierung

26 **to bridge** – überbrücken

33 **average** – durchschnittlich

43 **outlet** – *hier:* Ventil

Parents should ask for professional help if a teenager is often lost in music that has very destructive themes and if they see changes in behaviour (isolation, depression, alcohol or other 5 drug abuse).	Music is so powerful because it is a universal 25 language. It addresses universal human feelings and bridges gaps between cultures. Music brings people much closer together than languages do.
A survey found out that on average teenagers consider £6.58 a fair price for a CD album.	75 per cent of teenagers say that they have watched a music video online.
Music also plays a powerful social role: it brings young people with similar tastes 10 together.	30 Music is often a key part of a teenager's own personal world. It is quite common for teenagers to keep adults out of this world.
Record companies estimate that illegal peer-to-peer filesharing accounts for 95 per cent of all digital music downloads.	According to record companies, on average 43 per cent of the music owned and enjoyed by 35 teenagers has not been paid for.
Scientists say that music enhances brain 15 functioning. Playing music activates a variety of brain functions simultaneously: motor control, imagination, hearing, sight, memory, etc.	Many people agree that whatever you are doing becomes more intense when it is accompanied by music: a sporting event, a movie scene, a romantic situation, even driving your car.
Nearly 3/4 of 15–24s said they don't feel guilty about illegally downloading music.	40 60 per cent of 16–24 year olds would rather go without meeting friends for a week.
20 Especially for teenagers, music can serve as a source of moral or social guidance.	Music is generally believed to be a form of expression and an emotional outlet.
40 billion songs are downloaded illegally world-wide every year.	More than 80% of the teenagers interviewed 45 said that listening to music made them feel good.

a) 1. More than 80% of teenagers do not feel guilty about illegal downloads.
  2. Half of the teenagers say illegal downloads are acceptable.
  3. Nearly 75% of teenagers do not mind downloading music illegally.

b) 1. Teenagers often do not want to share their music with adults.
  2. Teenagers ask parents for advice if their music deals with destructive themes.
  3. Adults encourage teenagers to listen to music because it has a positive influence on them.

c) 1. Record companies say that nearly 40 billion songs are downloaded illegally every year.
2. Teenagers share passwords to download songs.
3. More and more adults download music illegally as well.

d) 1. Music makes you feel good whatever you do.
2. Whatever you do becomes more intense when you listen to music.
3. Music is suitable as an emotional outlet.

e) 1. Music makes it easier to get to know other people.
2. Only language is more powerful in bringing people together.
3. With the help of music, differences between cultures can be overcome.

f) 1. Some kind of music can even serve as emotional or moral guidance.
2. Whenever you listen to music, you feel better.
3. Music stimulates various activities in your brain.

g) 1. On average, teenagers spend £6.58 for music online every week.
2. Teenagers are not prepared to pay more than £6.58 for an album.
3. On average, teenagers say that £6.58 is a fair price for an album.

3 **Text production: Writing an email** → Writing an email, p. 118
A friend of yours called Marleen sends you the following email. Write an email in reply
giving Marleen some advice.

> Hi,
> You know that we've been playing in our band for the last couple of years now; you also know that we have
> never been that successful. For me it was crystal clear that music would be nothing more than a hobby …
> But then last year all of a sudden things started to change. We got more gigs than in the years before and
> now we have even been contacted by a record company. They want to offer us a contract on the condition
> that I stop school and become a full-time musician. I really don't know what to do … On the one hand,
> music is my life – but on the other hand, leaving college now means I would end up without any quali-
> fications at all. Can I please have your advice?
> Cheers,
> Marleen

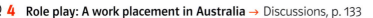

4 **Role play: A work placement in Australia** → Discussions, p. 133
After finishing school, you (aged 18) first want to do a work placement and then see what
comes next. So you have decided to work in the music industry for six months because music
is extremely important in your life. You have sent applications to a German record company
and an Australian music label. Now, both have offered you a placement, and they want a
decision soon. That's why you now find yourself in a discussion with your family and your
boyfriend / girlfriend.

a) You want to go to Australia because you believe this is a once-in-a-lifetime chance.

b) Your father / mother understands that you see this as a real chance but is worried
nevertheless.

c) Your boyfriend / girlfriend fears that your relationship will suffer if you go away for so long.

d) Your older brother / sister supports your plans and encourages you to go abroad.

Assessment test 3 – Diagnose

A1.45

1 **Listening comprehension: Teenagers as consumers** → Listening, p. 108
Listen to the text about teenagers as consumers and summarise the most important aspects in German.

2 **Comprehension** → Understanding non-fictional texts, p. 109
Copy and complete the table with information from the text.

Information about the study	Negative effects of working during school	Positive effects of working during school	Recommendations

5 to hamper – erschweren

7 delinquency – Kriminalität

14 sophomore – amerikanischer Student (2. Jahr)

19 decade – Jahrzehnt

22 attainment – Leistungen

23 substance abuse – Drogenmissbrauch

THE 10 O'CLOCK NEWS

HOME | NEWS | WEATHER | HEALTH | MONEY | SPORTS |

Search [   ] GO

Study: Too much part-time work harmful for students

A part-time job may seem like a sweet deal for teens raising money for college or wanting to buy their own things, but a new study warns that too many work hours may be harmful to a teen's development. The study, led by University of Washington researcher Kathryn
5 Monahan, suggested that working during the school year can hamper school performance and cause behavior problems like drug abuse and delinquency.
"Especially in a recessed economy, many adolescents may feel pressure to work during high school," Monahan told the *University of Washington*
10 *news service*. "The study suggests that working during the school year is perfectly fine, so long as the work hours for adolescents are restricted to fewer than 20 hours per week."
Monahan, a research scientist with UW's School of Social Work, used data from nearly 1,800 high school sophomores and juniors who were
15 followed for two years in the late 1980s. There was almost an even mix of boys and girls with ethnically and socio-economically diverse backgrounds from nine high schools in Wisconsin and northern California.
While the research was decades old, she said that work and teens have
20 not changed that much. The study, as reported by *USA Today,* showed that students who worked more than 20 hours a week had lower expectations for educational attainment and were less engaged in school. They also showed more problem behavior such as substance abuse.

At the same time, the same students had slightly higher grade point
25 averages than teens without jobs and were more independent in their
decision-making. *USA Today* said researchers attributed some of the
higher GPA to working students taking easier classes and spending less
time on homework. Even after the teens cut down their hours or stopped
working, *US News* and *World Report* said, the study showed that the
30 negative behavior still continued.
"Although working during high school is unlikely to turn law-abiding
teenagers into felons or cause students to flunk out of school, the extent
of the adverse effects we found is not trivial …," Monahan said. She said
parents, educators and employers should be careful about letting teens
35 work too many extra hours during the school year. The study is published
in the January/February issue of the journal *Child Development*. (382 words)

24 **grade point average (GPA)** – Notendurchschnitt

36 **issue** – Ausgabe

3 Comment → Writing a comment, p. 116
Write a text commenting on the advert "No money. No problem." which the Standard Bank uses to attract young people as customers. Take into account the slogan and also the text.

4 Role play: TweenPlus account
Standard Bank wants to start a large advertising campaign to promote their children's bank account, tweenPlus.

Here are the facts:

children (aged 11+) can open their own bank account with as little as £1 • earn credit interest – the more you save, the more interest you'll earn • StandardBank Cash Card for withdrawing up to £50 a day from cash machines • pay pocket money straight into your account • no monthly fee

Now prepare for the role play. There are four roles. Work on your own and collect arguments to prepare for the discussion.

a) You are a bank manager and defend your tweenPlus account.

b) You are a concerned parent and are worried that your child will end up in debt if they have an account of their own.

c) You are a member of a consumer watchdog organisation that criticises banks for massively targeting teenagers as potential customers.

d) You are a 16-year-old teenager and are all in favour of this kind of bank account.

Helping hand – Differenzierung

Topic 1

A 3 Role play → p. 8

Here are some arguments to start you off:

- The greater the number of young people who gather in one place, the more likely it is that the party will get out of control.
- There will always be some who go against the rules. In most cases, this means alcohol and drugs.
- Police operations on this scale cost the taxpayer a lot of money.
- You can't just go round having fun at someone else's expense.
- The partygoers certainly won't clean up when they leave.
- Especially younger people, who are under a lot of peer pressure, might easily be influenced by those who misbehave.
- Why can't you just have a bit more trust in young people? Always calling in the police beforehand shows what you think of them!
- As long as they celebrate in public places, everything is just fine.
- These parties are a brilliant way of getting to know other people.
- Where's the difference to your Schützenfest? Just because we're young?
- Adults just need to accept that life is changing because of the Internet. Everything is faster, more spontaneous, even freer.

A 4 Text production: Writing an email → p. 9

Here are some sentences you might want to use in your email:

- Dear …, on Facebook I just read that you are inviting people in California to a flash mob party at someone else's house – to the home of someone you do not know.
- Even though I do not know you and we will probably never meet, I would like to tell you what I think about this idea. Using someone else's property – in this case someone else's pool – is …
- Especially the fact that you cannot estimate how many people will eventually turn up …
- Have you thought about …
- You also might want to consider…
- Let me tell you about an incident which took place in Hamburg, Germany…
- So, all in all, I believe that your idea of inviting strangers to a stranger's house for a party is …

A 5 Mediation → p. 9

Follow these basic rules when doing a mediation task:

- Do not translate word for word.
- Just try to get the key message and the central ideas of the text across.
- Your new text can have a different line of argumentation or a different sequence.

For this task, you might want to include the following ideas:

- Menschen verbringen mehr Zeit auf Internetseiten von sozialen Netzwerken (Facebook, Twitter, MySpace usw.), Russen mehr als sechs Stunden im Monat, Deutsche etwa vier Stunden
- Facebook hat ca. 1 Milliarde aktive Mitglieder
- voraussichtliche Werbeausgaben auf diesen Seiten nur für die USA (2012) – 2,6 Miliarden Dollar

B 3 **Listening comprehension: Teens, cell phones and texting** → p. 11

These are the main topics which are mentioned in the audio text:

- American teenagers are increasingly using mobile phones and text messages to communicate with each other.
- Parents and schools find it difficult to set limits.
- Some teenagers already prefer texting to face-to-face conversations.

B 4 **Comment** → p. 11

Here are some ideas that might help you in your line of argumentation:

- There are those who admire teenagers for their ability to use digital communication with ease.
- They envy them for being able to stay in touch with the world around them effortlessly.
- There are those who say that teenagers are wasting their lives on social networking sites or on texting dozens of messages a day.
- They point out that teenagers are becoming increasingly technology-enslaved.
- Parents are worried that their children might be losing touch with the outside world as they replace it with a virtual one.
- They fear that today's teenagers might lose their ability to interact with people in the real world.
- Life is much more than digital communication. There is no substitute for authentic experience and real encounters.
- Digital communication offers huge advantages to those who have the knowledge and the skills to use it to fulfil their wishes.
- Digital communication is fast, easy, keeps people in touch and does not exclude people because of the way they look or speak. In this sense, it is fairer and more respectful.

E 3 **Analysis** → p. 17

Here are some ideas that might help you in your line of argumentation:

Chorus	Verses
words showing insecurity: don't know, fear	words showing determination, power and success: want, don't care, I'll, fucking, weapon, massive, winner
negative sentence: I don't know, question adressed to sb. else (When do you think …)	
repetition (When do you think it will all become clear? Cause I'm being taken over by fear) at the end of every verse	affirmative sentences: I want, I'll, I am

E5 **Comment** → p. 17

In your comment, the following phrases might help you:

- On the one hand Lily Allen's song portrays …
- The singer manages to show …
- The lyrics clearly emphasise what society …
- To many teenagers, the idea of their future consists of …
- On the other hand the dominant fear plays an important role …

- Hardly any teenager today believes that…
- While Lily Allen's song ends with …, for many teenagers …
- All in all I believe that you cannot say that teenagers today …
- There's no such thing as …

Topic 2

A3 **Analysis** → p. 25

The following sentences will help you with your analysis of the cartoon:

- The black-and-white cartoon shows …
- The father is … He is traditionally dressed and is …
- His son who is … is standing …
- There is a caption under the cartoon saying …
- This means that the public discussion of family matters on social media …
- A normal conversation or even an argument between family members …
- The father seems to be more concerned about his image on MySpace …
- For the son making his complaint public seems to be …
- So the cartoonist is making the point that …
- I think the cartoon is …

B4 **a) Text production: Writing an email** → p. 27

Your email to Sam's mother could include the following aspects and ideas:

- show an understanding for the shock she is feeling
- show an understanding for the difficulty of raising Sam alone
- say what you think of Sam's behaviour
- show some sympathy for her and acknowledge the fact that she may feel guilty or that she has made a mistake
- comment on how she talks to her son in front of other people
- offer advice on how she could behave in the future

C3   Mediation → p. 28

The following keywords might help you with your mediation:

- census by *Statistisches Bundesamt*, Germany
- traditional role model still valid today
- but: more working mothers, most work part-time
- fathers mostly breadwinners, mothers stay at home or work part-time (still most common role model in Germany)
- numbers of mothers working part-time have increased dramatically, this especially applies to single mothers
- generally speaking: more women than in the past feel that they must work part-time to make ends meet

C4   Listening comprehension: Miss World and women's rights go hand in hand → p. 29

Match the following jumbled clues with the headings in the table. This will help you understand the listening text.

Why Clara Belle was against beauty contests in the past	Reasons that made her change her view	Beauty contests and feminism	Clara Belle's views on contests and pageants in general
Rebecca Mordan's criticism: women are reduced to the "sum of their parts"	pageants and women's rights can go hand in hand; they celebrate the diversity of appearances; underline contestant's individuality contestant gains confidence, friendship and a broadened mind	she believed these contests were degrading and humiliating to the young women	she discovered people who • are motivated, shared a desire to contribute to their community and be a part of something positive • seek recognition • represent views or causes that are important to them

Topic 3

B4   Comment → p. 43

Here are some arguments for and against to help you write your newspaper article:

Arguments for	Arguments against
• financial benefits – for tourism industry + people living in tourist destinations • increased tourism = increased investment in infrastructure: good for tourists + local residents • culture, tradition, food, language, art of one local area is promoted around the world • everyone should see the world • new cultures, influences, opportunities	• local cultures are destroyed by influx of tourists • culture changed / watered down to suit visitors • visitors do not see 'real life' • mass tourism damages environment: long-haul flights, waste, etc. • sites of natural beauty ruined by overcrowding

C3 Analysis → p. 45

Here are some points to help you with the text analysis:

Examples from the text	Effect on the reader
• "… I was a criminal. Just like you." (l. 11) • "… Want more? I drank wine, spent money, …" (l. 40) • "And just like you – if you live in the Western world, and I have to assume you do, or how else would you be reading this?" (ll. 41 – 42)	• provoke the reader – ask the reader questions • awakens the interest of the reader • reader is challenged, involved • reader must make up their mind

D2 Analysis → p. 46

Here are some points to get you started:

Attitudes toward GM food in Europe	Comparison with USA
• support in Spain remained quite constant – high level • support in UK unstable – sharp decline from 1996 – 1999 and sharp increase from 1999 – 2002 • Germany: steady drop in support • Greece: extreme drop in support from 1996 – 2005: 49% – 12% • conclusion: support in Europe varies but decline is noticeable	• opposition to GM food has declined 10% • support for GM food stable • half US population against GM food, one third in favour • percentage of support for GM food higher in Spain, UK & Germany than in USA

Topic 4

C6 Composition → p. 59

Here are some ideas that might help you write the composition:

American suburbs	Life in Germany
• cities spread very fast, taking over what used to be inhabited land • very large suburbs • large distances between homes and shops, places of work, facilities, etc. • car is always necessary • lack of or poor public transport	• cities don't spread as fast; there is less uninhabited land in Germany • smaller suburbs • homes generally closer to shops, etc. • life without a car is more possible as you can walk to more places • public transport more widespread

F2 a) Comprehension → p. 64

Use the ideas below to help you answer the comprehension question:

- British people have their own unique way of writing about other countries and people
- tend to mock other cultures
- British writing seems to suggest that other countries are not as advanced/developed as Britain

F3 a) **Analysis** → p. 65

Your analysis should include the following points:

- excited as he had little knowledge of Britain
- full of anticipation – what would it be like?
- eager

Topic 5

A2 **Comprehension** → p. 73

Here are some points you might want to include:

LEFT OUT WIFE's problem:

- Her husband is chatting to other people on the Internet.
- He is spending a lot of time on the computer and less with her and their children.

FAMILY's answer:

- The wife should confront her husband with how she feels.
- They should have an honest, open discussion.

A3 **Text production: Writing an email** → p. 73

You might want to include the following arguments:

For	Against
• Technology allows you to see and hear your partner online. • People may be more honest and open when conversation isn't face-to-face.	• If you only write to one another you cannot see body language, facial expressions nor get a sense of emotions, so it is impossible to really get to know somebody. • It is easier to be untruthful online than it is face-to-face.

B3 **Classroom discussion** → p. 75

Here are some ideas to start you off:

Advantages	Disadvantages
• improves standards of handwriting • improves spelling skills • may increase students' vocabulary	• takes away time from "more important" subjects (languages, maths, etc.) • handwriting can be seen as an expression of "one's personality" • setting general standards could detract from uniqueness • boring, monotonous lessons

Grading grid – Bewertungsbogen für Englisch (Vorschlag)

Ebene	Aspekt	sehr gut (15, 14, 13)	gut (12, 11, 10)	befriedigend (9, 8, 7)	ausreichend (6, 5, 4)	mangelhaft (3, 2, 1)	ungenügend (0)
Wortebene	Allgemeiner Wortschatz	sehr differenziert, treffsicher und umfangreich, sehr hoher Grad an Korrektheit	differenziert und meist treffend, hoher Grad an Korrektheit	weniger differenziert bei vermehrter Fehlerzahl	begrenzt, teils ungenau, recht hohe Fehlerzahl	deutlich begrenzt, Verständlichkeit beeinträchtigt, hohe Fehlerzahl	stark begrenzt, Verständlichkeit erheblich beeinträchtigt, sehr hohe Fehlerzahl
Wortebene	Fachwortschatz, Funktionswortschatz	sehr differenziert, treffsicher und umfangreich, sehr hoher Grad an Korrektheit	differenziert und meist treffend, hoher Grad an Korrektheit	weniger differenziert bei vermehrter Fehlerzahl	begrenzt, teils ungenau, recht hohe Fehlerzahl	deutlich begrenzt, Verständlichkeit beeinträchtigt, hohe Fehlerzahl	stark begrenzt, Verständlichkeit erheblich beeinträchtigt, sehr hohe Fehlerzahl
Satzebene	Grammatische Strukturen	sehr hoher Grad an Korrektheit	hoher Grad an Korrektheit	grundlegende Beherrschung trotz vermehrter Fehlerzahl	noch angemessene Beherrschung, recht hohe Fehlerzahl	hohe Fehlerzahl, zum Teil auch bei elementaren Strukturen	durchgängige Verstöße, auch bei elementaren Strukturen
Satzebene	Satzbau und Satzverknüpfungen, Idiomatik	sehr differenziert und variantenreich, treffsichere Verwendung auch von idiomatischen Konstruktionen	differenziert und variabel, gelegentliche Verwendung von idiomatischen Konstruktionen; meist treffende Verwendung von Konstruktionen	eher einfache Konstruktionen, erkennbare Variabilität	meist einfache Konstruktionen, kaum Variabilität, gelegentliche Stilbrüche	sehr einfacher Satzbau, keine Variabilität, Verständlichkeit beeinträchtigt auch durch unidiomatische Wendungen und zahlreiche Stilbrüche	unzureichende Strukturierung, untypische Syntax, Text wirkt wie übersetzt, Verständlichkeit erheblich beeinträchtigt
Textebene	Aufbau / Gedankenführung	sehr stringent, komplex und differenziert, überzeugende Hervorhebung und Verbindung von Gedanken; sinnvoller und funktionaler Einsatz von Zitaten, in hohem Maße eigenständig, flüssig	klar, stringent, nachvollziehbare Schlussfolgerungen; überzeugende Darstellung von Aspekten; eigenständige Leistung, flüssig	Gliederung und gedankliche Zusammenhänge nachvollziehbar; zum Teil Anlehnung an Vorlage	Gliederungselemente und gedankliche Zusammenhänge erkennbar, Schwächen im logischen Aufbau, häufige Anlehnung an Vorlage	mangelnde oder widersprüchliche Gliederungselemente, teils zusammenhanglos, sehr enge Anlehnung an Vorlage	unzureichende Gliederung, Aufbau und Gedankenführung zusammenhanglos, übernommene Passagen
Textebene	aufgabenformattypische Versprachlichung	souveräne Beherrschung des zu erstellenden Textformats; überzeugende Anwendung der entsprechenden sprachlichen Konventionen	sichere Beherrschung des zu erstellenden Textformats, sprachliche Konventionen getroffen	angemessene Beherrschung des zu erstellenden Textformats, sprachliche Konventionen weitgehend getroffen bzw. dem Zieltext angemessen	durch Aufgabenformat vorgegebene Textsorte erkennbar, formattypische Merkmale stellenweise vorhanden	nur Ansätze der Konventionen der zu erstellenden Textsorte erkennbar	Versprachlichung insgesamt nicht der Textsorte entsprechend, erforderliche sprachliche Konventionen nicht beherrscht

Gewicht: Note / Punkte

Listening

As with all comprehension, watch out for **key words** and try to get the gist.

When you are involved in a **conversation** (e.g. on the telephone) or asked to interpret for someone, you can always request the speaker to **repeat or explain** what you haven't understood. When you not only hear but also see people talk, their **body language** helps you to understand what they say.

Announcements contain important information, usually in clear, simple language. They are often **repeated** several times to make sure everyone understands them.

Following **radio programmes** is more difficult because the only help you can get is from the speakers' **intonation**.

Be aware of the most important differences between **British and American English**, and be prepared for other variations such as **regional pronunciation**.

When you listen to **longer speeches or interviews**, take notes in a systematic way, e.g. in a grid or a checklist.

Useful phrases

> Excuse me, can you say that again, please? • Could you repeat that for me, please? • Sorry, I don't understand the word … • What does it mean? • Can you spell that for me, please? • Have I got that right? • Sorry, would you mind explaining that again, please?

Skimming

Skimming means finding the **main ideas in a text** in order to get an impression of its content.

- Read the title, the introduction or the first paragraph, the first sentence of every paragraph and any headings and sub-headings.
- Note any pictures, charts or graphs.
- Pay attention to any words or phrases in italics or bold print.
- Read the last paragraph, which often offers a short summary of the text.

Scanning

Scanning is useful for finding **specific information** quickly, e.g. you have a question in mind and read a passage to find the answer.

- Decide what **specific information** you are looking for. Ignore unrelated information.
- Look out for **relevant key words**. Stop when you find one and read that part of the text carefully. Make notes if necessary.
- How might the information be given in the text? For example, if you need a date, only look at the numbers in the text.
- **Headings** can help you to identify sections which might contain the information.
- **The first sentence** in a paragraph should indicate whether the information you need could be there, or not. Do not read the text in detail.

Understanding non-fictional texts

A **non-fictional text** is a text whose **content is based on facts**. The writer refers to people and places which really exist and incidents which really took place. Typical examples are **newspaper** or **magazine articles**, **essays**, **comments** or **advertisements**.

1 Reading a non-fictional text

- Read the text carefully.
- Look up unknown vocabulary if necessary, but try to concentrate only on key words that block your understanding of the text.
- Ask yourself the following questions and write notes:
  What type of text is it? • What is its central idea / main theme / message? Can you state it in a single sentence?
- Structure the text. Divide it into different units and underline important passages.

2 Understanding a non-fictional text

What kind of text is it?
- What kind of text is it? A newspaper / magazine article, an essay, etc.?
- Who is the author?
- When was it written?
- Where was it published? In a newspaper, on the Internet, etc.?
- Why was it written? What is the target group?

What is the text about?
- What is the central idea / main theme / message?
- What parts can it be divided into?
- What is the purpose of the text?
- What is the author's point of view / intention?
- What arguments or examples does the author use?
- What is special about the text?

Newspaper reports

We are confronted with a wide range of different newspapers from all around the world. On the one hand there are quality newspapers. They present the news in a neutral way and separate information from opinion so that the reader can form his/her own view. On the other hand, there are popular newspapers (tabloids). Their news reports are often sensational with big pictures and headlines. Popular newspapers often mix information and opinion, offering the reader a ready-made opinion.

Example:

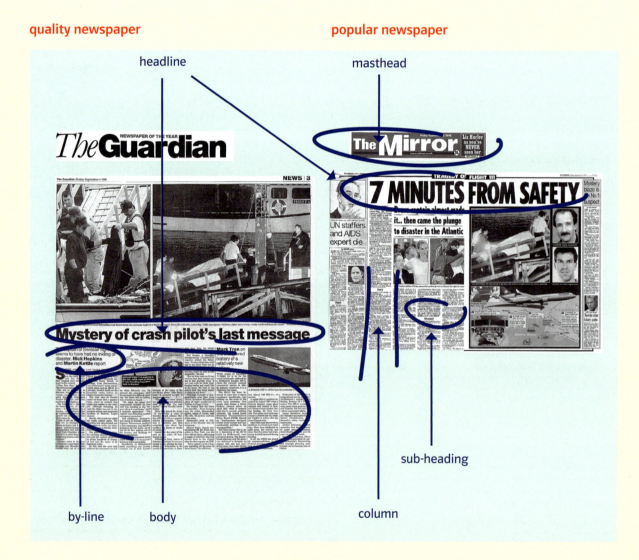

Understanding fictional texts

A **fictional text** is a literary work whose content is based on the **imagination of the author** and not necessarily on facts. There are three **literary genres: poetry** (poems, songs), **drama** (plays) and **fiction** (novels, short stories, fables, fairy tales, etc.).

By reading a fictional text, the reader is transferred into a different world and the author's intention is often a matter of interpretation. Pictures in the reader's mind are produced to create a new reality, and atmosphere and emotions are often more important than hard facts.

1 Reading a fictional text

- Read the text carefully.
- Look up unknown vocabulary if necessary, but try to concentrate only on key words that block your understanding of the text.
- Ask yourself the following questions and write notes:
  What is the story about? • What is its central idea/main theme/message? Can you state it in a single sentence?
- Structure the text. Divide it into different units and underline important passages.

2 Understanding a fictional text

When you analyse a text, you should follow these steps. Answer the questions and write notes.

What kind of text is it?
- What is the literary genre of the text? Poetry, drama or fiction?
- What kind of text is it (poem, song, short story, etc.)?
- Who is the author and when was it written?

What is the text about?
- What is the central idea / main theme / message?
- Who is the narrator?
- What is the setting?
- What is the plot?
- Who are the characters?

How we learn about the characters in a story:
- outward appearance
- language
- actions, behaviour, mood
- main traits
- motives, influences from the past
- roles, social background
- character's function in the constellation of characters

3 Character grid

outward appearance	athletic, attractive, blond, elegant, fat, tall, young, …
language	excited, gentle, polite, rude, …
actions, behaviour, mood	angry, embarrassed, emotional, irresponsible, terrified, upset, …
main traits	honest, intelligent, jealous, kind, show-off, shy, sympathetic, violent, …
roles, social background	boss, daughter, girlfriend, broken home, criminal, lonely, married, rich, …
function in the constellation of characters	enemy, friend, rival, …

4 Special features of the text

- What parts can it be divided into?
- Is there a turning point in the plot?
- What kind of language is used?
- What atmosphere is created and how?
- What else is special about the text?

The features of a short story

A **short story** is a short fictional prose text which is meant to be read in a single sitting. It can be as short as 500 and as long as 15,000 words. A lot of short stories follow different patterns but the following points apply to many of them.

- There may be one main **character** or a group of equally important characters.
- There is often only a single **setting** (i. e. the time and place of the action does not change). Longer short stories might have more than one setting.
- The setting helps to create a certain atmosphere.
- The reader may be led into the story through an **exposition**.
- In modern stories the action often starts in the first sentence.
- The action develops logically through **conflicts or crises**, reaching a climax or **turning-point** near or at the end (emphasis on action and suspense).
- Some stories concentrate on a decisive moment in the main character's life (emphasis on character and psychology).
- There is often a surprise **ending**, a happy / unhappy ending or an open ending.

The features of a play

Plays are very different from short stories or poems because they are not written to be read but to be **performed** and **watched**. Outside school or university, people do not normally sit down to read a play, unless they are planning a trip to the theatre. When a **playwright** or **dramatist** sits down to put pen to paper, he has **directors, stage managers** and **actresses / actors** in mind.

- A dramatic text usually consists of two parts: **dialogue** and **stage directions**. In a play, **dialogue** covers all the spoken language, not only the conversation of two characters.
- The **stage directions** give information about how to perform the play. This might refer to the setting, scenery, the characters' movements, tone of voice, etc.
- When you analyse a play, look at the **setting**, the **action** and the **characters** (→ Understanding fictional texts p. 111).
- Don't forget to describe the **atmosphere** of the play.
- Finally, give an **interpretation** of the play.

Dealing with poetry

Poetry may look shorter than other literary forms, but it can be more demanding. Here are some ideas on how to improve your feeling for and understanding of poetry.

- Read the poem and try to get the gist or message of the poem first. Then sum it up in your own words.
- Read the poem aloud to stress the relationship between certain words and ideas.
- Take a close look at structure and form:

  stanza: the way the lines of a poem are grouped together
  rhyme pattern: groups of words that rhyme
  repetition: when words or sounds are repeated

- Look for comparisons and contrasts (metaphors and similes). Identify images and symbols, and what impressions or ideas they give you.
- Find devices that are used to bring out certain feelings and to create an atmosphere, e.g. colours, sounds.
- Describe any characters who appear in the poem.
- Who is the speaker? What do we learn about the setting?

Example:

Films

Some films are sad – you watch them and cry.	A
You know that the hero is going to die.	A
Some films have spies – they fight, run and jump.	B
When they crash their cars, there's a very big bump!	B
Sometimes aliens come down from space.	C
That often means trouble for the human race.	C
And then there are ghost films – ghosts come out at night	D
And give everybody an awful fright.	D
But the worst films are love films where all the stars kiss.	E
Those are the films that I want to miss!	E

> **stanza:** five stanzas with two lines each
> **rhyme pattern:** AABBCCDDEE
> **repetitions:** some(times) (lines 1, 3, 5), you (lines 1, 2), films (lines 1, 3, 7, 9, 10)

William Sears

Useful phrases

The poem consists of / is divided into … stanzas / sections / lines … • It has an unusual layout. • It follows a clear rhyme scheme. • It is an example of unrhymed verse. • The rrangement of the rhymes is … (e. g. aabb). • A number of lines do not rhyme at all. • Lines x and y rhyme. • The poet aims to express a certain message poetically. • The vocabulary is simple / difficult. • The words mainly belong to the word field of … • The repetition of the words '…' creates a … atmosphere. • There is a strong contrast between '…' and '…'. The tone of the poem is serious / calm / sad / ironical / cheerful / … This is heightened by words such as …

Dealing with songs

Songs are **similar to poems**, but they additionally contain a **musical aspect**, which is particularly important. It is always useful to look for background information on the songwriter and / or the artist performing the song, who shouldn't be confused as they aren't necessarily the same person. Look at all the information you have got. If something is missing that could help you to understand the song better, try to find out more. The Internet is probably the best source of information for you. You can follow these steps:

Background information
- What is the title of the song?
- Who is / are the singer(s) / the band?
- Who wrote the lyrics? Who wrote the music?
- When was the song written?
- Was the song a success?

Music
- What kind of music is it?
- What instruments are used?
- What does it sound like?
- Can you describe the rhythm?
- What feelings are created by the music?
- What is the structure of the song (verses, chorus)?

Lyrics
- Examine the song text (verses and chorus). Look at form, structure and the language which is used (→ Dealing with poetry p. 113).
- Do the lyrics tell a story? What happens and what is the setting?
- What feelings are expressed by the words?
- Is there a message?

Comprehension questions

There is no general rule for answering comprehension questions. However, the following guidelines can be helpful:

- If the task refers to the text, **scan** the text for points you want to use, **take notes** and order them.
- For an **introductory sentence** it can be useful to refer to the words used in the task.
- Sometimes it is unavoidable to use the words from the text but you should try to use **your own words** as much as possible.
- Use **linking words** or **connectives** to show the logical development of different points, ideas or arguments of your answer.
- If your text is longer, divide it into **paragraphs**.
- Find a sentence that **concludes** your answer adequately and has the form of a general statement.

Text analysis

For all texts
- text type
- author
- target group
- purpose
- (historical) context
- structure
- language, register, style and tone
- relationship between style and content
- atmosphere
- other remarkable features
- effect on the reader
- your personal impression (if asked for)

For literary texts
- literary genre
- narrator and point of view
- setting
- characters (direct / indirect characterisation)
- main theme
- plot
- exposition, climax, turning point, rising / falling action, dénouement
- narrative techniques (chronology, frame story, suspense, tone, descriptions, comments, etc.)

Tips
- Secure your comprehension of the text by looking for keywords and taking notes.
- Considering background information about the text, its historical context, and its author can be helpful.
- Answer questions on the text precisely and to the point. Watch out for the way questions are asked: Do exactly as you are told when you are asked to *analyse, examine, describe, discuss, compare, summarise, interpret* or *comment* on things.
- Don't forget to relate the individual points to each other, i.e. look for similarities or contrasts in the characters, the atmosphere, the language, and find reasons for the author's choice of genre and style for a particular content.

- Explain everything in your own words, but use quotations from the text to support your statements, marking them clearly as quotations and giving line references.
- Clearly distinguish between facts and your interpretation.
- Avoid repetition.
- Never state your opinion without giving reasons, and only if you are asked.
- When you write about a text, think of using connectives and structuring devices as well as suitable adjectives and adverbs to give precise descriptions of characters, action and circumstances.

Writing a comment

An comment is a **clearly structured** piece of writing in which important arguments on a topic are presented.

Comments are generally written in the **simple present**. When you are asked to write a comment, always read the task carefully.

1 Preparation

- **Define** the topic clearly.
- **Brainstorm ideas**. Write down what you know about the topic in a word web, diagram or table.
- If necessary, **collect facts, arguments and other information**.
- Formulate your **opinion** on the topic.

2 Arranging your material

- Decide on the **most important facts, arguments or pieces of information** that you want to include.
- For each main argument try to think of two **supporting arguments**.
- Put your facts or arguments in a **logical order**. For example, you could:
  - start with general ideas and then go on to talk about details.
  - put things into chronological order.
  - start by giving all the arguments in favour and then give all the counterarguments.
  - follow each argument in favour with a counter-argument.

3 Writing your comment

The introductory paragraph
- The introductory paragraph should **introduce your topic** and catch the reader's interest.
- In your introductory paragraph you should also:
  - say clearly what your comment is going to be about in one or two sentences.
  - ask a question or questions which you will answer in your text.
  - give a **brief outline** of the problem / topic.

The main paragraphs
- Start a **new paragraph for each new idea**.
- Begin each paragraph with a **main idea or argument**.
- Write simple sentences.
- Arrange sentences in a logical order.
- Join sentences using suitable **connectives**.
- Use adverbs to emphasise points.
- Use **examples** where possible.

The conclusion
- Do not introduce new ideas!
- Make a **brief concluding statement** summarising what you have said in your comment.

4 Checking your comment

- Check that all your **sentences are complete** and that they make sense.
- Check your comment for **grammar, spelling and punctuation** mistakes.

5 Writing a model comment

Expressing your opinion To be quite honest, I do not think that/I cannot (fully) agree with …/I am not convinced by …/ I would like to question the view that …/I reject the idea that … • In my opinion/view this argument is wrong/weak/unconvincing because …	I do not think anyone would disagree • In fact/As a matter of fact, I believe it is fully justified to say that … • I am of exactly the same opinion as … • I share the view that … • To my mind, … • this argument is very strong/powerful/convincing/plausible
Making concessions To a certain extent, I can accept … • However, we shouldn't forget that … • Most of the arguments are hard to dismiss. • Yet there are experts who … • I agree in principle, but … • Personally, I would not go so far as to say that … • Although …, we should accept/must admit that … • In spite of all this, … • Admittedly, …, but …	**Giving arguments/reasons** One reason for my criticism/scepticism is that … • Another/A second/A further/An additional argument I would like to present is that … • I would also argue that … • Another point I would like to make is that … • The main reason, however, is that … • The most convincing argument is that … • That brings me neatly to my final and most important point: …

Your conclusion/summary
To sum up, … • In short, … • Considering all these arguments, … • I would conclude that … • I have come to the conclusion that … • It is safe to say that … • I would support the view that … • My suggestion is that … • My appeal to … is: … • In conclusion … • Having weighed up all the arguments, I would like to

Writing a newspaper/magazine article

The following steps can help you to write a newspaper or magazine article:

- Remember the **ABC of news writing**:
  Accuracy (be exact, all the facts have to be correct)
  Brevity (keep it short and to the point)
  Clarity (make sure everyone understands).
- Remember also the five Ws: **Who? What? When? Where? Why?** (sometimes How? and So what?)
- Give **answers** to these questions.
- Attract the **reader's attention** with the headline and the lead, which is usually the first word, sentence or paragraph of the story. The lead contains the most important, most exciting point and makes the reader go on reading.
- The **structure of a newspaper article** is basically an inverted pyramid: The most important thing is at the top, in the lead. More facts and additional details follow, the least important ones at the end, so that you can stop reading any time after the lead should you feel you have enough information. If the story is written well, however, or if you are interested in the details, you can read on till the end.
- Good news **style** is **active, informative, to the point**. Nothing is repeated and nothing is said that is not necessary. Everything must be logical and easy to understand.
- News articles often contain **anecdotes, examples and quotes**. If you use quotes when writing, make sure they express the speaker's intention. Without the right context, they may be misunderstood. Only use them when they make a point clearer.
- A **good ending** rewards the reader for finishing the article by making some kind of reference to the lead.

Writing an email

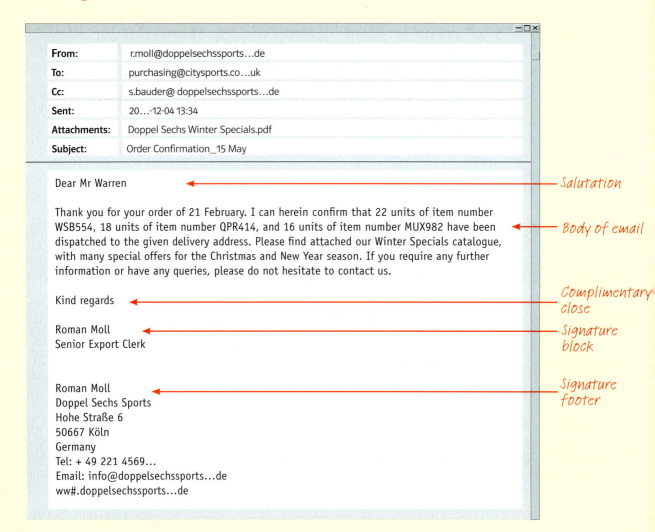

From:	The sender's email address will appear here automatically.
To:	Pay attention when writing the recipient's email address. One small typing mistake and the email will either be sent to the wrong person, or returned.
Cc:	This stands for 'carbon copy'. Here you enter the email address of anybody you would like to also receive the message.
Bcc:	This stands for 'blind carbon copy'. This has the same function as 'carbon copy' but the addresses under Bcc do not appear in the message header of the other recipients.
Sent:	This may also be labeled 'Date'. The correct date and time the message was sent will be added automatically.
Attachments:	Any kind of file, such as MS Word (.doc), MS Excel (.xls), PDF (.pdf) or pictures (.jpg) can be attached to an email.

Subject:	You should always mention the precise subject of your email. This will help all people involved deal with the mail, and will prevent it from being deleted.
Salutation:	Very formal salutations such as 'Dear Sirs' are not used in emails. Instead use 'Dear …' wherever possible. In the English-speaking world emails are personalised as often as possible – Dear Ms Dietrich, Dear Kevin, etc. To avoid 'Dear Sirs' you can use 'Dear East Slope Furnishings'.
Body of the email:	Begin the first word with a capital letter.
Compliment-ary close:	There are a number of expressions to choose from: Best/Kind regards Best wishes Regards Yours sincerely (considered very formal in emails)
Signature block:	Write your job title or department underneath your name.
Signature footer:	Write your company's full name, address and telephone number.

Writing a diary / blog entry

- When you write a diary or blog entry, it is often necessary to **slip into the role of a different character**.
- Try to put yourself into the character's situation (age, background, job, sex, etc.).
- Try to imagine **the character's thoughts, feelings and ideas**.
- Although in a diary entry the main focus is on the past, present emotions and dreams and hopes about the future may also play a role.
- Write your entry from the **first-person point of view**.

Writing a personal letter

A **personal letter** is a letter you write to someone you know well **on a personal basis**, e.g. a friend or relative. There are no special rules which you have to follow when you write to people you know well. The model letter below shows you what an informal letter generally looks like in English. You can use **informal language** in a personal letter, as if you were speaking to the person.

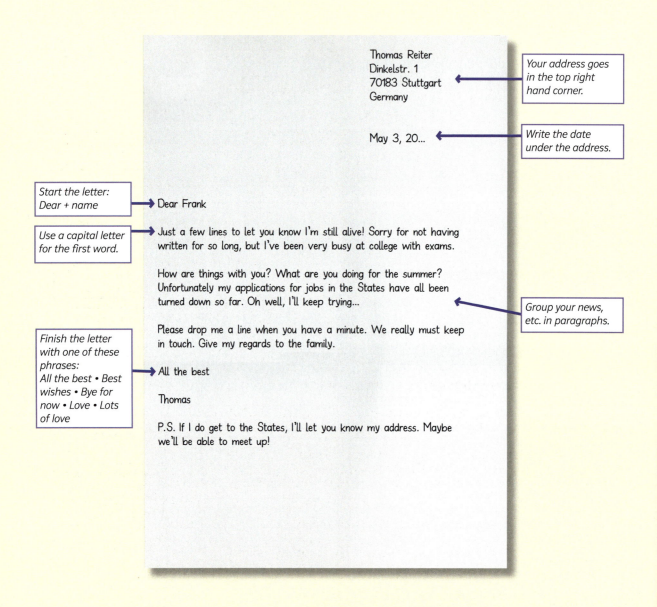

Thomas Reiter
Dinkelstr. 1
70183 Stuttgart
Germany

Your address goes in the top right hand corner.

May 3, 20...

Write the date under the address.

Start the letter: Dear + name

Dear Frank

Use a capital letter for the first word.

Just a few lines to let you know I'm still alive! Sorry for not having written for so long, but I've been very busy at college with exams.

How are things with you? What are you doing for the summer? Unfortunately my applications for jobs in the States have all been turned down so far. Oh well, I'll keep trying...

Group your news, etc. in paragraphs.

Please drop me a line when you have a minute. We really must keep in touch. Give my regards to the family.

*Finish the letter with one of these phrases:
All the best • Best wishes • Bye for now • Love • Lots of love*

All the best

Thomas

P.S. If I do get to the States, I'll let you know my address. Maybe we'll be able to meet up!

Writing a formal letter

A formal letter can be **a letter of application, a reservation, a request for information**, etc. **Commercial correspondence** refers to formal letters written in a business context, i.e. from one company to another. There are different ways of layouting these types of letters. The model letter below is in 'block form', which is probably the best to use because it is accepted everywhere. The parts in **blue** are only necessary in **commercial correspondence**.

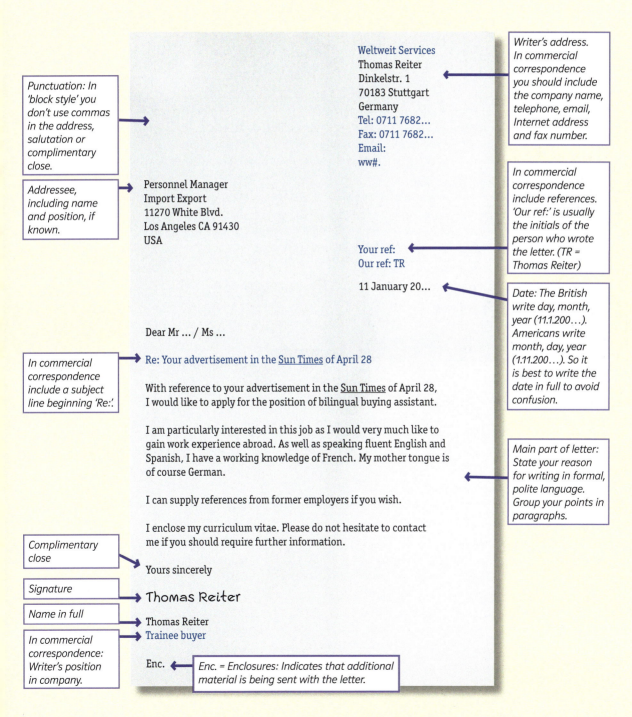

Writer's address. In commercial correspondence you should include the company name, telephone, email, Internet address and fax number.

Weltweit Services
Thomas Reiter
Dinkelstr. 1
70183 Stuttgart
Germany
Tel: 0711 7682...
Fax: 0711 7682...
Email: ww#.

Punctuation: In 'block style' you don't use commas in the address, salutation or complimentary close.

Addressee, including name and position, if known.

Personnel Manager
Import Export
11270 White Blvd.
Los Angeles CA 91430
USA

In commercial correspondence include references. 'Our ref:' is usually the initials of the person who wrote the letter. (TR = Thomas Reiter)

Your ref:
Our ref: TR

11 January 20...

Date: The British write day, month, year (11.1.200…). Americans write month, day, year (1.11.200…). So it is best to write the date in full to avoid confusion.

Dear Mr ... / Ms ...

In commercial correspondence include a subject line beginning 'Re:'.

Re: Your advertisement in the Sun Times of April 28

With reference to your advertisement in the Sun Times of April 28, I would like to apply for the position of bilingual buying assistant.

I am particularly interested in this job as I would very much like to gain work experience abroad. As well as speaking fluent English and Spanish, I have a working knowledge of French. My mother tongue is of course German.

Main part of letter: State your reason for writing in formal, polite language. Group your points in paragraphs.

I can supply references from former employers if you wish.

I enclose my curriculum vitae. Please do not hesitate to contact me if you should require further information.

Complimentary close

Yours sincerely

Signature

Thomas Reiter

Name in full

Thomas Reiter

In commercial correspondence: Writer's position in company.

Trainee buyer

Enc.

Enc. = Enclosures: Indicates that additional material is being sent with the letter.

Salutation	When used	Complimentary close
Dear Sir or Madam	to a company and when you don't know the person's name or sex	Yours faithfully
Dear Madam	to a woman, when you don't know her name	Yours faithfully
Dear Sir	to a man, when you don't know his name	Yours faithfully
Dear Mr Brown	to a man, whose name you know	Yours sincerely
Dear Ms / Mrs Brown	to a woman, whose name you know	Yours sincerely

Note: Nowadays the use of *Yours faithfully* and *Yours sincerely* is not always divided up as strictly as given above.

Useful phrases

Explaining the purpose of the letter
We are writing / I am writing … • in connection with … • … with reference / regard to … • … to advise you of … • … to confirm … • … to let you know … • … to tell you that … • … to ask / enquire (whether) … • …to inform you of … • … to request you to …

Stating a reference
Thank you for your mail of July 1st. • Many thanks for your letter dated 26th July. • We refer to your order for … • I have received your enquiry regarding … • Further to our telephone conversation today, … • With reference to your mail of June 5th, … • With regard to your enquiry of June 5th about …

Giving good news
I am delighted to tell you that … • You will be pleased to hear that …

Giving bad news
We regret to inform you that … • I am afraid that … • We are sorry to have to tell you that … • Unfortunately we are unable to …

Making a request
Please … • Please could you … ? • Could you possibly…? • We would be grateful if you could/would … • We would be much obliged if you could … • I would appreciate it if you could … • … would be very much appreciated.

Offering help
If you wish, we would be happy to … • Would you like us to …? • At your request we would gladly …

Giving information
We wish to advise you that … • We are pleased to inform you that … • For your information: …

Enclosing documents
I am enclosing … • Please find enclosed … • Please find attached … (= attachment / papers fixed to the letter with a paper clip / …)

Thanking
Thank you for sending me … • Many thanks for … • I am grateful to you for … • I am much obliged to you for sending me … (formal)

Useful phrases

Apologising

I am sorry about the delay in replying. • We were (very / extremely / most) sorry to hear about the problem. • We regret that this problem has occured. • We apologize for any inconvenience caused.

Assuring

Please rest assured that we will do our utmost to help you. • We assure you that we will do our best to put the matter right. • We promise to look into the matter immediately. • You can count on us to ensure smooth delivery in future.

Making concessions

We agree to reduce the price by (percentage / sum of money). • We are happy to grant you a discount of 3% on the goods. • We will let you have the goods at a reduced price of …

Closing remarks

If you have any questions, please do not hesitate to call me / us on (tel. no.). • Should you have any questions, feel free to contact me / us. • If you require further information, please do get in touch / ask. • Should you require further details, please contact us again. • If we can help in any way, we would be happy to be of assistance.

Referring to future contact

We look forward to hearing from you soon / meeting you next week / seeing you on the 29th. • We are looking forward to receiving your proposal / order.

Writing an enquiry

East Slope Furnishings
32 North Street
Brighton
BN1 2RG
Tel: + 44 1273 6307…
Email: purchasing@esfurnishings.co…uk
ww#.esfurnishings.co…uk

Möbelwelt GmbH
Gaußstraße 7
51503 Rösrath
Germany

Your ref:
Our ref: ELG/ag

17 November 20…

Dear Sir or Madam

Re: Product enquiry

Your address was passed on to us by a business partner who recommended your products. Our company, East Slope Furnishings, is a young and rapidly growing home furnishing company with outlets in six cities across the south of England. We supply affordable and stylish furniture and home accessories.

We have visited your website and were very impressed with your product range. Consequently, we are interested in adding a number of your products to our collection.

Could you please send us a copy of your latest brochure and an up-to-date price list? Please also supply us with information regarding your terms of payment, delivery times, possible discounts, as well as the minimum quantity for a trial order.

Thank you in advance and we look forward to hearing from you.

Yours faithfully

E. Lloréns Gómez
Elisabet Lloréns Gómez
Purchasing manager

Source of address

Introduce your company

Reason for enquiry

Ask for further information – sales literature, terms and conditions, delivery times, etc.

Polite ending

Writing an offer

Möbelwelt GmbH
Gaußstraße 7
51503 Rösrath
Germany
Tel: + 49 2205 4569…
Email: info@moebelwelt…de
ww#.moebelwelt…de

East Slope Furnishings
32 North Street
Brighton
BN1 2RG

Your ref: ELG/ag
Our ref: MD/jh

24 November 20…

Dear Ms Lloréns Gómez

Re: Your enquiry of 17 November 20…

Thank you very much for your enquiry of 17 November. We are pleased to hear of your interest in stocking our products in your store. ← *Reference to enquiry*

Please find enclosed, as requested, a copy of our latest brochure as well as an up-to-date price list. ← *Respond to enquiry / make offer*

Our prices are quoted DDP Brighton and Möbelwelt GmbH has a minimum order policy of 100 for deliveries to the United Kingdom. Nevertheless, trial orders can be arranged on an individual basis. Please also refer to our catalogue and website for special offers.

Our usual terms of payment are bank transfer to our account with the European Bank within 30 days from date of invoice. Regular customers are granted open account terms. ← *State terms of delivery and payment*

Standard delivery times to the United Kingdom are 2-3 working days, although express overnight delivery is available on some orders. ← *Refer to the delivery time*

Should you have any further questions or queries, please do not hesitate to contact us. ← *Polite ending / creating goodwill*

Yours sincerely

M. Dietrich

Meike Dietrich
Senior Export Clerk

Enc.

125

Writing an order

East Slope Furnishings
32 North Street
Brighton
BN1 2RG
Tel: + 44 1273 6307…
Email: purchasing@esfurnishings.co…uk
ww#.esfurnishings.co…uk

Möbelwelt GmbH
Gaußstraße 7
51503 Rösrath
Germany

Your Ref: MD/jh
Our ref: ELG/ag

30 November 20…

Dear Ms Dietrich

Re: Your offer of 24 November 20…

Thank you very much for sending us your brochure and price list. We also appreciate you outlining your delivery terms and conditions.

We have studied your catalogue and are very impressed with your products. We would like to order 16 units of item number AQW445 and 16 units of item number AQR457.

As agreed, we will make payment by bank transfer to the previously named bank within 30 days from date of invoice. Delivery is to be made DDP Brighton.

We look forward receiving the goods in time and to doing further business with you in the future.

Yours sincerely

E. Lloréns Gómez

Elisabet Lloréns Gómez
Purchasing manager

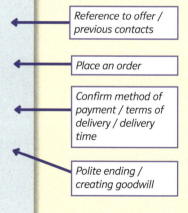

Reference to offer / previous contacts

Place an order

Confirm method of payment / terms of delivery / delivery time

Polite ending / creating goodwill

Writing a CV

CV is short for 'Curriculum Vitae'. There are no rules about how to write a CV in English. Use the following 'Dos and Don'ts' and the model CV below as a guide.

Dos
Do include skills and interests which are relevant to the job, if possible.
Do give the English equivalents of German terms, where possible.

Don'ts
Don't write more than one page.
Don't necessarily include a photo, unless asked to.
Don't use handwriting for your CV.
Don't sign your name at the end.

Curriculum Vitae

Name:	Ute Braun
Address:	Musterstraße 1, 50400 Köln, Germany
Telephone:	0211 / 2345…
Email:	u.braun@e-mail…de
Date of birth:	6.5.1988
Nationality:	German
Schools attended:	2004–2006: Language College, Stuttgart 1997–2004: Pfeiffer Realschule (Comprehensive)
Qualifications:	Diploma course as a bilingual secretary (English, Spanish)
Work experience:	July 2005 – September 2005: kitchen work at McDougall's July 2004 – September 2004: office assistant in the export department of Bosch
Skills, Interests and Experience:	fluent English and Spanish, a working knowledge of French; good computer skills (Word, Excel); clean driving license; tennis and member of the local repertory company (latest role: the Nurse in Romeo and Juliet)

Describing pictures

1 Types of pictures

photo(graph) • print • transparency • slide • painting • drawing • sketch • picture • illustration • image •
collage • electronic image • snapshot • skyline • panorama • close-up • action photo • still (from a film) •
scene • sequence

2 Describing a picture

First impression
- Where is the image from?
- What type of image is it?
- What does the image (roughly) show?
- Who created it?
- When and why was it drawn / taken?

Description
- Describe in detail what can be seen in the picture.
- Talk about what you can see in the foreground and in the background, from the left to the right and from the top to the bottom.
- Don't forget to look at the details. Describe the setting or situation, the quality of the picture, the characters and their appearance and body language.

Interpretation
- What message is given by the picture?
- Is it aimed at a particular target group?
- Did the person who created the picture intend it to have a certain effect on the viewer? If so, how is this achieved?

Evaluation
- Do you think the picture has the intended effect?
- Which elements are responsible for its success or failure?
- If it is a historical picture, compare the effect it might have had in its original context with the one it has on a viewer now.

Useful phrases

First impression
This is a photo / an illustration of … • This photo was taken in … • The illustration shows … •
In this illustration / photo you can see (that) … • My first thought when I saw the picture
was … • The photograph is shocking / disgusting / amazing / spectacular / special … • The
picture reminds me of … • It shows … • It was probably taken in / at … • The photograph
looks as if it was staged to achieve a certain effect. • It is a realistic picture.

Description
on the right-hand / left-hand side of the picture • in the centre • in the foreground • in the
background • at the top • at the bottom • in the upper right-hand corner • in the lower
left-hand corner • The picture was painted by … • It is a portrait / cartoon / still life / landscape / an oil / watercolour painting. • In the middle / centre of the picture there is … •
to the left / right of … • in the top left-hand / bottom right-hand corner • There is a contrast

Useful phrases

between … • … is clearly visible • The focus is on … • The field size is a close-up / medium shot / long shot • The colours are bright / dark. • … is seen from above / below / the front / the back • This creates a … atmosphere.

Interpretation

The person in the picture looks … (+ *adjective, e.g. happy*) • The photo / illustration supports the point made in the text that … • The photo / illustration gives you the impression that … • The illustration makes me feel … (+ *adjective: e.g. worried*) • The colours the artist has chosen make me feel … (+ *adjective: happy / sad / worried / …*) • In my opinion the illustration would be better, if … (+ *simple past: e.g. if it was more life-like*)

Evaluation

The artist aims to present … • The picture is (not) convincing because …

Describing cartoons

A cartoonist aims to be both **funny and critical**. When looking at a cartoon, the most important thing is to try to work out what point the cartoonist is making. Generally **the point is made by a combination of the text and the illustration**, so it is important to analyse and understand both. **Illustrations** generally show caricatures of **well-known people or particular stereotypes.** To understand a cartoon, you need to recognise and define the person or group of people illustrated.

To analyse a cartoon, you can follow the steps in the skill 'Describing pictures' → p. 128

Useful phrases

Describing the cartoon

The cartoon consists of an illustration of … • The illustration shows … • There is a caption under the cartoon, which says "…". • In the (first) speech bubble it says "…". • The text in the speech bubble is spoken by … • The figure is a stereotype / caricature of … • The drawing is detailed / clear / sketchy / abstract.

Talking about the point

The cartoonist is making fun of … • The cartoonist is satirising … • The cartoon is funny because of the misunderstanding between …

Giving your opinion

I think / I don't think the cartoon is (very) funny because … • I get the joke / point. / I don't get the joke / point. • I think / I don't think the cartoon is easy to understand because … • I agree / I don't agree with the point the cartoonist is making because …

Describing diagrams

As you know, **diagrams sum up a lot of statistics or information in very little space** and can make information easier to understand. The kind of diagram you choose to use (bar chart, pie chart, flow chart, line graph, etc.) depends on what you want to show.

A pie chart shows percentages of 100 %:

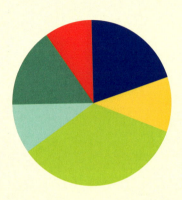

A bar chart is used to compare figures directly:

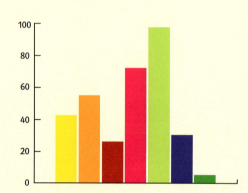

A line graph shows a development over a certain amount of time:

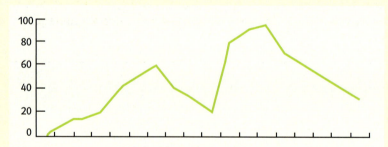

A flow chart shows the links between elements and their influence on each other. It is best used to describe processes that contain decisions at certain points, where alternatives need to be shown:

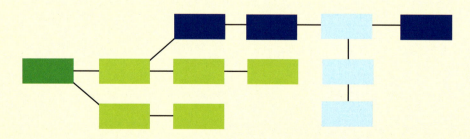

Useful phrases

Describing an increase
to rise • to increase • to have increased by • growth • an increase / a rise (in the number of …)

Describing a decrease
to decrease • to drop • to decline • a decrease • a decline • a drop (in the number of …) • a reduction (in the number of …)

Useful adjectives and adverbs
sharp(ly) • slow(ly) • steady / steadily • continuing / continual(ly) • gradual(ly) • significant(ly) • insignificant(ly) • negligible…negligibly • large • high • small

Expressing numbers & figures
the figures for the last year / the last month / … • the latest figures • the total number of … • a (significant/insignificant /…) number of … • a (high / …) percentage of … • the statistics • a majority / minority of …

Useful nouns
amount • proportion • sum • level • figure(s)

Useful verbs
to show that … • to indicate that … • to suggest that … • to give information about … • to make it clear that … • to illustrate … • to represent … • to depict

Qualifiers
a total of • over • under • nearly • more / less than • between • the same number as • the same amount of • from over / under … to just over / under • half • a third • two thirds • a quarter • (25) per cent • twice as many • three times as many • on average • averagely • roughly • exactly • precisely

Analysing advertisements

When you want to analyse an advertisement, you need to think of the following aspects:

- What is being advertised?
- What is the advertising medium (e.g. a poster, internet pop-up?)
- Who is the ad targeting? What is the product's target group? – men, women, older people, kids, etc.
- What image of the product does the ad try to give? – healthy, hi-tech, value-for-money, …
- How does it try to do this? What "devices" does it use? Think of pictures, text and layout. Ads can be complicated or simple, serious or funny, etc.
- What do you think of the ad? Do you think it is effective, entertaining, awful, clever, sexist, …?

Advertisers often use the AIDA formula to plan advertisements. Ads can also be analysed by using this formula:

Attention:	How does the ad attract your attention?
Interest:	How does the ad create interest in the product?
Desire:	How does the ad arouse desire?
Action:	How does the ad make you take action (i.e. buy the product)?

Useful phrases

Design

The advertisement is divided into … / consists of … • In the foreground / background … / On the left / right … • It features a … / It shows an image of … • The product is presented / depicted as a …

Impact

The design is colourful / simple / bold / … • It grabs / catches the reader's attention by … • The eye is drawn towards … • The arrangement of text and images has the effect of … • The most striking feature is … • The use of … conveys an impression of … • The choice of font creates a retro / modern look

Product and target market

The product / service being advertised is … • It might appeal to people who … • The advert seems to be directed / aimed at … • It appeals to the desire for status / prestige / security / …

Claim and message

The slogan / strapline promises the customer … • It claims to … • The claim is supported with statistics / endorsements / … • The hidden / underlying message seems to be that … • It makes fun of … / It plays with the idea of … • The language is flowery / plain / straightforward / … • It makes use of alliteration / pun / wordplay / irony … • It prompts / urges the reader to …

Mediation

Mediation means **communicating the main points of a text**, written in one language, **in another language.** For example, the text may be in English and you have to formulate the main points in German, or the text may be in German and the text you produce should be in English. Mediation is not a word-for-word translation. Instead, it is about **getting a message** or **the main points of a text** across in a different language.

Tips

- Read the **task description** carefully to understand what you are supposed to do.
- Read the text and **underline the words** you need to look up in a dictionary.
- Read the text again and **mark the most important points** based on the task description. You can also write **key words** in the margin.
- Pay attention to words such as 'but', 'however', and other signals which indicate a new point.
- You do not normally need to include examples in your mediation text as these usually only illustrate the main points in the original text.
- **Plan the structure** of your mediation text: Think of a good introduction to your text. Which points will you start with? Do you want to include a conclusion?
- Your mediation does not need to have the same structure as the original text.

Discussions

1 Rules for a discussion

- Always be polite!
- Look at the person / the people you are talking to but don't stare at them.
- Don't interrupt unless you feel it is really necessary.
- Listen carefully to what other people are saying.
- Keep to the point.
- Don't talk too much.

2 The role of a discussion leader

A discussion leader makes sure the **discussion is held in an orderly way** and that participants are always polite to each other. He / She always remains neutral (i.e. doesn't give his / her own opinion).

Useful phrases

Introducing the topic and the participants
(As you know,) our discussion today is about… • On my right / left I have … *(name of person or group),* who is / are in favour of / against …

Choosing whose turn it is to speak
Who'd like to open the discussion? • … , would you like to open the discussion? • The next person to speak is … , followed by … and then …

Making sure everyone has an equal chance to speak, including people who are shy
Is there anything you'd like to say, …?

Making sure no one person monopolises the discussion
I'm sorry to interrupt you, but I'm afraid you'll have to stop there. • Sorry, but I must give the others a chance to put forward their arguments now.

Making sure that only one person speaks at a time
Please wait your turn, you'll have a chance to speak in a minute! • If you'd just let … finish, please.

Noting down the most important points and summarising the discussion at the end
Time is running out, so I'd like to sum up what we've been discussing. • We heard from … that …

Thanking everybody at the end
Thank you for taking part in the discussion! • And finally I'd like to thank all the participants for holding a fair / friendly / … discussion.

Making a suggestion
Let's consider … • I suggest/propose that you / we … • I suggest/propose (+ -ing form) • What do you think about …? • If I were you, I'd …

Responding to a suggestion
That's a good idea! / Fine! • OK / Yes, why not? • OK, if you want, I don't really mind. • I think it would be a better idea to talk about / consider … • Couldn't we look at this / do this another way? • What about …? • I'm not sure. How about …?

Useful phrases

Asking for an opinion
What do you think / feel about …? • What is your view / opinion on / about …? • What would you say? • I'd like to hear what you think about …

Giving an opinion
As far as I'm concerned … • I think / feel / believe / am of the opinion that … • To my mind … • In my opinion … • In my view …

Agreeing
You're (quite / absolutely) right. • That's a very good point! • Absolutely! / Exactly! • I agree (with you / Susie / …). • You have a point there. • You might / could be right. • I think you're right to a certain extent / up to a point.

Disagreeing
I disagree (entirely). • I'm sorry, but I completely disagree. • Stop exaggerating! • I think you're oversimplifying things. • That's an interesting point, but … • That's not the point. • You've missed the point (entirely).

Interrupting someone
Sorry to interrupt, but could you please explain / repeat the point you've just made. • Excuse me for interrupting, but I don't understand what you've just said. • Sorry for interrupting but …

Dealing with being interrupted
Can I just finish what I was saying, please? • Just a second. I haven't quite finished. • Would you let me / allow me to make my point, please. • You could at least let me finish my sentence!

Changing the subject
There is something else that I'd like to say … • Have you ever thought of / considered …? • On the other hand … • Try looking at things another way / from a different angle. • I'd like to bring up another point.

Returning to the original subject
Let's get back to what we were saying / discussing. • Let's get back to the point. • As I was saying before, … • Getting back to what we / you / … said earlier …

Asking for a further explanation
Did I get that right? • Do you really mean that …? • Did I understand correctly that you think …? • Could you explain what you just said / the point you just made / … again, please? • Could you give me / us a concrete example, please?

Saying that a point has been misunderstood
That's not what I meant to say (at all)! • You've got me (completely) wrong. • You've (completely) misunderstood me. • That's not what I was trying to say! • I didn't make myself clear. I'll try and explain again.

Tips for everyday conversation

Always make sure your **language and behaviour is appropriate for the situation** at hand. If it's a formal situation and you know what will be talked about, prepare by looking up useful words and facts.

When you are talking to older or more **experienced people or to your boss**, you should use more **polite phrases** and not be too direct. With **people of the same age or people you know really well**, you probably feel more at ease and can **be a little more direct**. In any case, always show that you are interested in what the person has to say and that you respect him / her.

Give **precise and clear information** and remember to **be tactful** when telling people something that affects them personally.

Always pick up on what your conversation partners have said to show that you **respect and sympathise** with them, that you are listening carefully and judging the content fairly. Use **supportive intonation and body language** as well as the following phrases, where appropriate.

Useful phrases

please • thank you • you're welcome • don't worry • not at all • Could I …? • Would you …? • May I …? • I'd like … • Yes, I will • No, I don't • Yes, that's true, but … • I agree, but … • It's just … • of course • I see • you know • I mean … • Really? • Are you sure? • What a pity. • That's very kind of you. • I appreciate that.

Small talk

Small talk is **light (casual) conversation**. It is a way of showing interest in others, communicating in a friendly way and avoiding conflict at all times! At a **social event**, such as a party, you might spend the whole time in casual conversation. At a **business meeting, on the phone, at an interview, etc.** you can start (and end) with **a little small talk**.

Topics for small talk

- The weather (especially popular in Britain!)
- A journey (to or from the place where you are)
- Where you live / Where your conversation partner lives
- Your family and / or your conversation partner's family (if you know them)
- A recent / well-known TV programme or film
- Tips about what to see and do in a certain town or city (i.e. cultural events, attractions, restaurants, local specialities, etc.)
- Sport (e.g. a current sports event)
- A vacation
- Where you / your conversation partner went to school or university
- What you do for a living / what your conversation partner does for a living
- Hobbies and interests
- An experience / event that you and your conversation partner are both currently involved in or have been involved in
- A non-controversial item in the news

Useful phrases

Starting a conversation
Hi! / Hello! • What are you up to? • Do you mind if I join you? • Nice to see you (again)! • How are you? • How are you doing? • How are things?

Finding a topic
Did you see … on TV last night / at the weekend / …? • Have you seen the new … film yet? • Did you read about … in the newspaper this morning? • Terrible / Beautiful weather, isn't it? • How was your journey? • How did you get here? • What made you decide to come here? • Have you ever been here before? • Who do you think is going to win … this evening?

Making plans
Shall I pick you up? • Let's arrange to meet at … • Sorry, I can't manage Friday. I'm meeting … then. • I've got an appointment with … at … • Thursday would suit me better / best. • That's no good, I'm afraid. What about …? • I've got a date with … on … • I'm seeing … then. • Shall we book seats / tickets / a table? • When does the performance start? • It starts at … • If there's a problem, call me.

Responding & showing surprise
Really? • I don't believe it! • That's incredible! • Well, I've never heard of anything like that before! • That's the funniest / most interesting / strangest thing I've heard in ages! • I've never thought of it like that before. • I couldn't agree more! • That's funny! Exactly the same thing happened to me the other day / two weeks ago / … .

Finishing a conversation
It was nice talking to you! • Goodness / Oh no, is that the time? • Excuse me, / What a shame, I've got to go now. • Hope to see you again soon. • Hope you get home safely. • Take care. • Give my regards to … . • Don't forget to say hello to … for me!

Making phone calls

1 Preparing a phone call

- **Prepare yourself** thoroughly. Make **notes in English** or write out a rough draft of the main things you want to say. This is especially important when making formal or business calls.
- If possible **find out the name and number** of a direct contact person in advance.
- **Think of things** the contact person is likely **to ask or say** and work out responses.
- **Be prepared to spell words**, especially people's names and names of places.

2 During the phone call

- **Speak clearly and slowly**. State your requests clearly and to the point.
- Don't worry about making mistakes.
- **Be polite!** Say *please* when you ask for information and *thank you* when you receive help.
  Remember: *please = bitte* • *you're welcome / not at all = bitte schön; gern geschehen*
- When making a social call, give your first name only.
- When making a formal / business call, give your first name and surname.

- **Address people** you know well by their first names. In a formal / business situation address people using *Mr, Mrs* or *Ms* [mz] + surname.
- **State telephone numbers** as single digits. When the same number occurs twice consecutively, you can say *double* (e.g. *33 = double 3*). *0 = Oh* (BE & AE) or *zero* (AE)
  Example: *07145 14406: Oh / zero – seven – one – four – five – one – double four – oh / zero – six*
- **Ask the caller to spell names**, etc. for you to avoid confusion.
- **Repeat important information** (times, names, addresses, prices, etc.) to be sure that you have understood everything correctly.
- Don't expect to understand every single word that is said.
- If you are not sure if you have understood something:
  - **Ask the person to repeat** what they have just said: *Could you repeat that, please?*
  - **Ask the person to explain** something in a different way: *So what you're saying is …?*
  - **Ask the person to speak more slowly**: *Could you speak a little more slowly, please?*
- If you can't hear the caller properly, **ask the caller to speak more loudly**.
- If you think you've got the wrong number, check and apologise. Don't just hang up.
- If the caller has got the wrong number, explain politely. **Don't just hang up**.

Useful phrases

> **The kind of things you may want to say**
> Hello. Is that Mr Brown speaking? • Could I speak to Mr Brown, please? • This is … I'm calling from Germany. • I'm calling about … • I'd like to enquire about … • I hope I'm not calling at an inconvenient time. • I've got a few questions / a complaint about … • I'd like to make an appointment to see the doctor / dentist / … • Shall I ring back later? • Could you take a message / give him / her a message, please? • What time would be most convenient? • Could you repeat that, please? • I'm afraid the line's very bad / we've got a bad connection.
>
> **What you may hear at the other end of the line**
> Brown and Wilson Car Rentals. Can I help you? • Speaking! • I'll just fetch him. Hang on a moment, please. • I'm afraid he's not available / he's in a meeting. I'm afraid the line is engaged at the moment. • Could you call back later? • Can I take a message? • I'll give you his extension. • I'll put you through to the … department… • I'll connect you. Please hold the line. • Sorry. I think you've dialled the wrong number. • The person you are calling is not available at the moment. Please leave a message after the tone. • If you wish to contact the sales… complaints…customer service department, please press ONE…TWO…

A job interview

If a company finds your letter of application and CV interesting, their human resource department may invite you for an interview. For the interviewee, the interview process starts beforehand with **good preparation**.

1 Preparation

- **Find out about the business or institution** where you will have your interview.
- **Think of questions** that you might be asked, and come up with **suitable answers**.
- Have a friend ask you the questions (plus some surprise ones) and give you a constructive feedback on how you answered them.
- **Think of questions to ask the interviewer** about the business or institution. You want to show that you already know something about them.
- **Dress nicely and arrive early** so that you can collect your thoughts before the interview.

2 During the interview

- **Smile and maintain eye contact** with your interviewer (although it isn't a good idea to stare).
- The interviewer knows that you are nervous, so he or she might try to lighten the atmosphere with **small talk** (→ Small talk p. 135). Be prepared to chat with him or her.
- **Speak clearly and not too quickly!** It is perfectly alright to pause for a moment and think about what you want to say.
- If necessary, ask the interviewer to repeat or explain a question. This also gives you more time to think!
- **Do not answer questions with only *yes, no,* or *I don't know*.** However, keep answers clear and concise. This is your chance to convince the interviewer that you are the right person for the job!
- If possible, **ask the question(s) about the business or institution** that you thought of.
- **Thank** your interviewer at the end.

3 After the interview

- After a short time, **send a short, follow-up mail** thanking your interviewer and expressing interest in the position again. If you haven't been told when the decision will be made, ask politely when you can expect a reply.
- **If you don't get the job, don't worry!** Think of what you can do better next time, and work on these points. As with any other skill, the more interviews you do, the better you will get!

Useful phrases

> As you can see from my CV … • I trained in … • I graduated / will be graduating from school in … • I enjoy dealing with clients / working with people. • I have excellent … skills / good knowledge of … • I'm PC literate. • I'm accustomed to working hard. • I'm prepared to work overtime. • During my time at school I did internships at …

Word webs

Word webs are useful for **collecting and organising a large amount of information** about a certain topic. You can make a word web for yourself or as a group. The basic structure of a word web is always the same.

1 How to make a word web

- **Use a pencil** so that you can easily delete things or change their position, if necessary.
- Write your main topic in the middle of a page and draw a circle around the word or phrase. (Fig. 1)
- Think of **important things** directly related to the main topic. Write each idea (subtopic) in a **circle** around the outside of your first circle. **Draw lines** connecting the subtopics to the main topic. (Fig. 2)
- Now add more circles with related ideas around the subtopics. (Fig. 3) Instead of drawing circles you can use lines with 'branches' for subtopics. (Fig. 4)

2 Ways of using word webs

- To **brainstorm for ideas on a given topic:** Write the topic heading in the centre circle and add all new and related aspects.
- To **organise information from a text** (or other source): Start with the most important point in the text, add the main subtopics, then add relevant detailed information or quotations from the text.
- To **develop word fields**: Start with the generic term and add all related words.
- To **organise arguments**: Start with the topic of discussion. Add a branch or circle: 'for' and another one 'against'. Continue by adding further branches / circles with arguments 'for' and 'against'.

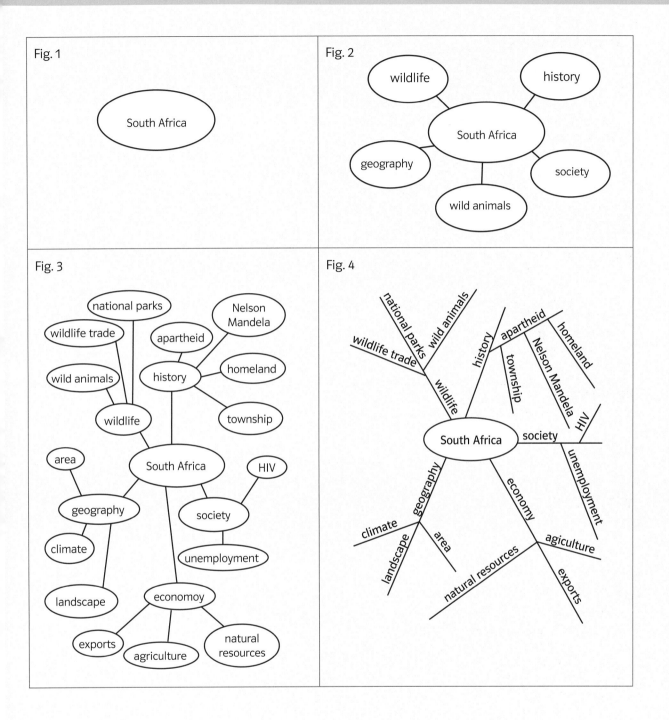

Fig. 1

South Africa

Fig. 2

wildlife · history · South Africa · geography · society · wild animals

Fig. 3

national parks · wildlife trade · wild animals · apartheid · Nelson Mandela · homeland · history · township · wildlife · area · South Africa · HIV · geography · society · climate · unemployment · landscape · economoy · exports · agriculture · natural resources

Fig. 4

national parks · wildlife trade · wild animals · history · apartheid · homeland · township · Nelson Mandela · HIV · wildlife · South Africa · society · unemployment · geography · economy · agiculture · climate · area · landscape · natural resources · exports

Brainstorming

Brainstorming is the first step when you want to **collect ideas on a specific topic**. You can brainstorm on your own, with a partner or in a group.

1 Individual brainstorming

- First write down **each idea that comes to mind** when you think of the topic.
- In a second step, go through your collection of ideas and choose those which you really want.
- **Structure** your ideas in a grid or a word web.

2 Brainstorming in a group (placemat)

- Form groups of four. Write down the topic in the middle of a big sheet of paper (placemat). Each of you works in one corner.
- Collect your ideas on the topic and write them down in your corner.
- Discuss all ideas and decide on the ones you find best or most important. Write them in the middle of your placemat.

Example:

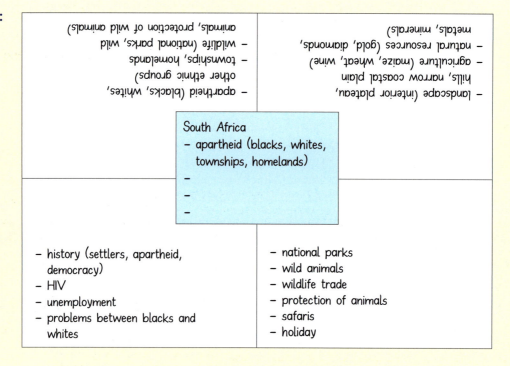

Taking notes

Taking notes means writing down information from a spoken source (speech, interview, etc.) in short form.

- Only write down the **most important information**. It is impossible to note down everything.
- Only write down **key words**, never complete sentences. Key words are often names, times, numbers and places.
- Try to order your notes systematically. If possible, use headings, sub-headings or grids.
- Use **symbols** for certain relationships, for example: = ≠ →
- Make sure that you can read your handwriting!

Marking up a text

When you read a text, it can be useful to mark up **information that you will need later** for answering questions, etc. Remember that you can only mark up texts **in photocopies or in books that belong to you**.

- When you read the text, keep in mind **which information** you are looking for.
- Mark relevant information by **underlining, circling or highlighting** the words or phrases.
- If you want to mark different kinds of information, choose **different colours**.
- You can also write down **key words in the margins**.
- When you read the text again later, you can **concentrate on the marked words** and phrases and on your notes in the margins.

Example:

The struggle against apartheid

Apartheid (meaning *separateness* in Afrikaans) was a system of legalised racial segregation in South Africa. Apartheid had its roots in the history of colonisation and settlement of southern Africa.
   The first Europeans who settled in South Africa were the Dutch in 1652. In 1806 the British arrived. The discovery of diamonds in 1867 and gold in 1886 led to increased immigration and brought wealth which, however, native Africans were denied. The Union of South Africa was formed in 1910 and racial segregation was generally accepted although the policy of apartheid didn't become official until 1948, when the National Party came to power.
   Apartheid classified inhabitants and visitors into racial groups (black, white, coloured, and Indian or Asian). South African blacks had to move to small and economically unproductive areas of the country known as 'homelands'. Blacks who worked in factories and mines had to live in 'townships', i.e. poor and underdeveloped living areas which were built around the major cities. The government also segregated education, medical care and other public services. The services for black people were greatly inferior to those of whites and the black education system was designed to prepare blacks for life in the labouring class.

Margin notes:
- definition and roots
- first settlers
- apartheid
- examples

141

Guessing new words

Don't be afraid of texts containing new words. You already know many different ways of guessing their meanings. After applying your guessing technique there will still be some words you don't know, but don't worry, you will probably understand the most important points in the text.

Guessable words	Examples:
• Words that are used in a German context.	*bestseller, boycott, clown, laptop, track, …*
• Words that are similar to German words → but watch out for false friends!	*individuality, inner, install, parallel, to wander, …*
• Words that are similar to words you know from another foreign language (French, Latin, Spanish, Italian) → but watch out for false friends!	*academic, announcement, artificial, descendant, dignity, disrespect, individuality, junior, minor, pasta, phase, …*
• Compounds of words you already know.	*handwriting, heartfelt, mixed ability, single-sex, washing machine, wholeheartedly, …*
• Words from a word family you already know.	*adventurous, announcement, importation, to mirror, nationalism, relevance, …*
• Words you already know, but with a different meaning, the new meaning being guessable from the context.	*to admit, light, plain, pretty, to report sb…*
• Words whose meaning you can guess from the context.	*(he) dozed off (in his chair); (it's old-fashioned) out of date*

Working with a dictionary

1 English-German, German-English

When using an English-German or German-English dictionary, make sure to check the following information in your dictionary.

- What part of speech is the word?
- What does it go together with?
- What topic or word field does it belong to?
- How is it pronounced?
- Are there irregular forms?
- What translations are given?
- Which of the translations can only be used in a limited context (*AE, formal, slang*, etc.)?
- Which of the translations fits the context?

Example:

fo·cus[ˈfəʊkəs] <pl **focuses, foci**> [pl ˈfəʊsaɪ] s ➊ (MATH OPT) Brennpunkt m ➋ (fig) Brennpunkt, Herd m, Zentrum nt; ~ (un)scharf eingestellt; ~ scharf einstellen vt ➊ (OPT PHOT) einstellen (on auf) ➋ (fig) konzentrieren (on auf); **focus group** s (in marketing) [ausgewählte] Test-

2 English-English

This type of dictionary is best used for **writing an English text** when you are not quite sure which is the best word in a given context. The more English you read, the more you will improve your language! An English-English (monolingual) dictionary provides you with the following information:

- What part of speech is the word?
- What does it go together with?
- What topic or word field does it belong to?
- How is it pronounced?

- Are there irregular forms?
- What synonyms and / or definitions are given?
- Which of the given meanings fits the context?
- Examples show how the word is typically used.

Tips for using an English-English dictionary

- Before looking up a word identify whether it is a verb, noun, adjective, adverb, etc.
- When you have found the entry for the word, make sure you look at the meaning for the correct class of word.
- Read any additional information which the dictionary gives you about the word.
- Take your time to read the entry carefully.
- Make sure you find the entry which matches the use of the word in the given context.

Example:

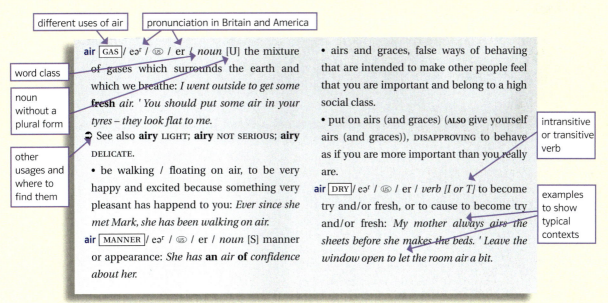

different uses of air

pronunciation in Britain and America

word class

noun without a plural form

other usages and where to find them

air GAS / eəʳ / ⓤⓢ / er / *noun* [U] the mixture of gases which surrounds the earth and which we breathe: *I went outside to get some* **fresh** *air.* ' *You should put some air in your tyres – they look flat to me.*
⮌ See also **airy** LIGHT; **airy** NOT SERIOUS; **airy** DELICATE.
- be walking / floating on air, to be very happy and excited because something very pleasant has happend to you: *Ever since she met Mark, she has been walking on air.*
air MANNER / eəʳ / ⓤⓢ / er / *noun* [S] manner or appearance: *She has* **an** *air* **of** *confidence about her.*

- airs and graces, false ways of behaving that are intended to make other people feel that you are important and belong to a high social class.
- put on airs (and graces) (ALSO give yourself airs (and graces)), DISAPPROVING to behave as if you are more important than you really are.
air DRY / eəʳ / ⓤⓢ / er / *verb [I or T]* to become try and/or fresh, or to cause to become try and/or fresh: *My mother always airs the sheets before she makes the beds.* ' *Leave the window open to let the room air a bit.*

intransitive or transitive verb

examples to show typical contexts

Working with films

An interesting way of dealing with a specific topic is by watching and analysing related films. A film usually tells a story, so you **can analyse the plot, setting, characters and narrative techniques** exactly the way you do with a fictional text (→ Understanding fictional texts p. 111). In addition to the content, you can analyse the **audiovisual aspects** of the film.

1 Important film genres

action • adventure • comedy • crime • drama • epic / historical • horror • musical • science fiction • war • western • fantasy • romance • melodrama

2 Choosing a film

- If you are looking for a film that deals with a specific topic, you can search on the Internet. Use a search engine or check the *International Movie Database*.

3 Analysing a film

- **Choose a scene** from the film.
- Make a **list of the types of camera shots**.
- Say what effect each shot creates, e. g. it shows a character's emotions, it includes the viewer in the scene, it shows where the action is going to take place, etc.
- If you have access to **different versions of the film**, compare the same scene in both. What similarities / differences do you notice?
- If the film is **based on a novel, short story or play**: How much of the original plot has been used in the film? Have characters been cut out / added in? Why is this the case, do you think? Compare the message of the film with that of the original text. Which do you prefer – the book or the film? Why?
- Is the **music** memorable? Does it create a particular atmosphere? What effect does the music have on the scenes?
- If you have the film on DVD, also watch the **special features** (director's commentary, interviews, cut-out scenes, trailers, etc.)
- If you have got the **film script**, compare it to the film version, concentrating on one or two scenes. What changes were made in the film?
- Choose two actors / actresses from the film. Find out about other films they acted in. Then say whether you found them suitable in their role in the film you are analysing.
- Describe the **film poster and / or film trailer**. What aspects of the film does it emphasise? Most modern films have homepages which include the poster and trailer.
- Write a **review** of the film in which you **outline the plot and the roles** played by the actors. Say whether you liked the film and would recommend it or not.
  Explain why.
- Check the Internet for online reviews and comments by people who have seen the film. Compare their evaluation with yours.

4 Camera operations

Field size
(Bildausschnitt/Bildgröße)

long shot (Totale): people/objects shown from distance

full shot: shot of the whole body/object

medium shot: upper body/part of an object

close-up (Nahaufnahme): head and shoulders

extreme close-up: (Detailaufnahme) face only; detailed shot

Camera movements

static shot: camera does not move

to pan left/right (horizontal schwenken); to tilt up/down (vertikal schwenken)

crane shot (Kranfahrt): camera moves flexibly in all directions on a crane

to zoom in on/out of s.th. (e.g. a face)

tracking shot (Kamerafahrt): camera is on a vehicle moving on the ground

Camera positions

E.g. A point-of-view shot is seen through a character's eyes. Other examples are:

establishing shot: shows location (long shot/pan) at the start of a scene

overhead shot: bird's eye view

over-the-shoulder shot

reverse-angle shot: from the opposite side, usually shows a dialogue partner

Camera angles

high-angle shot (from above)

eye-level shot

low-angle shot (from below)

5 Important aspects of one or more film scenes

setting	contemporary / historical? • science fiction? • city / country? • exterior / interior?
characters	how many? • who? • appearance? • costumes? • body language?
story and storyline	dialogue? • interaction? • fight? • narrative structure?
camera	field size? • view? • zooming? • panning? • tracking?
light	colours? • brightness / darkness? • atmosphere?
cut	tempo? • rest? • correspondence with actions?
sound and music	voices? • atmosphere?
special effects	animation? • slow / fastmotion?

6 Presenting a film in class

- **Start by giving your audience more information** than just the title:
  - Who directed it?
  - Who acted in it?
  - Who produced it?
  - When was it made?
  - Who wrote the music?
  - Was it a success?
  - If the film is based on a literary text, say which one.
- Then briefly **introduce the setting and the characters and sum up the plot.**
- Say what is **good or bad** about the film and why you like it or not.
- **Present a scene** that has an important function in the film. The scene should enable you to say something about the characters, their relationship with each other, their role in the plot, their language and body language, the atmosphere of the film and what is typical of the way it tells its story. You should also be able to say at what point in the film it comes and what its function is.

Useful phrases

In the foreground / background there is … • The camera takes a long / medium / close-up / extreme close-up shot. • This brings us close to … / creates a distance between … • The camera position is … • The view of … is frontal / from above / below / behind. • The focus is on a … detail. • The camera zooms in / out of … • The camera pans from … to … • … is introduced in a panning shot. • The movement of … is followed in a tracking shot. • The shots follow each other quickly. / The … shot lasts for a while. This creates a / an … atmosphere. • … is shown in slow / fast motion.

Internet research

1 Subject searches and key word searches

- Browse a **subject guide or directory**, e.g. *Yahoo*, to choose a category, then a subcategory and so on, e.g. *travel > travel guides > United States > Las Vegas*.
- Use a **search engine**, e.g. *Google*, to look for certain key words, e.g. *history apartheid Mandela*.
- Most of the search engines use OR as a default. This means that you will get a list of sites that include any one of any of the key words you entered, e.g. you will get sites for South Wales (in Britain) as well as New South Wales (in Australia) if you enter *new south wales*.
  With most search engines you can **use + or – signs in front of certain key words** to make sure they are included or excluded from your search, e.g. *+martin +luther -king*. If you look for a certain phrase, like the title of a book, put it in **inverted commas**, e.g. *"lord of the rings"*.
- To get better results, it may help to put the **most unusual or relevant word first**.
- If you don't get many hits, check your spelling, try similar key words or use fewer words.
- If you get too many hits, be more specific and add some words.

2 Bookmarks *(Favoriten)*

- To make it easier to return to a site you like, you can add a **bookmark** either by clicking on the bookmarks *(Favoriten)* menu, by pressing Control-D *(Strg-D)* or by clicking on your right mouse button.
- If you forgot to add a bookmark, you can go back to sites you have visited during the last few sessions by using the forward or back buttons or by pressing Control-H *(Strg-H)*.

3 Evaluating your results

- Don't believe everything you read! Remember that anyone can publish anything on the Internet. **Judge the reliability** of a website before using information from it. Is it similar to *www.harvard.edu* or more like *www.aol/users/joedoe*?
- Is it a commercial website? Then it might be interested in selling something rather than giving objective information.
- Does it contain **facts or just opinions**?
- Is the **author** someone who is likely to know something about a subject, e.g. a university teacher or a journalist?
- Also check if the website has been **updated recently**, especially if you are looking for the latest news on a topic.

Projects and group work

1 Finding information

Set up an **'information centre'** in your classroom (or of your own) in which you keep a record of where to find information. Find and keep a record of:

- The name, address, email address, telephone and fax number of:
  - your local library
  - the nearest university or college library
  - your twin-town association (if your area has one)
  - the nearest newsagent or bookshop which stocks English newspapers and magazines. (Tip: Try your nearest main station.)
- The **website addresses** of search engines, schools and colleges, youth organisations, political parties, newspapers, magazines, government agencies in America and the UK.
- The names of classmates who have **contacts** (penfriends, relatives, friends, etc.) **in the English-speaking world**, and who might be willing to help you.
- The names of classmates or people in your neighbourhood who have an **English-speaking parent / parents** and who might help you. Collect **brochures** from travel agencies and tourist information bureaus. Collect material while you are on holiday (leaflets, magazines, postcards, advertisements, menus, timetables, etc.). Add information and addresses to your files when you find new material.

2 Doing a project

- Read the information you are given about the **project task** carefully.
- In your groups, **brainstorm** to find ideas about:
  - what you all already know about the topic.
  - which aspects you want to concentrate on.
  - where you can find information.
- If necessary, **decide which points are more important** (concentrate on these) and which are less important (and can possibly be left out).
- Decide **which tasks each member of the group are going to do**. Make sure the workload is divided equally.
- If not specified in the task, decide how you want to **present your material**.
  You can produce: a talk using visual aids • a video • a CD • a leaflet • a brochure • a file of written information • a written report • a poster or wall chart • a website.
- Remember to **keep a record of your sources**, i.e. where you found material, where quotes or extracts from original material were taken from, etc.

Questionnaires and surveys

1 Before doing a survey

- It is important to have a clear idea of **what kind of information** you hope to get from your survey.
- Write one or two **sentences describing your topic** and explaining why you are doing the survey. (Later you can include these sentences at the start of your questionnaire so that the people you ask (interviewees / participants) have a clear idea of what the survey is about.)
- Briefly **state what you expect the results of your survey to be** – or give alternatives.
- Decide **how many people** you want to interview and **which social groups** they should belong to. For example, is the age of participants important? Should they be male or female? Should they have a certain job or hobby?

2 The questionnaire

- The success of a survey depends largely on **how good your questions** are.
  If possible, ask an independent person to answer your questions before you carry out the survey to make sure your questions are clear.
- Decide what **type of questions** you want to ask. The most common types of questions are described in the box below.
- Your questions need not all be of the same type, but it is best not to include too many different types.
- Always keep the **aim of your survey** in mind when you are formulating questions.
- Word your questions **clearly and concisely**. Use formal language.
- **Don't ask too many questions** (between 10 and 15 is usually enough).
- Put your questions in **logical order**.
- Group questions relating to particular aspects together.
- Start off with simpler, more general questions and then go on to more detailed questions.
- Your last question can be an open-ended question.

3 Types of questions

Multiple choice questions	Yes / No questions
The interviewee chooses from given answers.	Questions that can be answered with 'Yes' or 'No'.
Which of the following do you own? *a) a TV* ☐ *b) a DVD player* ☐ *c) an MP3 player* ☐ *d) a CD player* ☐	*Do you exercise more than three times a week?* ☐ *YES* ☐ *NO*
Graded questions	**Open-ended questions**
The interviewee has to choose to what extent they agree / disagree with, like / don't like / … something.	Questions to which the interviewees must give their own answer. The questions usually begin with a question word: who, what, when, where, why or how.
How often do you eat fruit or vegetables on average per day? ☐ *never* ☐ *less than three times* ☐ *more than three times*	*How, in your opinion, could the recycling system in your area be improved?* _____

4 Presenting the results

- When you summarise and present your results, always **think of your aims**, for example:
  - proving a certain expectation right or wrong
  - comparing the answers of different groups
  - giving the majority opinion
  - presenting the most surprising results.
- Never forget to say **how many and what kind of people took part** in your survey! Most answers can be turned into statistics straight away, so you can present your statistics as percentages and use diagrams to support the presentation visually.

Example:

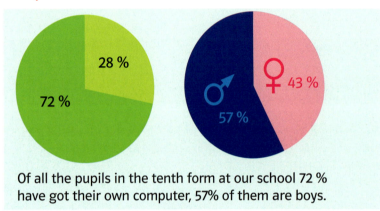

Of all the pupils in the tenth form at our school 72 % have got their own computer, 57% of them are boys.

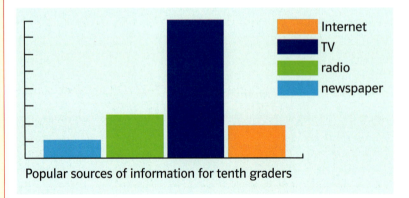

Popular sources of information for tenth graders

- Ratings may require a different **form of presentation**, e.g.:
  When asked about the importance of foreign languages, 26 out of 30 people answered that foreign languages were generally very important to them, 3 out of 30 thought foreign languages were only important in some situations, and only one person said they were not important at all.
- Presenting **answers to open-ended questions**, you may be able to make a top three, five or ten using similar answers or you may quote the most surprising ones, e.g.:
  The top three breakfast favourites in our class are: 1. rolls 2. cereals 3. jam.

Presentation

1 Preparation

Gather material on your topic:
- Brainstorm to find ideas on the topic and make a word web.
- Find information from relevant sources (library, school books, the Internet, newspapers, etc.)

Choose which main points you want to talk about.

Make a set of prompt cards in English, which you can look at during your talk to remind you of what you want to say (→ prompt cards p. 152).
- Write down the key words, phrases and vocabulary which you will need.
- Note down any examples or quotations.
- Note down any visual aids (OHPs, photographs, posters, flip charts, etc.) which you plan to use.

Arrange your prompt cards in logical order. You could present points:
- in terms of importance, from the most to the least important (or vice versa)
- chronologically
- with all those in favour first, followed by all those against.

Make a prompt card for your introduction (→ card 1 p. 152). Catch the listeners' attention with:
- an interesting question or fact
- a quote or joke
- a picture or cartoon on an OHP transparency.

Make a prompt card for your conclusion (→ card 7 p. 152):
- Note the point(s) you want to emphasise.
- Write down key words and phrases.
- Make a note of a final quotation or an example you wish to use.

2 Giving a talk or presentation

- **Practise your talk or presentation** out loud, preferably in front of a mirror, or ask a friend/relative to listen to you!
- **Speak slowly and clearly!**
- Use short, clear sentences.
- **Vary your voice** so that you don't sound boring. For example, emphasise particularly important points by speaking a little more loudly.
- **Look at your audience** as often as possible. Don't look at your prompt cards all the time.
- Try not to make distracting movements such as waving your hands, etc.
- **Smile!** (But don't laugh nervously!)
- **Start by introducing yourself** (if necessary) and your topic. **Finish by thanking** your audience for listening. Ask if anyone has any questions.

3 A market place

- **Form groups** and **prepare** your product.
- Choose a **speaker** for your group.
- **Present** your product in the classroom. Your classmates walk around and look at the different products. The **speaker** presents the product to the people who pass by and answers their questions.
- **Discuss** the products in class.

4 A gallery walk

- **Prepare** your product (on your own or in a group).
- Prepare an **evaluation sheet** in class.
- **Present** your product in the classroom and give the evaluation sheets to your classmates.
- Your **classmates** walk around, look at the different products and **fill in the evaluation sheet**.
- **Discuss** the results of the evaluation sheets in class.

5 Prompt cards

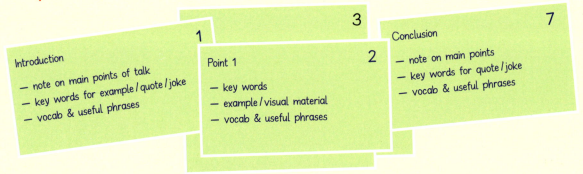

Introduction
— note on main points of talk
— key words for example / quote / joke
— vocab & useful phrases

1

Point 1
— key words
— example / visual material
— vocab & useful phrases

3

2

Conclusion
— note on main points
— key words for quote / joke
— vocab & useful phrases

7

Useful phrases

Good morning / afternoon, my name is … • Today I'm going to talk about … • The subject of my talk today is … • Can everyone hear me alright? • Can everyone see the board / screen / etc.? • I'd like to begin by (+ -ing form) … • Let me start by saying a few words about … • Let me give you an example. • As you can see on the chart / graph / cartoon … • I'd like to finish / conclude by (+ -ing form) … • Let me finish by (+ -ing form) … • Finally … • Thank you very much for your attention. • I hope you all enjoyed my talk. • I'd be happy to answer any questions

Tenses

Simple present

Positive sentences	Negative sentences	Questions
I play football. You play football. He/she/it plays football. We play football. You play football. They play football.	I don't play football. You don't play football. He/she/it doesn't play football. We don't play football. You don't play football. They don't play football.	Do I play football? Do you play football? Does he/she/it play football? Do we play football? Do you play football? Do they play football? Questions with question word: Why do I play football? Why do you play football? Why does he/she/it play football? Why do we play football? Why do you play football? Why do they play football?
! Be careful with these verbs: be, have		

Examples of typical use:

1. Facts and general statements: Cats eat mice.

2. Everyday activities or habits: Our team plays football on Sundays.
Tense markers: always, often, sometimes, never, usually, every day/week/month/year, on Mondays/…, at 7 o'clock/…

3. A set sequence of events or actions: The two knights fight, the Queen screams, and then the King saves her.

4. For scheduled future events with an adverbial phrase of time: The train leaves at 14:35.

Present progressive

Positive sentences	Negative sentences	Questions
I am singing. You are singing. He/she/it is singing. We are singing. You are singing. They are singing.	I'm not singing. You aren't singing. He/she/it isn't singing. We aren't singing. You aren't singing. They aren't singing.	Am I singing? Are you singing? Is he/she/it singing? Are we singing? Are you singing? Are they singing?

Positive sentences	Negative sentences	Questions
		Questions with question word: What am I singing? What are you singing? What is he/she/it singing? What are we singing? What are you singing? What are they singing?
❗ Some verbs are never used in the progressive form, especially those which express feelings or belief: believe, love, hate, seem, have (in the sense of own), can, mean, want to, feel, notice, realise		

Examples of typical use:

1. An activity that is going on right now and will continue for a certain limited or temporary period of time:
   Greg is cooking dinner (now).
   Tense markers: now, just now, at the moment

2. Planned future events with an adverbial phrase of time: They are visiting us in three weeks.

Simple past

Positive sentences	Negative sentences	Questions
I played football. You played football. He/she/it played football. We played football. You played football. They played football.	I didn't play football. You didn't play football. He/she/it didn't play football. We didn't play football. You didn't play football. They didn't play football.	Did I play football? Did you play football? Did he/she/it play football? Did we play football? Did you play football? Did they play football? Questions with question word: Why did I play football? Why did you play football? Why did he/she/it play football? Why did we play football? Why did you play football? Why did they play football?
❗ Be careful with irregular verbs		

Examples of typical use:

1. For activities that began and ended at a specific time in the past: They returned from Canada a week ago.
   Tense markers: yesterday, ago, last week/month/year, in 2007/…, on Tuesday/…

2. For a series of events in the past as in a story, often called the 'narrative past':
   As the train left the station, Helen looked around the compartment. There was no one else in sight. She took out the letter and started to read it.

Past progressive

Positive sentences	Negative sentences	Questions
I was singing. You were singing. He/she/it was singing. We were singing. You were singing. They were singing.	I wasn't singing. You weren't singing. He/she/it wasn't singing. We weren't singing. You weren't singing. They weren't singing.	Was I singing? Were you singing? Was he/she/it singing? Were we singing? Were you singing? Were they singing? Questions with question word: What was I singing? What were you singing? What was he/she/it singing? What were we singing? What were you singing? What were they singing?

Examples of typical use:

1. An activity in the past that was already in progress when something else happened:
   They were cleaning the house when the guests arrived.

2. Several activities or events that were happening at the same time in the past:
   While Patty was mowing the lawn, Sid was cleaning the windows.

Present perfect simple

Positive sentences	Negative sentences	Questions
I have finished. You have finished. He/she/it has finished. We have finished. You have finished. They have finished.	I haven't finished. You haven't finished. He/she/it hasn't finished. We haven't finished. You haven't finished. They haven't finished.	Have I finished? Have you finished? Has he/she/it finished? Have we finished? Have you finished? Have they finished? Questions with question word: What have I finished? What have you finished? What has he/she/it finished? What have we finished? What have you finished? What have they finished?
! Be careful with irregular verbs With the present perfect simple the result of the action is usually more important than the action itself. Never use the present perfect with adverbs of past time, e.g. yesterday, last week, three years ago, in 2007.		

Examples of typical use:

1. Activities that happened recently, and whose effects are still felt in the present:
   They have moved to Stratford and they are still living there.

2. With certain adverbs: just, so far, ever, never, recently, lately, today, this week, already, (not) yet
   The test results have just arrived. – I have had good marks so far this year. – Have you ever been to New York?

3. With for and since, for activities that started in the past and are continuing:
   I haven't eaten chocolate for three weeks! – I haven't seen Melanie since 2008.

Present perfect progressive

Positive sentences	Negative sentences	Questions
I have been waiting.	I haven't been waiting.	Have I been waiting?
You have been waiting.	You haven't been waiting.	Have you been waiting?
He/she/it has been waiting.	He/she/it hasn't been waiting.	Has he/she/it been waiting?
We have been waiting.	We haven't been waiting.	Have we been waiting?
You have been waiting.	You haven't been waiting.	Have you been waiting?
They have been waiting.	They haven't been waiting.	Have they been waiting?
		Questions with question word:
		Why have I been waiting?
		Why have you been waiting?
		Why has he/she/it been waiting?
		Why have we been waiting?
		Why have you been waiting?
		Why have they been waiting?

Examples of typical use:

1. Activities that have either been going on either continuously or at intervals up to the present, often with adverbials of time such as all day, for a week, etc.: We have been looking for a camping site all day.

2. With no mention of time, the activity has taken place very recently and the result is clearly visible:
   It has been raining.

Past perfect simple

Positive sentences	Negative sentences	Questions
I had finished.	I hadn't finished.	Had I finished?
You had finished.	You hadn't finished.	Had you finished?
He/she/it had finished.	He/she/it hadn't finished.	Had he/she/it finished?
We had finished.	We hadn't finished.	Had we finished?
You had finished.	You hadn't finished.	Had you finished?
They had finished.	They hadn't finished.	Had they finished?

Positive sentences	Negative sentences	Questions
		Questions with question word:
		What had I finished?
		What had you finished?
		What had he/she/it finished?
		What had we finished?
		What had you finished?
		What had they finished?
! Be careful with irregular verbs		

Examples of typical use:

1. An activity that happened before another activity in the past, showing the connection between the two activities:
   When we arrived at the station, the train had already left.
   After I had watched the news, I decided to go out.

2. In reported speech, when the original statement is in the past or present perfect:
   Jane said that she had forgotten to do her homework.

Past perfect progressive

Positive sentences	Negative sentences	Questions
I had been waiting.	I hadn't been waiting.	Had I been waiting?
You had been waiting.	You hadn't been waiting.	Had you been waiting?
He/she/it had been waiting.	He/she/it hadn't been waiting.	Had he/she/it been waiting?
We had been waiting.	We hadn't been waiting.	Had we been waiting?
You had been waiting.	You hadn't been waiting.	Had you been waiting?
They had been waiting.	They hadn't been waiting.	Had they been waiting?
		Questions with question word:
		Why had I been waiting?
		Why had you been waiting?
		Why had he/she/it been waiting?
		Why had we been waiting?
		Why had you been waiting?
		Why had they been waiting?

Examples of typical use:

1. A past activity that occurred before another where there is a direct relation to the activity that followed:
   He was tired because he had been working so hard.

2. In reported speech, when the original statement is in the present perfect progressive:
   He said that he had been working hard.

Going to-future

Positive sentences	Negative sentences	Questions
I am going to leave early. You are going to leave early. He/she/it is going to leave early. We are going to leave early You are going to leave early. They are going to leave early.	I'm not going to leave early. You're not going to leave early. He/she/it's not going to leave early. We're not going to leave early. You're not going to leave early. They're not going to leave early.	Am I going to leave early? Are you going to leave early? Is he/she/it going to leave early? Are we going to leave early? Are you going to leave early? Are they going to leave early?

Examples of typical use:

1. For an action in the future that has already been planned or prepared:
   They're going to buy Tom a new computer for his birthday.

2. For a prediction about the future, when you can see that something is about to happen:
   Look at those clouds. It's going to rain soon.

Future simple (will-future)

Positive sentences	Negative sentences	Questions
I will play football. You will play football. He/she/it will play football. We will play football. You will play football. They will play football.	I won't play football. You won't play football. He/she/it won't play football. We won't play football. You won't play football. They won't play football.	Will I play football? Will you play football? Will he/she/it play football? Will we play football? Will you play football? Will they play football? Questions with question word: Why will I play football? Why will you play football? Why will he/she/it play football? Why will we play football? Why will you play football? Why will they play football?

> **!** English will = German werden
> English want = German wollen

Examples of typical use:

1. Things that are likely to happen at a defined or undefined time in the future:
   You'll be a great movie star some day.

2. For forecasts, such as the weather forecast: On Saturday, there will be rain for most of the day.

3. In 'if'-clauses Type 1 – future situations that are probable/possible:
   If the weather is fine, I'll play football.

Future progressive

Positive sentences	Negative sentences	Questions
I will be singing. You will be singing. He/she/it will be singing. We will be singing. You will be singing. They will be singing.	I won't be singing. You won't be singing. He/she/it won't be singing. We won't be singing. You won't be singing. They won't be singing.	Will I be singing? Will you be singing? Will he/she/it be singing? Will we be singing? Will you be singing? Will they be singing? Questions with question word: What will I be singing? What will you be singing? What will he/she/it be singing? What will we be singing? What will you be singing? What will they be singing?

Example of typical use:

Events – often planned – that will be going on at a certain time in the future when another event occurs:
You will be sleeping by the time I get home.

Future perfect simple

Positive sentences	Negative sentences	Questions
I will have finished. You will have finished. He/she/it will have finished. We will have finished. You will have finished. They will have finished.	I won't have finished. You won't have finished. He/she/it won't have finished. We won't have finished. You won't have finished. They won't have finished.	Will I have finished? Will you have finished? Will he/she/it have finished? Will we have finished? Will you have finished? Will they have finished? Questions with question word: When will I have finished? When will you have finished? When will he/she/it have finished? When will we have finished? When will you have finished? When will they have finished?
! Be careful with irregular verbs		

Example of typical use:

Future activities that take place before other future activities to show a relation between them. The simple present is used for the other activities:
Joanna will have finished the college course by the time she is 20.

Future perfect progressive

Positive sentences	Negative sentences	Questions
I will have been waiting.	I won't have been waiting.	Will I have been waiting?
You will have been waiting.	You won't have been waiting.	Will you have been waiting?
He/she/it will have been waiting.	He/she/it won't have been waiting.	Will he/she/it have been waiting?
We will have been waiting.	We won't have been waiting.	Will we have been waiting?
You will have been waiting.	You won't have been waiting.	Will you have been waiting?
They will have been waiting.	They won't have been waiting.	Will they have been waiting?

Example of typical use:

Used in the same way as the future perfect simple but placing more emphasis on the activity:
They will have been studying English for eight years before they take the exam.

Conditional I

Positive sentences	Negative sentences	Questions
I would play football.	I wouldn't play football.	Would I play football?
You would play football.	You wouldn't play football.	Would you play football?
He/she/it would play football.	He/she/it wouldn't play football.	Would he/she/it play football?
We would play football.	We wouldn't play football.	Would we play football?
You would play football.	You wouldn't play football.	Would you play football?
They would play football.	They wouldn't play football.	Would they play football?
		Questions with question word:
		Why would I play football?
		Why would you play football?
		Why would he/she/it play football?
		Why would we play football?
		Why would you play football?
		Why would they play football?

Examples of typical use:

1. For suggestions, polite questions and requests:
   Which ring would you take? – Well, I would take that ring.
   Would you like a drink?
   Would you help me, please?

2. In 'if'-clauses Type 2 – future situations that are improbable/unlikely:
   If you studied hard, you would pass the exam.

Conditional II

Positive sentences	Negative sentences	Questions
I would have helped. You would have helped. He/she/it would have helped. We would have helped. You would have helped. They would have helped.	I wouldn't have helped. You wouldn't have helped. He/she/it wouldn't have helped. We wouldn't have helped. You wouldn't have helped. They wouldn't have helped.	Would I have helped? Would you have helped? Would he/she/it have helped? Would we have helped? Would you have helped? Would they have helped? Questions with question word: Why would I have helped? Why would you have helped? Why would he/she/it have helped? Why would we have helped? Why would you have helped? Why would they have helped?
! Be careful with irregular verbs		

Example of typical use:

In 'if'-clauses Type 3 – past situations that are unreal/impossible/hypothetical:
If you had studied hard, you would have passed the exam.

If-clauses

There are three main types of 'if'-clauses (or conditional sentences) in English. They are basically used in the same way as conditional sentences in German. You can put the 'if'-clause at the beginning or at the end of the sentence.

1. Type 1 - Future situations (probable/possible):

a.	'if'-clause: simple present – main clause: 'will'-future If you study hard, you will pass the exam. Wenn du fleißig lernst, wirst du die Prüfung bestehen.
b.	'if'–clause: present perfect – main clause: 'will'- future If you have studied hard, you will pass the exam. Wenn du fleißig gelernt hast, wirst du die Prüfung bestehen.
c.	'if'-clause: simple present – main clause: can + infinitive If you study hard, you can pass the exam. Wenn du fleißig lernst, kannst du die Prüfung bestehen.
d.	'if'-clause: simple present – main clause: might + infinitive If you study hard, you might pass the exam. Wenn du fleißig lernst, wirst du eventuell die Prüfung bestehen.

2. Type 2 – Future situations (improbable/unlikely)

a. 'if'-clause: simple past – main clause: conditional I (would + infinitive)
   If you studied hard, you would pass the exam.
   Wenn du fleißig lernen würdest, würdest du die Prüfung bestehen.

b. 'if'-clause: simple past – main clause: could + infinitive
   If you studied hard, you could pass the exam.
   Wenn du fleißig lernen würdest, könntest du die Prüfung bestehen.

3. Type 3 – Past situations (unreal/impossible/hypothetical)

a. 'if'-clause: past perfect – main clause: conditional II (would + have + past participle)
   If you had studied hard, you would have passed the exam.
   Wenn du fleißig gelernt hättest, hättest du die Prüfung bestanden.

b. 'if'-clause: past perfect – main clause: could + have + past participle
   If you had studied hard, you could have passed the exam.
   Wenn du fleißig gelernt hättest, hättest du die Prüfung bestehen können.

c. 'if'-clause: past perfect – main clause: might + have + past participle
   If you had studied hard, you might have passed the exam.
   Wenn du fleißig gelernt hättest, hättest du eventuell die Prüfung bestanden.

! Exceptions to the rules:

1. The present tense is used in both clauses in general statements and for repeated activities or habits:
   If plants don't get enough water, they die. – If she has time, she goes to the fitness club.

2. For recommendations and advice use 'were' in the 'if'-clause and conditional I in the main clause:
   If I were you, I would study a bit harder.

3. 'If' can be left out when the order of the verb and subject are reversed:
   Had I studied harder, I would have passed the exam.

! Frequently made mistakes:

1. Be careful with commas. If you start with an 'if'-clause, use a comma. Don't use a comma if you start with the main clause:
   If you study hard, you will pass the exam.
   You will pass the exam if you study hard.

2. Don't use 'will' in the 'if'-clause, except to express willingness:
   They can come to Britain if they'll work.

3. Don't use 'would' in the 'if'-clause except when you are making a polite request:
   I would be grateful if you would hand in your homework on time in future.

The passive

The passive is often used when the action is more important than who or what performed it. The passive is frequently used in scientific and technical writing. The passive can be formed with or without an 'agent'. The 'agent' is the person or thing that causes an action to occur.

Form the passive using a form of 'to be' + past participle (+ by + agent)

Bank robbers often steal money.

Money is often stolen by bank robbers.

Simple present	Present progressive
I am invited to the party. You are invited to the party. He/she/it is invited to the party. We are invited to the party. You are invited to the party. They are invited to the party.	I am being terrorised by the neighbours. You are being terrorised by the neighbours. He/she/it is being terrorised by the neighbours. We are being terrorised by the neighbours. You are being terrorised by the neighbours. They are being terrorised by the neighbours.
Simple Past	Past progressive
I was invited to the party. You were invited to the party. He/she/it was invited to the party. We were invited to the party. You were invited to the party. They were invited to the party.	I was being terrorised by the neighbours. You were being terrorised by the neighbours. He/she/it was being terrorised by the neighbours. We were being terrorised by the neighbours. You were being terrorised by the neighbours. They were being terrorised by the neighbours.
Present perfect	Modal verbs
I have been invited to the party. You have been invited to the party. He/she/it has been invited to the party. We have been invited to the party. You have been invited to the party. They have been invited to the party.	I can be found in the office. You must be informed. He/she/it mustn't be informed. We needn't be informed. You ought to be informed. They should be informed.
Future	Future perfect
I will be invited to the party. You will be invited to the party. He/she/it will be invited to the party. We will be invited to the party. You will be invited to the party. They will be invited to the party.	I will have been invited to the party. You will have been invited to the party. He/she/it will have been invited to the party. We will have been invited to the party. You will have been invited to the party. They will have been invited to the party.
❗ Be careful with irregular verbs	

Relative clauses

Relative clauses are used to describe people or things. A relative clause usually begins with a relative pronoun.

Relative pronoun	refers to
who	people (subject or object)
whom	people (object), formal English
which	things
that	people or things (subject or object)
whose	possessions

1. Defining relative clauses:
   A defining relative clause is important for the meaning of the sentence. Without the relative clause the sentence would not make sense. Defining relative clauses are not set off from the rest of the sentence by commas:
   The house that/which we live in is very old.
   This is the woman who(m) I saw yesterday.
   This is the boy whose bike was stolen.

   The pronoun 'that, which, who(m)' can be left out if the pronoun is the object of the relative clause. This type of relative clause is known as 'contact' clause:
   The house we live in is very old.
   This is the woman I saw yesterday.

2. Non-defining relative clauses:
   In non-defining relative clauses the information is additional descriptive information. The sentence is clear even without a relative clause. These relative clauses are separated with commas:
   My grandmother, who will be 85 in December, walks her dog every morning.

Adjectives

Adjectives describe people and things: the tall man – bright lights

1. The comparison of adjectives

Positive form	Comparative form	Superlative form
cold	colder	the coldest
hot	hotter	the hottest
funny	funnier	the funniest
modern	more modern	the most modern
❗ Remember the irregular forms:	good – better – the best much – more– the most bad – worse – the worst far – further – the furthest	

2. Making comparisons:

Use more/-er than, not as … as and as … as to make comparisons:

The black car is more modern than the red car.

The blue car is newer than the red car.

The red car is not as new as the blue one.

The white car is as new as the blue one.

3. Adjectives used as collective nouns:

Adjectives can be used as collective nouns. In such cases, the + adjective refers to a particular group of people as a whole:

We raised money for the blind.

The very young and the very old are particularly at risk.

4. Participles as adjectives:

The present participle (-ing form) and past participle of verbs can often be used as adjectives:

an interesting book

the finished report

5. Verbs followed by adjectives:

Verbs are usually followed by adverbs, however some verbs are followed by adjectives:

to be	Sally was tired.
to become	Anne became ill.
to feel	Thomas felt happy.
to get	The child got dirty.
to look	Mary looks sad.
to seem	Her new boyfriend seems very nice.

Adverbs

Adverbs are formed by adding -ly/-ily to an adjective.

Adjective	Adverb
safe	safely
happy	happily
real	really
reasonable	reasonably
! Remember the irregular forms:	good – well fast – fast hard – hard

1. Adverbs which describe actions (verbs):   He walked quickly.
   She spoke slowly.

2. Adverbs before other adjectives: This is an extremely good essay.

3. Adverbs before other adverbs: He was driving incredibly fast.

4. Adverbs before past participles: Credit cards are frequently accepted.

5. The comparison of adverbs:

Positive form	Comparative form	Superlative form
fluently	more fluently	the most fluently
! Remember the irregular forms:	well – better – the best badly – worse – the worst fast – faster – the fastest	

6. Some useful adverbs: always, usually, often, frequently, sometimes, seldom, rarely, never, recently, soon, lately, in the past, in the future, largely, for the most part, partly, probably, possibly, hardly, definitely, obviously, clearly, basically, consequently, as a result

Question tags

A question tag is added to the end of a sentence turning it into a question. In German you use expressions like '…, nicht wahr?' and '…, oder?' in a similar way.

1. If the statement is positive, the questions tag is negative:
   He likes chocolate, doesn't he?

2. If the statement is negative, the question tag is positive:
   He doesn't like chocolate, does he?

3. The subject of the verb is the same in the statement and in the question tag:
   He likes chocolate, doesn't he?

4. If the statement is in the simple present or simple past tense, the question tag uses 'do/don't' or 'did/didn't':
   He likes chocolate, doesn't he?
   He went to England, didn't he?

5. If the statement uses an auxiliary verb (to be, to have, will, etc.) or a modal (can, must, etc.), use the modal or auxiliary in the same tense in the tag:
   Tom is here, isn't he?
   Roger has bought a new car, hasn't he?
   Jill will be at the party, won't she?
   You can speak English, can't you?

Modal auxiliaries

1. Will/would/can/could/may:

Asking someone to do something: Will/Would/Can/Could you do me a favour?
Asking for permission/giving permission: May I use your phone? – Yes, of course, you may.
Talking about abilities: She can speak English.

2. Must/mustn't/needn't:

Instructing someone to do something or not to do something: You must wear a safety helmet. You mustn't smoke in the office.
Talking about a necessity or duty: I must finish the project by Friday. You needn't pay in advance.

3. May/might/could/must/will:

Expressing a possibility or probability: It may/might/could/will rain. You must be Mr Jones.
Making a suggestion: We could go to that new Spanish restaurant.

4. Should/ought to/shouldn't/ought not to:

Giving advice: You should/ought to use a dictionary. You shouldn't arrive late for the interview.

5. Modal auxiliaries only have a present and/or past tense form. For other tenses substitutes are used:

Modal auxiliary	Substitutes	Examples
can/could	be able to	He won't be able to lift the piano.
may/mustn't	be allowed to not be allowed to	We were allowed to visit the church. We weren't allowed to see the pope.
must/needn't	have to not have to	The Millers will have to sell their house. We didn't have to wait long.

-ing forms

An -ing form can be either a present participle or a gerund.

The present participle

1. The present participle is used in the progressive tenses (present progressive, past progressive, etc.):
   Mary is playing the guitar. – The plane was flying at a height of 10,000 metres.

2. The present participle can be used as an adjective: the winning party – a growing child

3. The present participle can be used to shorten clauses, often after a conjunction, e.g: after, while, before, when
   I was riding my bike to work when I met her. → While riding/Riding my bike to work, I met her.
   I saw a woman who was wearing a silly hat. → I saw a woman wearing a silly hat.
   After we had eaten a burger, we went home. → After eating a burger, we went home.
   Read the text before you answer the questions. → Read the text before answering the questions.
   Although I felt tired, I couldn't sleep. → Although feeling tired, I couldn't sleep.

The gerund

1. The gerund is used after prepositions: You're very good at speaking English.

2. The gerund is often used after certain verbs: like, hate, enjoy, love, mind, prefer
   I don't mind watching TV but I prefer reading and I also enjoy playing computer games.

3. The gerund can be used as a noun: Laughing is good for you. – Studying is very important.

4. Some verbs have the construction verb + preposition + gerund:
   to be afraid of, to look forward to, to feel like, to talk about, to insist on, to decide against, to think about/of, to succeed in, to apologise for
   I'm afraid of flying.

5. When the following expressions are followed by a verb, use the gerund:
   There's no point in waiting any longer.
   It's not worth going to see the new James Bond film.
   A waste of money/time: It's a waste of time talking to you.
   To spend/waste/time/money: He spent all his money playing on the fruit machines.

Reported speech

Reported speech (or indirect speech) is used to report what someone has said without quoting them.

1. Start the reported speech with a reporting verb:

   a. Statements: say (that), tell sb. (that), answer, mention, explain, reply, etc.
   "I'm tired." → She says (that) she's tired.

   b. Questions: ask, want to know
   "Are you hungry?" → She asks me if I'm hungry.
   "Where do you go to school?" → She wants to know where I go to school.

   c. Commands: tell sb. to + infinitive
   "Leave me alone!" → She told me to leave her alone.

2. If the reporting verb is in the present, present perfect or future tense, the tense stays the same:

"Watching TV is bad for your eyes".   → Mr Jones says watching TV is bad for our eyes.

→ Mr Jones has said watching TV is bad for our eyes.

→ Mr Jones will say watching TV is bad for our eyes.

3. If the reporting verb is in the past tense, the tense of the reported speech changes:

simple present "I walk the dog every day."	→	simple past She said she walked the dog every day.
present progressive "I'm walking the dog."	→	past progressive She said she was walking the dog.
simple past "I walked the dog last night."	→	past perfect She said she had walked the dog last night.
past progressive "I was walking the dog."	→	past perfect progressive She said she had been walking the dog.
present perfect "I have walked the dog."	→	past perfect She said she had walked the dog.
present perfect progressive "I have been walking the dog."	→	past perfect progressive She said she had been walking the dog.
past perfect "I had walked the dog."	→	past perfect She said she had walked the dog.
past perfect progressive "I had been walking the dog."	→	past perfect progressive She said she had been walking the dog.
will future "I will walk the dog every day."	→	conditional I She said she would walk the dog every day.

4. Questions follow the same tense changes as statements:

"Where did you park the car?" → The policeman asked the man where he had parked the car.

5. Some adverbs of time also change in reported speech, for example:

now	→	then
yesterday	→	the day before/the previous day
here	→	there
last year	→	the year before/the previous year
today	→	that day
tomorrow	→	the next day

6. Statements involving truths and facts do not have to change:

"Cats eat mice". → The teacher said that cats eat mice.

Videotraining: Englische Aussprache

Perfekte englische Aussprache leicht gemacht: Mit dem Lernprogramm zur englischen Lautschrift können Sie alle Laute einüben. Wählen Sie einfach in der Navigation rechts den entsprechenden Reiter (*Vowels* oder *Consonants*) aus und dann klicken Sie auf das gewünschte phonetische Symbol. Sprechen Sie die Wörter laut nach.

Unter www.klett.de geben Sie einfach den Online-Link 808201-1000 ein. Von dort aus können Sie die Webanwendung online starten.

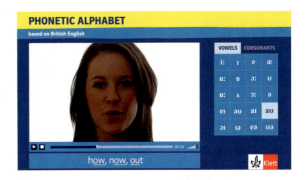

Abkürzungen

etw.	= etwas	sb.	= somebody	BE	= britisches Englisch
jmdm	= jemandem	coll.	= umgangssprachlich	AE	= amerikanisches Englisch
jmdn	= jemanden	sg	= Singular	fml	= formal
sth.	= something	pl	= Plural	infml	= informal

Pronunciation

In this book the following phonetic symbols are used:

Consonants		Vowels		Diphthongs	Additional symbols
[ŋ] morning	[ʃ] she	[ɑ:] father	[i] happy	[aɪ] I, my	['] Primary stress on the following syllable
[r] red	[tʃ] lunch	[ʌ] but	[i:] teacher, she	[aʊ] now, house	
[s] this	[ð] the	[e] pen	[ɒ] got	[eə] there, pair	[ˌ] Secondary stress on the following syllable
[z] is	[θ] thanks	[ə] a sister	[ɔ:] ball	[eɪ] name, they	
[ʒ] television	[v] video	[ɜ:] girl	[ʊ] book	[ɪə] here, idea	[‿] Link between two words
[dʒ] page	[w] wow, one	[æ] flat	[u] January	[ɔɪ] boy	
		[ɪ] it	[u:] too, two	[əʊ] hello	[x] Pronounced like the German ach**t**
				[ʊə] sure	

All other letters are pronounced roughly the way they are written, e.g [b], [j], [l] etc.

The page numbers refer to the first occurrence of the word.

A

to abandon [əˈbændən] verlassen 24
abundant [əˈbʌndənt] reichlich 42
abuse [əˈbjuːs] Missbrauch 37
abused [əˈbjuːzd] missbraucht 44
access [ˈækses] Zugang 42
to access [ˈækses] erreichen 10
accessible [əkˈsesəbl] zugänglich 71
to accompany [əˈkʌmpəni] begleiten 96
to accumulate [əˈkjuːmjəleɪt] anhäufen, (sich) ansammeln 24
to achieve [əˈtʃiːv] erreichen 16
acid rain [ˌæsɪd ˈreɪn] saurer Regen 57
acquaintance [əˈkweɪntəns] Bekannte(r) 23
to acquire [əˈkwaɪə] erwerben 12
addiction [əˈdɪkʃn] Sucht 13

additive [ˈædɪtɪv] Zusatzstoff 47
adolescent [ˌædəˈlesənt] Heranwachsender 11
to adopt [əˈdɒpt] annehmen 94
adventurous [ədˈventʃərəs] abenteuerlich 49
adverse [ˈædvɜːs] widrig 99
advice [ədˈvaɪs] Rat 96
affair [əˈfeə] Affäre 24
to affect [əˈfekt] betreffen, beeinflussen 14
affection [əˈfekn] Zuwendung 24
ambitious [æmˈbɪʃəs] ehrgeizig 42
ancient [ˈeɪnʃənt] antik 44
to announce [əˈnaʊns] ankündigen 42
annually [ˈænjʊəli] jährlich 30
appeal [əˈpiːl] Anziehung(skraft) 14
to appeal [əˈpiːl] ansprechen 49

to apply [əˈplaɪ] anwenden 84
to appreciate sth. [əˈpriːʃieɪt ˌsʌmθɪŋ] etw. schätzen 25
appreciation [əˌpriːʃiˈeɪʃn] Wertschätzung 60
approach [əˈprəʊtʃ] Ansatz 42
appropriate [əˈprəʊpriət] angemessen, passend 8
approximately [əˈprɒksɪmətli] ungefähr 45
arid [ˈærɪd] trocken, dürr 57
to assess [əˈses] beurteilen, bewerten 48
association [əˌsəʊʃiˈeɪʃn] Verbindung 36
attempt [əˈtempt] Versuch 46
attitude [ˈætɪtjuːd] Haltung 11
audience [ˈɔːdiəns] Publikum 24
authorities [ɔːˈθɒrətiz] Behörden 9
average [ˈævrɪdʒ] durchschnittlich 96

B

to back up [bæk ˈʌp] absichern 43

to ban [bæn] verbieten 8

to banish [ˈbænɪʃ] verbannen 24

barely [ˈbeəlɪ] kaum 10

battery farm [ˈbætərɪ ˌfɑːm] Legebatterie 39

to be at a loose end [bɪ ˌət ə ˌluːs ˈend] nicht wissen, was man mit sich anfangen soll 20

to belong to [bɪˈlɒŋ tuː] gehören zu 25

benefit [ˈbenəfɪt] Vorteil 30

to be struck by sth. [bɪ ˈstrʌk] von etwas beeindruckt sein 69

beverage [ˈbevrɪdʒ] Getränk 47

biased [ˈbaɪəst] voreingenommen 53

bill [bɪl] Rechnung 12

billion [ˈbɪljən] Milliarde 30

binding [ˈbaɪndɪŋ] bindend 42

biodiversity [ˌbaɪəʊdaɪˈvɜːsətɪ] Artenvielfalt 41

to blame sb. [bleɪm] jmdm die Schuld geben für 20

to blush [blʌʃ] rot werden 11

to boast [bəʊst] angeben 11

to boost [buːst] stärken, erhöhen 60

boundary [ˈbaʊndrɪ] Grenze 41

branch [brɑːntʃ] Sektor 47

to bridge [brɪdʒ] überbrücken 96

broadband [ˈbrɔːdbænd] Breitband 10

to broadcast [ˈbrɔːdkɑːst] übertragen, senden 9

brochure [ˈbrəʊʃə] Prospekt, Broschüre 76

to bully [ˈbʊlɪ] mobben 36

burden [ˈbɜːdn] Last 25

C

capability [ˌkeɪpəˈbɪlətɪ] Möglichkeit, Fähigkeit 43

capital [ˈkæpɪtl] Hauptstadt 63

carbon dioxide [ˌkɑːbndaɪˈɒksaɪd] Kohlendioxid 40

carriage [ˈkærɪdʒ] Wagen (eines Zuges etc.) 68

cash machine [ˈkæʃ məˌʃiːn] Bankautomat 99

to cater for [ˈkeɪtə fə] sorgen für 49

censorship [ˈsensəʃɪp] Zensur 95

characteristic [ˌkærəktəˈrɪstɪk] Merkmal, Charakteristikum, Eigenschaft 26

climate change [ˈklaɪmət ˌtʃeɪndʒ] Klimawandel 40

coastline [ˈkəʊstlaɪn] Küstenlinie 42

coincidence [kəʊˈɪnsɪdəns] Zufall 27

to collapse [kəˈlæps] einstürzen 60

combustion [kəmˈbʌstʃn] Verbrennung 43

to commission [kəˈmɪʃn] in Auftrag geben 74

commitment [kəˈmɪtmənt] Bindung, Engagement 49

common [ˈkɒmən] normal, üblich 94

compassion [kəmˈpæʃn] Mitgefühl 30

to compensate [ˈkɒmpənseɪt] entschädigen 49

to compile [kəmˈpaɪl] zusammenstellen 48

conclusion [kənˈkluːʒn] Schlussfolgerung 68

confidence [ˈkɒnfɪdəns] Selbstvertrauen, Sicherheit 15

confidential [ˌkɒnfɪˈdenʃl] vertraulich 94

consciousness [ˈkɒnʃəsnəs] Bewusstsein 44

to console [kənˈsəʊl] trösten 31

to constitute [ˈkɒnstɪtjuːt] darstellen, bilden 24

consumption [kənˈsʌmpʃn] Verbrauch 16

contemporary [kənˈtemprərɪ] zeitgenössisch 11

content [ˈkɒntent] Inhalte 95

contest [ˈkɒntest] Wettbewerb 29

contract [ˈkɒntrækt] Vertrag 97

to convey [kənˈveɪ] vermitteln 74

core [kɔː] Kern 12

to counter [ˈkaʊntə] erwidern, dagegen sprechen 53

counterpart [ˈkaʊntəpɑːt] Gegenstück 32

crowd [kraʊd] (Menschen)menge 9

crucial [ˈkruːʃl] entscheidend 65

curious [ˈkjʊərɪəs] wissbegierig 49

current [ˈkʌrənt] aktuell, gegenwärtig 41

custody [ˈkʌstədɪ] Gewahrsam 9

to cut ties [kʌt ˌtaɪz] Verbindungen lösen 56

cynical [ˈsɪnɪkl] zynisch 49

D

damage [ˈdæmɪdʒ] Schaden 45

data protection [ˈdeɪtə prəˌtekʃn] Datenschutz 39

to debrief [ˈpækɪdʒ] einen Einsatzbericht abgeben 79

debts [dets] Schulden 12

decade [ˈdekeɪd] Jahrzehnt 98

declaration [ˌdekləˈreɪʃn] Erklärung 56

to decline [dɪˈklaɪn] sinken, zurückgehen, abnehmen 36

to decrease [dɪˈkriːs] zurückgehen, sinken 15

to dedicate [ˈdedɪkeɪt] widmen 12

deliberate [dɪˈlɪbrət] absichtlich 53

delinquency [dɪˈlɪŋkwənsɪ] Straffälligkeit 98

delivery times [dɪˈlɪvrɪ ˌtaɪmz] Lieferzeiten 76

demand [dɪˈmɑːnd] Anforderung 73

to demand [dɪˈmɑːnd] verlangen, fordern 48

densely [ˈdenslɪ] dicht 63

depression [dɪˈpreʃn] (hier:) Tiefdruckgebiet 63

depth [depθ] Tiefe 24

desertification [dɪˌzɜːtɪfɪˈkeɪʃn] Versteppung 57

desire [dɪˈzaɪə] Wunsch 25

destination [ˌdestɪˈneɪʃn] (Reise-)ziel 48

destructive [dɪˈstrʌktɪv] zerstörerisch 96

to detain [dɪˈteɪn] in Gewahrsam nehmen 9

determined [dɪˈtɜːmɪnd] bestimmt, entschlossen 12

to devalue [ˌdiːˈvæljuː] abwerten 33

development [dɪˈveləpmənt] Entwicklung 58

to devise [dɪˈvaɪz] erfinden 65

discomfort [dɪsˈkʌmfət] Unannehmlichkeit 64

discount [ˈdɪskaʊnt] Rabatt, Nachlass 77

to discourage [dɪsˈkʌrɪdʒ] abschrecken, abhalten 14

to dismiss sth. [dɪsˈmɪs] etw. als … abtun 53

to dispel [dɪsˈpel] verbannen 36

to dissolve [dɪˈzɒlv] auflösen 47

distributed [dɪˈstrɪbjuːtɪd] verteilt 43

diverse [daɪˈvɜːs] unterschiedlich, vielfältig, verschieden 49

doable [ˈduːəbl] machbar 42

donation [dəʊˈneɪʃn] Spende 60

drenched [drentʃt] durchnässt 68

drought [draʊt] Dürre 41

duty [ˈdjuːtɪ] Pflicht 8

E

ease [i:z] Erleichterung, Bequemlichkeit 33

effect [ɪ'fekt] Auswirkung 40

elaborate [ɪ'læbrət] kompliziert 70

electricity grid [ˌelɪk'trɪsəti ˌɡrɪd] Stromnetz 43

embedded [ɪm'bedɪd] tief verwurzelt 36

emerging [ɪ'mɜːdʒɪŋ] neu 43

to emigrate ['emɪɡreɪt] auswandern 56

emission [ɪ'mɪʃn] Emission, Ausstoß 40

to emit [ɪ'mɪt] ausstoßen 40

emitter [ɪ'mɪtə] Erzeuger 57

empathic [em'pæθɪk] einfühlsam 33

empathy ['empəθɪ] Empathie, Mitgefühl 32

to employ a strategy [ɪm'plɔɪ] (hier:) eine Strategie anwenden 17

encounter [ɪn'kaʊntə] Begegnung 20

to encourage sb. [ɪn'kʌrɪdʒ] jdn ermutigen, animieren 14

endangered [ɪn'deɪndʒəd] gefährdet; (hier:) vom Aussterben bedroht 59

enemy ['enəmɪ] Feind 45

to engage in sth. [ɪn'ɡeɪdʒ] sich an etw. beteiligen 21

to enhance [ɪn'hɑːns] verbessern 75

enquiry [ɪn'kwaɪərɪ] Anfrage 76

to ensure [ɪn'ʃɔː] sicherstellen, garantieren 42

entitlement [ɪn'taɪtlmənt] Anrecht, Anspruch 32

envious ['envɪəs] neidisch 65

epidemic [ˌepɪ'demɪk] Epidemie, Seuche 32

to eradicate [ɪ'rædɪkeɪt] beseitigen 36

to establish [ɪ'stæblɪʃ] aufbauen 73

estimate ['estɪmət] Schätzung 40

to estimate ['estɪmeɪt] schätzen 30

even ['iːvn] gleichmäßig 98

event [ɪ'vent] Ereignis, Veranstaltung 8

evidence ['evɪdəns] Beweis 8

to exceed [ɪk'siːd] übertreffen 42

excessive [ɪk'sesɪv] übermäßig 53

executive [ɪɡ'zekjətɪv] Führungskraft 60

exhaustive [ɪɡ'zɔːstɪv] erschöpfend, umfassend 25

to expend in [ɪk'spend] aufwenden für 30

to expose [ɪk'spəʊz] aussetzen (einer Gefahr, einem Risiko) 84

to expose sth. [ɪk'spəʊz ˌsʌmθɪŋ] etw. enthüllen 52

exposure [ɪk'spəʊʒə] Aussetzen 33

to extend [ɪk'stend] verlängern, ausdehnen 68

extent [ɪk'stent] Ausmaß 40

to extinguish [ɪk'stɪŋgwɪʃ] löschen 9

F

facade [fə'sɑːd] Fassade 69

face value [ˌfeɪs 'væljuː] Nennwert, eingetragener Wert 25

to facilitate [fə'sɪlɪteɪt] erleichtern 11

famine ['fæmɪn] Hungersnot 56

fault [fɒlt, fɔːlt] Fehler 12

to feature ['fiːtʃə] (als Besonderheit) aufweisen, groß herausbringen 85

to feel guilty [ˌfiːl 'ɡɪltɪ] sich schuldig fühlen 96

fertilizer ['fɜːtɪlaɪzə] Dünger 57

to forecast ['fɔːkɑːst] voraussagen 42

foremost ['fɔːməʊst] führend 58

fossil fuel [ˌfɒsl 'fjʊəl] fossiler Brennstoff 40

fossil-fuelled [ˌfɒsl'fjuːld] fossil befeuert 42

to found [faʊnd] gründen 56

free-range [ˌfriː'reɪndʒ] Freiland- 39

to frown [fraʊn] die Stirne runzeln 25

full-time [ˌfʊl'taɪm] Vollzeit 97

fungus ['fʌŋɡəs] Pilz 56

G

gate [ɡeɪt] Tor 20

to gather ['ɡæðə] zusammenkommen 60

gender ['dʒendə] Geschlecht 33

genuinely ['dʒenjʊɪnlɪ] echt, aufrichtig, von Grund auf 24

to get out of control [ɡet ˌaʊt ˌəv kən'trəʊl] außer Kontrolle geraten 9

glacier ['ɡlæsɪə, 'ɡleɪʃə] Gletscher 40

to glue [ɡluː] kleben 94

GM food [ˌdʒiː'em ˌfuːd] gentechnisch verändertes Lebensmittel 39

to gossip ['ɡɒsɪp] tratschen, lästern 11

to grind sb. down [ɡraɪnd ˌdaʊn] jmdn zermürben 68

guess [ɡes] Vermutung 26

H

habit ['hæbɪt] Gewohnheit 84

habitat ['hæbɪtæt] Lebensraum 41

hallmark ['hɔːlmɑːk] Kennzeichen 74

to hang on to sth. [ˌhæŋ ˌɒn tə] etw. behalten 74

to harm [hɑːm] schädigen, schaden 49

harvest ['hɑːvɪst] Ernte 56

hazardous ['hæzədəs] gefährlich 39

heap [hiːp] Haufen 60

to hijack ['haɪdʒæk] entführen 60

to hinder ['hɪndə] behindern 84

hole [həʊl] Loch 13

horrified ['hɒrɪfaɪd] entsetzt 60

host [həʊst] Gastgeber(in) 49

to humiliate [hjuː'mɪlɪeɪt] demütigen 25

to hurl [hɜːl] schleudern 22

I

immigration [ˌɪmɪ'ɡreɪʃn] Einwanderung 56

impact ['ɪmpækt] Auswirkung 36

to improve [ɪm'pruːv] besser werden, sich verbessern 15

improvement [ɪm'pruːvmənt] Verbesserung 42

inadequates [ɪ'nædɪkwəts] sozial Benachteiligte 10

in advance [ɪn əd'vɑːns] im Voraus 8

incentive [ɪn'sentɪv] Anreiz 43

inconvenience [ˌɪnkən'viːnɪəns] Unannehmlichkeit 30

inconvenient [ˌɪnkən'viːnɪənt] ungünstig 52

to increase [ɪn'kriːs] (an)steigen, steigern, erhöhen 11

independence [ˌɪndɪ'pendəns] Unabhängigkeit 56

indigenous [ɪn'dɪdʒɪnəs] einheimisch 49

inevitable [ɪ'nevɪtəbl] unvermeidlich 37

ingredient [ɪn'ɡriːdɪənt] Zutat 47

inhospitable [ˌɪnhɒs'pɪtəbl] ungastlich 65

initial [ɪ'nɪʃl] erste(r,s) 60

to injure ['ɪndʒə] verletzen 60

innocent ['ɪnəsnt] harmlos 72

instant ['ɪnstənt] sofort 47

to integrate ['ɪntɪɡreɪt] integrieren 94

intended [ɪn'tendɪd] (hier:) bestimmt 76

interconnected [ˌɪntəkə'nektɪd] vernetzt 43

interest ['ɪntrəst] Zinsen 99

to interfere with [ˌɪntə'fɪə] sich einmischen; (hier:) verhindern 59

to intervene [ˌɪntə'viːn] sich einschalten 8

intimacy ['ɪntɪməsɪ] Intimität, Nähe 24

invoice ['ɪnvɔɪs] Rechnung 77

Dictionary

issue [ˈɪʃuˌɛ] Thema 40

itinerary [aɪˈtɪnərərɪ] Reiseroute, Reiseplan 65

J

janitor [ˈdʒænɪtə] Hausmeister 60

juncture [ˈdʒʌŋktʃə] Punkt 80

justifiable [ˈdʒʌstɪfaɪəbl] gerechtfertigt 49

juvenile [ˈdʒuːvənaɪl] Jugendliche(r) 20

K

key [kiː] wesentlich 96

to kid [kɪd] Spaß machen 68

kidney [ˈkɪdnɪ] Niere 10

L

to label [ˈleɪbl] beschriften, nennen 22

a lack of sth. [ˈlækˌəv] fehlend, Mangel an 32

law-abiding [ˈlɔːəˌbaɪdɪŋ] gesetzestreu 99

likelihood [ˈlaɪklɪhʊd] Wahrscheinlichkeit 94

literacy [ˈlɪtrəsɪ] Lese -und Schreibfähigkeit 74

literate [ˈlɪtrət] lese- und schreibkundig 74

loads [ləʊdz] Mengen von 10

lot [lɒt] Grundstück 59

M

magnitude [ˈmæɡnɪtjuːd] Ausmaß, Größe 60

to maintain [meɪnˈteɪn] aufrechterhalten 73

majority [məˈdʒɒrətɪ] Mehrzahl, Mehrheit 76

to make amends [ˌmeɪkəˈmendz] etw. wiedergutmachen 78

to make sth. worth one's while [meɪk ˌsʌmθɪŋ ˌwɜːθ wʌnz ˈwaɪl] jmdn für etw. belohnen 30

to manoeuvre [məˈnuːvə] manövrieren 74

mass transit [ˌmæs ˈtrænzɪt] öffentliche Verkehrsmittel 58

to match [mætʃ] übereinstimmen 37

mate [meɪt] Kumpel 24

maturity [məˈtjʊərətɪ] Reife 15

mayhem [ˈmeɪhem] Chaos 20

mayor [meə] Bürgermeister(in) 8

means of communication [ˌmiːnz əv kəˌmjuːnɪˈkeɪʃn] Kommunikationsmittel 70

mediocre [ˌmiːdɪˈəʊkə] mittelmäßig 65

to meet [miːt] erreichen 42

memorial [məˈmɔːrɪəl] Denkmal 61

might [maɪt] Macht 31

to miss out on sth. [ˌmɪsˈaʊtˌɒn] etw. verpassen 74

monitoring [ˈmɒnɪtərɪŋ] Kontrolle, Überwachung 8

mother-in-law [ˈmʌðərɪnˌlɔː] Schwiegermutter 22

mountain range [ˈmaʊntɪn ˌreɪndʒ] Bergkette 63

N

narcissism [ˈnɑːsɪsɪzm] Selbstverliebtheit 32

natural resource [ˌnætʃərl rɪˈzɔːs] Bodenschatz 42

necessity [nəˈsesətɪ] Notwendigkeit 42

need [niːd] Bedürfnis 11

O

obesity [əˈbiːsɪtɪ] Fettleibigkeit 59

obsessed [əbˈsest] besessen 72

obsession [əbˈseʃn] Obsession, Besessenheit 13

occasionally [əˈkeɪʒənlɪ] gelegentlich 49

offer [ˈɒfə] Angebot 76

offshore [ˌɒfˈʃɔː] vor der Küste 43

ongoing [ˌɒnˈɡəʊɪŋ] in Gang befindlich, laufend 24

to opt out [ɒpt ˈaʊt] aussteigen 20

order [ˈɔːdə] Bestellung, Auftrag 76

outstanding [aʊtˈstændɪŋ] herausragend 48

to outstrip [ˌaʊtˈstrɪp] übersteigen 43

overwhelming [ˌəʊvəˈwelmɪŋ] überwältigend 25

P

painstakingly [ˈpeɪnzˌteɪkɪŋlɪ] gewissenhaft, sorgfältig 74

to participate [pɑːˈtɪsɪpeɪt] teilnehmen 43

passionate [ˈpæʃənət] leidenschaftlich 13

peer [pɪə] Gleichaltrige(r) 36

peer pressure [ˈpɪə ˌpreʃə] Gruppenzwang 15

performance [pəˈfɔːməns] Leistung 98

persecution [ˌpɜːsɪˈkjuːʃn] Verfolgung 56

pesticide [ˈpestɪsaɪd] Pestizid, Schädlingsbekämpfungsmittel 57

phenomenon [fəˈnɒmɪnən] Phänomen 8

placement [ˈpleɪsmənt] Praktikum 97

polluting [pəˈluːtɪŋ] umweltverschmutzend 49

population [ˌpɒpjəˈleɪʃn] Bevölkerung 63

population density [ˌpɒpjəleɪʃn ˈdensɪtɪ] Bevölkerungsdichte 63

pre-booking [ˌpriːˈbʊkɪŋ] Vormerkung 68

to predict [prɪˈdɪkt] vorhersagen 58

predictable [prɪˈdɪktəbl] vorhersehbar 42

pre-industrial [ˌpriːɪnˈdʌstrɪəl] vorindustriell 40

prejudice [ˈpredʒʊdɪs] Vorurteil 28

to preserve [prɪˈzɜːv] bewahren 58

pressure [ˈpreʃə] Druck 15

prevalent [ˈprevələnt] vorherrschend 10

to prevent sth. from happening / sb. from doing sth. [prɪˈvent] verhindern 43

previous [ˈpriːvɪəs] vorherig 61

pricy [ˈpraɪsɪ] teuer 68

privacy [ˈpraɪvəsɪ] Privatsphäre 76

to proceed [prəˈsiːd] fortfahren 76

profoundly [prəˈfaʊndlɪ] stark 61

progress [ˈprəʊɡres] Fortschritt 76

to prohibit [prəʊˈhɪbɪt] verbieten 8

to promote [prəˈməʊt] fördern, unterstützen 99

property [ˈprɒpətɪ] Grundbesitz 59

to propose [prəˈpəʊz] vorschlagen 44

public order [ˌpʌblɪk ˈɔːdə] öffentliche Ordnung 8

punctuation [ˌpʌŋktʃʊˈeɪʃn] Interpunktion 74

purpose [ˈpɜːpəs] Zweck, Absicht 46

to put at risk [ˌpʊt ət ˈrɪsk] gefährden 8

Q

quotation [kwəʊˈteɪʃn] Angebot, Kostenvoranschlag 76

R

to rage [reɪdʒ] toben 11

to raise money [ˌreɪz ˈmʌnɪ] Geld beschaffen 98

recent [ˈriːsənt] kürzlich, letzte/r/s 8

to reckon [ˈrekən] vermuten 10

recommendation [ˌrekəmenˈdeɪʃn] Empfehlung 98

to recover [rɪˈkʌvə] sich erholen 15

to release [rɪˈliːs] entlassen, veröffentlichen 32

relentless [rɪˈlentləs] gnadenlos, (hier:) unablässig 58

reluctantly [rɪˈlʌktəntlɪ] zögerlich 56

to remain [rɪˈmeɪn] bleiben 76

renewable energy [rɪˌnjuːəblˈenədʒɪ] erneuerbare Energie 39

rent [rent] Miete 12

to replace [rɪˈpleɪs] ersetzen 95

to require [rɪˈkwaɪə] benötigen 42

researcher [rɪˈsɜːtʃə] Forscher(in) 25

residential neighborhood [ˌrezɪˈdenʃl] Wohngebiet 59

to resolve [rɪˈzɒlv] lösen 11

resource [rɪˈzɔːs; ˈriːsɔːs] Vorrat, Rohstoff 57

to respond to [rɪˈspɒnd] (hier:) reagieren auf 60

to restrict [rɪˈstrɪkt] begrenzen 14

retirement [rɪˈtaɪəmənt] Ruhestand 42

to retreat [rɪˈtriːt] zurückgehen 40

to reveal [rɪˈviːl] bekannt geben, enthüllen 25

to revise [rɪˈvaɪz] wiederholen, noch einmal durchsehen 10

to reward [rɪˈwɔːd] belohnen 49

ridiculous [rɪˈdɪkjələs] lächerlich 73

risk [rɪsk] Risiko 94

row [raʊ] Auseinandersetzung 13

rubbish [ˈrʌbɪʃ] Müll 9

rudely [ˈruːdlɪ] unhöflich 68

runoff [ˈrʌnɒf] Sickerwasser 57

rural [ˈrʊərəl] ländlich 58

S

sacrifice [ˈsækrɪfaɪs] Opfer 61

to sample [ˈsɑːmpl] ausprobieren 20

scale [skeɪl] Ausmaß, Umfang 42

scarce [skeəs] knapp 41

sceptic [ˈskeptɪk] Skeptiker(in) 52

screen [skriːn] Bildschirm 10

secretive [ˈsiːkrətɪv] geheimnisvoll 72

to seek [siːk, sɔːt, sɔːt] versuchen 49

selective [səˈlektɪv] wählerisch 49

self-absorbed [ˌselfəbˈzɔːbd] mit sich selbst beschäftigt 32

selfish [ˈselfɪʃ] egoistisch 73

self-respect [ˌself rɪˈspekt] Selbstrespekt 25

self-worth [ˌselfˈwɜːθ] Selbstwert 25

sensible [ˈsensɪbl] vernünftig 49

shameless [ˈʃeɪmləs] schamlos 16

shift [ʃɪft] Veränderung 37

to shift [ʃɪft] sich verschieben 41

shortcut [ˈʃɔːtkʌt] Kurzform 84

sick leave [ˈsɪk ˌliːv] Fehlzeit durch Krankheit, Krankenstand 81

significance [sɪgˈnɪfɪkəns] Bedeutung 36

single-handedly [ˌsɪŋglˈhændɪdlɪ] im Alleingang 30

to slaughter [ˈslɔːtə] schlachten 53

slope [sləʊp] Hang 57

small-scale [ˌsmɔːlˈskeɪl] in kleinem Umfang 49

social networking site [ˌsəʊʃl ˈnetwɜːkɪŋ ˌsaɪt] Internetseite eines sozialen Netzwerks 8

social worker [ˈsəʊʃl ˌwɜːkə] Sozialarbeiter(in) 9

sociogram [ˈsəʊsɪəʊgræm] Soziogramm 22

source [sɔːs] Quelle 96

to spoil (a child) [spɔɪl] verwöhnen 45

stereotype [ˈsterɪətaɪp] Stereotyp, Klischee 28

to stigmatise [ˈstɪgmətaɪz] brandmarken 36

straightforward [ˌstreɪtˈfɔːwəd] geradlinig, unkompliziert 10

to strengthen [ˈstreŋkθn] verstärken 95

strife [straɪf] Streit 31

strike [straɪk] Schlag 60

to strike [straɪk] treffen 60

stunned [stʌnd] betäubt 60

to stunt [stʌnt] hemmen 43

subsidised [ˈsʌbsɪdaɪzd] subventioniert 53

substitute [ˈsʌbstɪtjuːt] Ersatz 71

to suffer [ˈsʌfə] leiden, erleiden 25

supply [səˈplaɪ] Vorrat, Angebot 41

to surmise [səˈmaɪz] mutmaßen 33

survey [ˈsɜːveɪ] Umfrage 36

to swap [swɒp] tauschen 10

swiftly [ˈswɪftlɪ] schnell 68

T

to tackle [ˈtækl] etw. angehen 14

to take sth. for granted [ˌteɪk fə ˈgrɑːntɪd] etw. als selbstverständlich/gegeben hinnehmen 42

to take pride in [ˌteɪk ˈpraɪd ˌɪn] auf etw. stolz sein 84

target [ˈtɑːgɪt] Ziel 42

to target [ˈtɑːgɪt] zielen auf 99

taste [teɪst] Geschmack 96

tax bill [ˈtæks ˌbɪl] Steuerabrechnung 58

to tease someone [tiːz] jmdn hänseln 11

temperate [ˈtempərət] gemäßigt 63

theft [θeft] Diebstahl 94

threadbare [ˈθredbeə] schäbig 20

tidal [ˈtaɪdl] Gezeiten- 43

tough [tʌf] (hier:) hart, schwer 61

to track [træk] verfolgen 24

track record [ˈtræk ˈrekɔːd] Erfolgsgeschichte 79

tranquil [ˈtræŋkwɪl] ruhig, friedlich 69

to trap sth. [træp] etw. auffangen 40

to trash [træʃ] verwüsten 20

to trust sb. [trʌst] jmdm vertrauen 24

twice [twaɪs] zweimal 10

U

ultimately [ˈʌltɪmətlɪ] schließlich 60

unchecked [ʌnˈtʃekt] ungehindert, unkontrolliert 58

to underwrite [ʌndəˈraɪt] Risiko übernehmen, versichern 43

unfortunate [ʌnˈfɔːtʃənət] bedauernswert 27

unharmed [ʌnˈhɑːmd] unbeschädigt 47

unimaginably [ˌʌnɪˈmædʒɪnəblɪ] unvorstellbar 48

unintelligible [ˌʌnɪnˈtelɪdʒəbl] unverständlich 65

unique [juːˈniːk] einzig, einmalig 49

unprecedented [ʌnˈpresɪdəntɪd] beispiellos 41

unrecognizable [ʌnˈrekəgnaɪzəbl] unerkennbar 36

unruly [ʌnˈruːlɪ] wild, ungebändigt 69

urban [ˈɜːbən] städtisch 63

urgency [ˈɜːdʒənsɪ] Dringlichkeit 31

V

vacant [ˈveɪkənt] leer stehend, frei 59

vice versa [ˌvaɪsˈvɜːsə] umgekehrt 46

volunteer [ˌvɒlənˈtɪə] Freiwillige(r) 60

to vow [vaʊ] schwören 60

W

weapon [ˈwepən] Waffe 16

to witness [ˈwɪtnəs] mitansehen 60

worthwhile [ˌwɜːθˈwaɪl] lohnend 49

Y

yearning [ˈjɜːnɪŋ] Verlangen 25

Bild- und Textnachweise

Textquellennachweis

8/9 © DW Deutsche Welle, 2011; **10/11** Teenagers and technology: 'I'd rather give up my kidney than my phone', Jon Henley, 16 July © Guardian News & Media Ltd. 2010; **12/13** From: Willy Russell, The Wrong Boy, p. 80–82 © Black Swan edition 2001; **14/15** What teenagers think about binge drinking, Poppy Robertson © Guardian News & Media Ltd. 2010; **16/17** The Fear Text: Allen, Lily/Kurstin, Gregory Allen © EMI April Music Inc./Kurstin Music/Universal Music Publishing Ltd./ EMI Music Publishing Germany GmbH & Co. KG, Hamburg/ Universal Music Publ. GmbH, Berlin; **20/21** What's wrong with today's youth?, Idle hands, idle minds, Cristina Odone, The Observer, 6 January 2002 © Guardian News & Media Ltd. 2002; **24/25** From: Friends ain't friends... How social media has changed the way young people form friendships. By Philip Jenkinson © Copyright Young Life Australia.; **26/27** From: Klett English editions, ISBN 579822 © Original: Puffin Books, 2007; **28/29** From: Das bisherige Rollenmodell bleibt etabliert, Armin Lehmann © Der Tagesspiegel; **30** © Network for Good; **31** © Kenneth R. Thompson; **32/33** Source: www.psychologytoday.com / BLOGS What The Wild Things Are © 2010, Samantha Smithstein, Psy. D; **36/37** Homophobia is declining in schools, study claims, Tracy McVeigh, The Observer, 3 March © Guardian News & Media Ltd 2012; **40/41** Source: National Environment Research Council Brochure, June 2007, www.nerc.ac.uk/publications; **42/43** Juliet Davenport, Britain could be running on 100% renewable energy by 2050, 14 December 2010 © Guardian News & Media Ltd. 2010; **44/45** From: T.C. Boyle, A Friend of the Earth © Penguin, 2000; **46/47** © 2007 BBC Focus, Bristol Magazines Ltd.; **48/49** What it means to travel green, John Vidal, 20 February © Guardian News & Media Ltd 2010; **52/53** From: New film exposes unsavoury side of US food industry by Leonard Doyle, 14 Jun 2009 © Telegraph Media Group Ltd.; **58/59** What Urban sprawl costs you, Used with permission of the Orlando Sentinel © 2006; **60/61** © 2009 Advameg, Inc.; **64/65** Extract from THE KINGDOM BY THE SEA by Paul Theroux. Copyright © 1983, Paul Theroux, used by permission of The Wylie Agency (UK) Limited; **68/69** Adapted from: www.helium.com © 2002-2010 Helium, Inc. All rights reserved.; **72/73** From: 'FAMILY MATTERS: Time spent chatting online is time lost with family' Posted: February 25, 2010 by Jim May, Midland Reporter-Telegram. Source: MyWestTexas.com © Copyright 2011, Mywesttexas.com; **74/75** A fifth of children have never received a letter', Rachel Williams, 21 May 2010 © The Guardian News & Media Ltd., 2010; **78-81** From: Martin Lukes, Who Moved My BlackBerry? © Penguin Books Ltd., 2006; **84/85** From: The University of Alabama Computers and Applied Technology Program (2009). Technology education: A series of case studies. Available at http://www.bamaed.ua.edu/edtechcases.; **94/95** © Daily Mail, London 2011; **98/99** © EndPlay, Inc.

Bildquellennachweis

4 Thinkstock (iStockphoto), München; **4** shutterstock (Patrizia Tilly), New York, NY; **4** Fotolia.com (Alexander), New York; **5** iStockphoto (Anna Bryukhanova), Calgary, Alberta; **5** Thinkstock (iStockphoto), München; **5** Video(s) supplied by BBC Motion Gallery, London; **6** Fotolia.com (diego cervo), New York; **6** iStockphoto (Karen Mower), Calgary, Alberta; **6** Thinkstock (iStockphoto), München; **6** Fotolia.com (Monkey Business), New York; **6** shutterstock (My Portfolio), New York, NY; **6** iStockphoto (craftvision), Calgary, Alberta; **7** www.CartoonStock.com (Jonny Hawkins), Bath; **10** BigStockPhoto.com (monkeybusinessimages), Davis, CA; **10** Copyright Guardian News & Media Ltd 2011, London; **12** www.willyrussell.com, Whiston, Merseyside; **14** iStockphoto (Piotr Marcinski), Calgary, Alberta; **16** dreamstime.com (Wanderlust), Brentwood, TN; **20** iStockphoto (Luca Cepparo), Calgary, Alberta; **21** Cagle Cartoons (Dave Granlund), Santa Barbara, CA; **22** Thinkstock (Monkey Business), München; **22** shutterstock (Patrizia Tilly), New York, NY; **22** iStockphoto (Chris Gramly), Calgary, Alberta; **23** Thinkstock (Monkey Business), München; **23** iStockphoto (Logorilla), Calgary, Alberta; **23** Fotolia.com (Thomas Pajot), New York; **25** www.CartoonStock.com (Delgado, Roy), Bath; **26** iStockphoto (GYI NSEA), Calgary, Alberta; **28** shutterstock (Robert Adrian Hillman), New York, NY; **29** www.CartoonStock.com (Bacall, Aaron), Bath; **31** Ullstein Bild GmbH (Wolter), Berlin; **31** FEMA (PD/Greg Henshall), Washington, D.C.; **31** Alamy Images (Jeremy Hoare), Abingdon, Oxon; **31** www.bilderbox.com (www.BilderBox.com), Thening; **32** iStockphoto (Joan Vicent Cantó Roig), Calgary, Alberta; **35** nach: Statistisches Bundesamt, Wiesbaden 2011; **36** Alamy Images (Peter Marshall), Abingdon, Oxon; **37** nach: Journal of Adolscent Health, 2006 (http://www.sprc.org/sites/sprc.org/files/library/SPRC_LGBT_Youth.pdf); **38** Fotolia.com (Alexander), New York; **38** shutterstock (MarcelClemens), New York, NY; **38** iStockphoto (narvikk), Calgary, Alberta; **39** iStockphoto (Jani Bryson), Calgary, Alberta; **39** iStockphoto (eskaylim), Calgary, Alberta; **39** iStockphoto (Bart Coenders), Calgary, Alberta; **39** iStockphoto (Lucía Cóppola), Calgary, Alberta; **39** iStockphoto (Maridav), Calgary, Alberta; **41** iStockphoto (Andy Green), Calgary, Alberta; **42** Copyright Guardian News & Media Ltd 2011, London; **42** Federal Coordinator, Alaska Natural Gas Transportation Projects, 2012; **44** Corbis (Lynn Goldsmith), Düsseldorf; **46** Avenue Images GmbH (Stockbyte), Hamburg; **47** MEV Verlag GmbH, Augsburg; **48** ifotoStock (Frank Sánchez), Madrid; **48** Copyright Guardian News & Media Ltd 2011, London; **49** Madden, Chris, ..; **52** Telegraph Media Group Limited, London; **52** Fotolia.com (Eky Chan), New York; **54** iStockphoto (Richard Semik), Calgary, Alberta; **54** Fotolia.com (chasingmoments), New York; **54** shutterstock (Palette7), New York, NY; **54** Fotolia.com (Birgit Urban), New York; **54** iStockphoto (S. Greg Panosian), Calgary, Alberta; **54** shutterstock (Jiri Moucka), New York, NY; **55** shutterstock (Timo Kohlbacher), New York, NY; **55** Thinkstock (iStockphoto), München; **55** shutterstock (Brendan Howard), New York, NY; **55** Thinkstock (Ron Chapple Studios), München; **55** iStockphoto (Mark Stay), Calgary, Alberta; **55** Fotolia.com (sumikophoto), New York; **56** akg-images, Berlin; **58** www.CartoonStock.com (Andrew Toos), Bath; **60** iStockphoto (Charles Daniel Howell), Calgary, Alberta; **62** www.CartoonStock.com (Robert Thompson), Bath; **62** Pauline Ashworth, Stuttgart; **63** iStockphoto (Bob Duffy), Calgary, Alberta; **64** Getty Images (Ulf Andersen), München; **64** iStockphoto (Ismail Akin Bostanci), Calgary, Alberta; **68** Fotolia.com (oscity), New York; **69** Thinkstock (iStockphoto), München; **69** shutterstock (QQ7), New York, NY; **70** iStockphoto (Daniel Laflor), Calgary, Alberta; **70** The Cartoonist Group (Dan Piraro), Seattle; **70** iStockphoto (Anna Bryukhanova), Calgary, Alberta; **71** iStockphoto (Sanne Berg), Calgary, Alberta; **71** [Lichtenstein, Roy: Oh, Jeff... I love you, too... but...] © VG Bild-Kunst, Bonn 2012. ddp images GmbH (AP Photo/Courtesy the Estate of Roy Lichtenstein via The Art Institute of Chicago), Hamburg; **71** iStockphoto (HultonArchive), Calgary, Alberta; **72** iStockphoto (Jacob Wackerhausen), Calgary, Alberta; **73** www.CartoonStock.com (Love, Jason), Bath; **74** iStockphoto (Aldo Murillo), Calgary, Alberta; **75** www.CartoonStock.com (McPherson, John), Bath; **76** iStockphoto (Blend_Images), Calgary, Alberta; **76** iStockphoto (Lise Gagne), Calgary, Alberta; **77** www.CartoonStock.com (Fran), Bath; **78** iStockphoto (Daniel Laflor), Calgary, Alberta; **84** iStockphoto (TommL), Calgary, Alberta; **85** www.CartoonStock.com (Bucella, Marty), Bath; **86** BBC Information and archives, London; **87** BBC Information and archives, London; **88** Video(s) supplied by BBC Motion Gallery, London; **89** BBC Information and archives, London; **99** TBWA \ HUNT \ LASCARIS, Johannesburg; **110** The Guardian, London; **110** The Mirror, London; **171** Klett-Archiv, Stuttgart

Sollte es in einem Einzelfall nicht gelungen sein, den korrekten Rechteinhaber ausfindig zu machen, so werden berechtigte Ansprüche selbstverständlich im Rahmen der üblichen Regelungen abgegolten.